The People Solutions Sourcebook

Also by Neil Thompson:

Loss, Grief and Trauma in the Workplace
Promoting Equality: Working with Diversity and Difference
    (third edition)*
People Skills (third edition)*
Effective Communication (second edition)*
Crisis Intervention
*Grief and its Challenges**
*People Management** – coming soon!

* Also published by Palgrave Macmillan

The People Solutions Sourcebook

Neil Thompson

First edition published as *People Problems* 2006
Reprinted three times
Second edition 2012

Palgrave Macmillan in the UK is an imprint of Macmillan Publishers Limited, registered in England, company number 785998, of Houndmills, Basingstoke, Hampshire RG21 6XS.

Palgrave Macmillan in the US is a division of St Martin's Press LLC, 175 Fifth Avenue, New York, NY 10010.

Palgrave Macmillan is the global academic imprint of the above companies and has companies and representatives throughout the world.

Palgrave® and Macmillan® are registered trademarks in the United States, the United Kingdom, Europe and other countries

ISBN: 978-0-230-29147-8

This book is printed on paper suitable for recycling and made from fully managed and sustained forest sources. Logging, pulping and manufacturing processes are expected to conform to the environmental regulations of the country of origin.

A catalogue record for this book is available from the British Library.
A catalog record for this book is available from the Library of Congress.

10   9   8   7   6   5   4   3   2   1
21   20   19   18   17   16   15   14   13   12

Printed and bound in Great Britain by
the MPG Books Group, Bodmin and King's Lynn

For Bernard

Contents

PART 3   Guide to further learning

Illustrations

About the author

Neil Thompson is an independent writer, trainer, consultant and international conference speaker, working with Avenue Consulting Ltd
(www.avenueconsulting.co.uk). He has held full or honorary professor-
ships at four UK universities and has established himself as one of the
leading thinkers and writers in his field. He has over a hundred and fifty
publications to his name, including several bestselling textbooks. His
recent books include:

> *The Critically Reflective Practitioner* (with Sue Thompson, Palgrave
> Macmillan, 2008);
> *Loss, Grief and Trauma in the Workplace* (Baywood, 2009);
> *People Skills* (3rd edn, Palgrave Macmillan, 2009);
> *Effective Communication* (2nd edn, Palgrave Macmillan, 2011);
> *Crisis Intervention* (2nd edn, Russell House, 2011);
> *Promoting Equality* (3rd edn, Palgrave Macmillan, 2011); and
> *Grief and its Challenges* (Palgrave Macmillan, 2012).

He has also produced a number of education and training DVDs
(including one on *Creative Problem Solving*), self-help audio
programmes, training manuals and e-books (see www.avenuemedia
solutions.com for more details).

Neil has over thirty-four years' experience as a practitioner, manager,
educator, consultant and expert witness in the human services. He is
very well respected for his ability to communicate complex ideas in an
accessible way without oversimplifying them.

He has been a speaker at seminars and conferences in the UK,
Ireland, Greece, the Netherlands, Norway, Italy, Spain, the Czech
Republic, Turkey, Hong Kong, India, Canada, the United States and
Australia, and has qualifications in social work, management (MBA),
training and development, mediation and dispute resolution, as well as
a first-class honours degree in Social Sciences, a doctorate (PhD) and
a higher doctorate (DLitt).

Neil is a Fellow of the Chartered Institute of Personnel and
Development; the Royal Society of Arts (elected on the basis of his

contribution to workplace learning); and the Higher Education Academy; and a Life Fellow of the Institute of Welsh Affairs. In addition, he is a member of the International Work Group on Death, Dying and Bereavement.

He has served as the editor of the US-based international journal *Illness, Crisis & Loss*, and currently edits the free *Well-being* BULLETIN e-zine (www.well-being.org.uk). He set up the online resources, *Social Work Focus* (www.socialworkfocus.com), *humansolutions* (www.human solutions.org.uk) and *Grief Challenges* (www.griefchallenges.com).

He is now a sought-after workshop facilitator, consultant and international conference speaker. His website (with a blog and a free 'tip of the week' facility) is at www.neilthompson.info.

Preface

This revised and extended edition of what, in its earlier incarnation, carried the title of *People Problems* attempts to build on the strengths of the original. This has been achieved by updating some of the ideas and references, adding new ideas and insights here and there and, perhaps most significantly of all, extending the number of problem-solving tools from 50 to 88. The additional 38 problem-solving methods therefore offer an even wider range of potential ways of tackling problems, and thereby provide even greater flexibility in terms of the approach we use to helping people to meet their needs by addressing the problems that are standing in their way.

In the six years since I wrote the first edition, I have continued to work (as a trainer or consultant) with a wide range of people across a wide range of organizations. Despite this variety, there has continued to be considerable continuity about the issues I am called upon to help people address. As a result of this I am even more convinced now of the value of this book and the need for members of the people professions – broadly defined – to have a good understanding of people and their problems. I am therefore delighted to be able to offer this second, revised, expanded and updated edition which should offer even more insights into how we can play a positive role in helping people to tackle the problems they face and rise to the challenges their lives involve.

It has also been good to learn, based on feedback from people who bought the first edition of the book, that it can help readers to cast light on their own problems. Several people have commented to me that they found the book useful not only for their professional roles, but also for dealing with their own problems and life challenges – an added bonus that I had not considered when I wrote the first edition!

Of course, it remains the case that no book can provide all the answers, nor should a book attempt to do so. There are no easy or magic answers to the problems we encounter in the people professions, there are just various challenges and various ways of tackling those challenges. This book does not offer answers, but it does provide a foundation of understanding and insights based on my 34 years of experience and the learning from so many other people and so many other sources that I have been privileged to gain. My hope is that those insights will serve as a sound foundation for you to build up your own understanding and repertoire of tools and techniques you can use. But, the emphasis must be on *foundation*. The knowledge to be gained from this book is far from comprehensive. It needs to be emphasized that this is very much an introduction and will not provide you with enough knowledge in itself (which is why Part Three of the book is a guide to further learning).

Good luck in building on the ideas presented here. They should stand you in good stead in your efforts to tackle the 'people problems' you are likely to encounter.

Acknowledgements

In the acknowledgements to the first edition of this book, I expressed my gratitude to: Duncan Pritchard, Principal of Aran Hall School; Graham Thompson, Bangor University; Bernard Moss and Mark Savage, Staffordshire University; John Bates, Liverpool Hope University; and Rob Kennett, Kent Constabulary. I also thanked Susan Thompson for her support in so many ways, Maggie Holloway for her excellent typing skills and Judy Marshall for the excellent job she did in preparing the typescript for publication and, for their invaluable support, Beverley Tarquini and Catherine Gray at the publishers. I remain deeply indebted to all those people for helping me lay the sound foundations of the first edition on which this new edition is now built. I am now also very grateful to Penny Simmons for the excellent copy-editing job she has done, as with so many of my other books.

Two other people I thanked at that time are sadly no longer with us. Jo Campling was for many years a trusted friend and mentor and a tremendous source of support for my publishing efforts. Although not directly involved in this new edition, Jo's influence is still very much a part of my work in general and this book in particular. Jo was delighted to welcome the publication of the first edition and saw it as a reflection of the success of my *People Skills* book which was another project which owed much to her support. I believe that she would have been even more delighted to see the publication of this new, revised, updated and expanded edition of the original book, recognizing this as an acknowledgement of the important contribution to successful professional practice that this text can make.

Sheree Keep of the publishers has also passed away in the time since the first edition of the book saw the light of day. She was a joy to work with and is no doubt sadly missed by everyone who knew her. It is people like Sheree who make me feel that wrestling with the complexities of human problems is worth it, that there is such a positive side to humanity that makes struggling with the negatives worth the investment of time, effort and energy.

Introduction: who, why, what and how

Who is the *People Solutions Sourcebook* for?

Any people whose work brings them into contact with others, regardless of the nature of the job itself, are likely to find themselves in situations where they would benefit from having a range of problem-solving tools to use as and when required.

What unifies this diverse range of people who could potentially benefit from this book is the very real set of challenges we face when we are involved in helping people who are experiencing problems or trying to tackle situations where some people's behaviour is causing problems for others. This book, in tandem with my *People Skills* book (Thompson, 2009a), can therefore provide a very helpful platform for developing the knowledge, skills and confidence needed to be sufficiently well equipped to rise to those challenges.

For people who work with children and young people, the insights to be gained here can be very valuable indeed. However, it will be necessary for each worker to take into account the level of development of the child(ren) or young person(s) concerned before using a particular tool or approach.

Why should I use the book?

Working in the 'people professions' can be a source of great satisfaction and enjoyment. However, it is no exaggeration to state that, where there are people, there are problems. Indeed, it would be very naïve to assume that you could bring large numbers of people together in workplaces or in society more broadly without there being difficulties of some description. However, this is not a reason for pessimism or negativity. Rather, it is an acceptance of the challenge that, when we work with people, we need to have well-developed problem-solving skills. Putting those skills to good use can be an excellent source of satisfaction and pleasure in their own right. Adopting a position of realism means that we have to avoid the unhelpful extremes of, on the one hand, a destructive pessimism that sees no hope and, on the other, a naïve optimism that sees the world through rose-tinted spectacles. The reality is that working with people has very many positives, but there will inevitably be problems as well. A key aim of this book is to help equip you to turn some of those problems into successes and sources of satisfaction by helping you to develop the skills and strategies that can play such an important role in working with people and their problems.

What does it cover?

The book is divided into three main parts: Part One can be seen as an extended essay on what is involved in problem solving. This entails looking at some key issues that can help us to understand some of the complexities involved. In effect, Part One fulfils two roles: on the one hand, it provides a theoretical backdrop for the set of tools presented in Part Two to help deepen our understanding of the range of ideas on which the tools are based. On the other hand, it also provides an important analysis in its own right of the knowledge, skills and values involved in problem solving in a variety of settings.

Part Two presents 88 methods, techniques or tools. Some of these are new, based on my own work over the years; others are not so new, but none the less offer important insights. The aim is not to provide detailed step-by-step instructions for you to follow, as that would be a gross over-simplification of the complexities involved in this demanding, but rewarding type of work. Rather, the idea of tools is that they provide a bridge between theory and practice, a basis for critically reflective practice (Thompson and Thompson, 2008). Tools will not do the job for you, but they will give you a framework to work to, to enable you to draw on the wisdom to be gleaned from the research and other people's experience in this area – so that you do not have to start from scratch with only your own experience to rely on. Part Two should help you to incorporate your own experience with the knowledge and understanding that we have gained from a long history of working with people and their problems. Each method or technique is explained so that you can develop an understanding of what is involved, in what circumstances it could possibly be used and with what objectives in mind. The ideas presented will not, of course, guarantee success in any particular venture but, if used appropriately, should increase the chances of a positive outcome.

For convenience the tools are presented in alphabetical order, but, of course, different tools will be applicable in different situations and some can be used in different ways, depending on the circumstances. Some tools are particularly useful for clarifying our thinking (for example, six thinking hats; SWOT analysis); some are helpful for promoting change (culture audit; using dissonance); some are 'self management' tools designed to help us deal with our own pressures (the CIA framework; tuning in); some are good for facilitating interpersonal interactions (confronting without being confrontational; SOLER); while others involve raising awareness (recognizing grief; the three Rs), but they should all provide a framework or structure that can help bring a degree of order and understanding to what are often confused and confusing – if not downright chaotic – problem situations.

Part Three is a shorter section comprising the guide to further learning. It includes references to further reading where appropriate, plus details of relevant websites and other learning resources where suitable ones exist that I am aware of. It is intended to act as a foundation for further learning, recognizing that this is very much an introductory text that lays the foundations for more advanced learning and skill development.

How should I use the book?

There is no single definitive way to use the book. There is much to be gained from the conventional approach of starting at the beginning and working your way through, close reading Part One before focusing on the tools in Part Two. Part Three would then be the next step to prepare you for taking your learning further, but that is not the only option. You could also read quickly through Part Two to get the feel of the range of methods available and then read Part One fully. You could then re-read Part Two more thoroughly, concentrating on those tools that particularly appeal to you. You can then read Part Three as a launch pad for developing your knowledge further.

With either of these options you will have Part Two as a reference source to come back to from time to time, especially when you have problems that you are struggling with and you are looking for ideas and inspiration. However, one approach that I would strongly advise you not to adopt is to miss out Part One altogether and simply use Part Two as an A to Z of problem-solving tools to be used as appropriate. If you do not have the understanding of problem solving that Part One is

designed to help you develop, then you are unlikely to get the full benefit of the specific tools that make up Part Two and you may even find
yourself in a situation where the inappropriate use of tools is making
the situation worse. So, please do resist the temptation to save time by
jumping straight into the toolbox without developing key elements of
knowledge you need to be able to put the tools to good (and safe) use.

There is a focus throughout the book on 'use of self'. What this
means is that the tools are of no use on their own and can, in fact, be
dangerous if not used properly (just as a saw, hammer or screwdriver
can). We need to draw on our own personal resources (knowledge,
skills and values) to be able to put these tools to good use. Having a
method or tool to draw upon does not give us an easy answer. In undertaking this type of work, we still need to draw on a good understanding
of what makes people tick (this is a point we shall explore in more detail
in Part One).

One further important point to recognize is that some problems are
not resolvable – that is, there are no guarantees that these tools or,
indeed, any approach to a particular problem will be successful. This is
important to note because, if we do not take this on board, we can, in
effect, set ourselves up for stress. What I mean by this is that, if we set
ourselves unrealistic targets, we create unrealistic expectations, something that is recognized as a significant source of stress (Thompson,
1999). Learning to be realistic about what can and cannot be achieved
is an important part of professional development in the people professions. This is because we must avoid the disruptive extremes of: (i)
being defeatist and cynical and assuming that progress cannot be made
in circumstances where (with the right input from a skilled worker)
progress may indeed be possible; and (ii) as mentioned earlier, setting
ourselves up for stress by having unrealistic expectations.

It is to be hoped that, in conjunction with the discussion of skills
in *People Skills*, this book will help to equip you to tackle some of the
very significant challenges that arise in working with people and their
problems.

PART 1

Understanding people and their problems

Introduction

As mentioned in the Introduction, Part One of this book is an extended essay which has the aim of (i) providing a general introduction to the subject matter of problem solving in relation to people, and (ii) setting the scene for Part Two and the various tools, methods and techniques to be found there. Many people can work in the people professions without realizing that problem solving is a key part of what they do. For example, I have come across many managers who complain of people getting in the way of their doing their job – as if they fail to grasp that helping people solve their problems (so that they can achieve their maximum level of quality and quantity of work) is a key part of any manager's role. Similarly, I have come across many social workers who get bogged down in 'providing services', who lose sight of the rationale for providing such services – that is, to solve a problem or meet a need (Thompson, 2009b). Many more examples could be provided of managers and professionals engaged in a wide range of settings who have fallen into the trap of failing to appreciate the problem-solving nature of their work.

For some people, problem solving is an explicit part of their role – for example, a community psychiatric nurse trying to work with somebody with mental health problems to avoid an eviction from their flat, or a debt advice worker trying to help a family to resolve financial problems that are spiralling out of control. For others, however, direct problem solving may not be a key part of their role, but problem-solving skills are required to enable them to do their bread and butter work. For example, a youth worker may be trying to develop a particular scheme or project, but finds that there are obstacles in the way of doing so (perhaps a conflict between two or more of the participants). Problem-solving skills will then need to be drawn upon, even though direct problem solving is not the object of the exercise. For people involved in management roles, both sides of this particular coin can be seen to apply – that is, a manager will have responsibility for certain areas of work and will, at times, need to adopt a problem-solving approach in order to achieve the particular objective. However, he or she is also quite likely to become involved in problem-solving activities as a direct

3

part of the managerial role – for example, in dealing with grievances, disciplinary matters and so on.

An important distinction to draw is that between people problems and problem people. By people problems, I mean the sort of difficulties and complications that arise when people come together – for example, conflict, stress, communication breakdowns. This is not to be confused with 'problem people'. 'Problem people' is a term I prefer not to use because of its unhelpful connotations. It implies that somebody is 'by their very nature' difficult or a problem. This is a gross oversimplification of some very complex issues about how problems arise and how best they can be dealt with. To label individuals as problem people is to indulge in a judgemental attitude. This is a situation to be avoided because adopting a judgemental attitude means making a value judgement about an individual's worth and assuming that they are responsible for the problems concerned. There are a number of reasons why we should steer clear of this sort of reaction:

1. *It is often not fair.*   For example, someone may be labelled as lazy, but this is likely to mask underlying issues of motivation which are just as much a managerial responsibility as that of the individual (this is not to say that people are never lazy but, rather, that it is much more appropriate to try and find out why their motivation is so low rather than just write them off as a 'lazy person').
2. *It is rarely effective.*   Being judgemental simply does not help. It does not take us any further forward in our problem-solving activities and, in fact, can often act as a block to such activities.
3. *It can be counterproductive.*   Tensions and conflicts can be generated by adopting a judgemental attitude. Applying a negative label to somebody can actually, in some circumstances, encourage them to adopt the behaviour you are implicitly criticizing. For example, labelling somebody as 'obstructive' may actually make that person less co-operative, rather than more.
4. *It fails to see the situation from the point of view of the person concerned.*   I shall be arguing below that the important part of effective problem solving is the ability to put yourself in other people's shoes, to see the situation from their point of view (that is, to have empathy). Being judgemental about somebody prevents us from doing this. If we fail to take account of the individual's point of view, then we are likely to generate resistance, rather than commitment, to making progress. This relates to the important concept of motivation, an issue that we shall explore in more detail below.

Problem solving is not simply a matter of trying to cure people of their ills, to recognize some sort of pathology within them and try to address it. In reality, problem solving is a complex, multifaceted undertaking, and the more understanding of the complexities we have, the better equipped we will be to undertake such activities. Simply labelling certain individuals as 'problem people' certainly does not do justice to intricacies involved in the development, management and resolution of problems.

What is a problem?

Before going any further it is important to clarify what I mean by 'problems', given that the book is about problem-solving strategies. For the purposes of this book, a problem is anything that either brings about negatives (pain, suffering distress, anxiety and so on) or blocks positives (health, fulfilment, satisfaction, progress in achieving our goals and so on) or a mixture of the two. In a sense, having a problem can be defined as being in a situation that we want to get out of. Problem-solving methods are therefore tools we can use to help people get out of such situations.

Problems can come in all sorts of shapes and sizes and varying degrees of severity or intensity. They can reinforce one another and one can be the root cause of others – the issue of cause and effect is not a simple one. Sometimes problems can be manageable on their own, but in combination they can prove overwhelming. Problems are certainly not entirely subjective, but there is none the less an important subjective dimension. That is, if somebody perceives a situation as a problem, then it *is* a problem, in so far as that is how it will be experienced by the person(s) concerned – *as a problem*. As it was expressed quite some time ago now, 'the definition of the situation is real in its consequences' (Thomas and Znaniecki, 1958). For example, if someone is worried about something, even if this worry is unrealistic, it does not alter the fact that he or she is experiencing worry and thus has a problem (as defined above). It would be a serious mistake to disregard this problem by assuming that it is not a 'real' problem. If it is perceived as 'real', it will be experienced as 'real' and will therefore be 'real in its consequences'.

There is a close relationship between problems and unmet needs (Thompson, 2009b), and it is a two-way relationship. That is, unmet needs can cause problems, and experiencing problems can lead to our needs not being met. An example of the former would be someone's need for affection leading to low self-esteem, while an example of the latter might be an aggressive manner leading to a need for affection not being met.

What this reflects is that suffering is part of what it means to be human (as recognized in the nineteenth century by the existentialist philosopher, Friedrich Nietzsche – Magnus and Higgins, 1996). Human experience is not a matter of pursuing the holy grail of a problem-free life; rather it is a series of problems and challenges – and the opportunities that go with them.

What is a 'people' problem?

As noted above, problems come in all shapes and sizes and can have different causes. They can be technical (the new software is incompatible with the existing software we use), financial (outgoings exceed income) or logistical (the equipment we need is not where we need it to be) and so on. While problems such as these will generally have human consequences (frustration, poverty or other such negative outcomes), what I refer to as 'people' problems have not only human consequences, but also human causes for the most part. This is primarily, but not exclusively, a question of relationships. Relationships can be wonderful and a great source of strength and joy (and an important spiritual resource, as recognized in the concept of 'connectedness'). However, they can also be terrible and a source of great pain and problems (as Sartre, 1989, put it, 'hell is other people'). Difficulties can arise because of the nature of the relationship, a change in it or the ending of it.

Relationships are not only individual matters, of course. Problems arise because of relationships between groups or other 'factions' (genders, ethnic or religious groups and so on). We should therefore be wary of adopting too narrow a perspective on this.

Relationships involve a number of dimensions, but four in particular merit our attention here:

1. *Power.* We should be wary of seeing power as something an individual either has or does not have. Power is, by and large, a matter of relationships (Thompson, 2007). For example, a manager may have power over an employee in the workplace, but that relationship may be reversed outside work if, for example, that employee is a special constable. Power is a very complex issue, but for present purposes we should

note that it is an important dimension of relationships (and relationships are an important dimension of power).

2. *Conflict.* A common mistake is for people to assume that conflict is what occurs when relationships break down. However, in reality, relationships can be characterized by conflict over a very long period of time without ever breaking down. Conflict, or at least the potential for conflict, is present in all relationships.

3. *Communication.* Relationships exist through communication and are also a major channel of communication (consider, for example, how much of your communication is with people you are in some sort of relationship with, compared with communicating with people who are peripheral to your network of relationships).

4. *Identity.* Our sense of who we are arises, in part at least, from our relationships. For example, being a parent is not only a status, it is also a relationship. (In my own case, my identity as a parent stems from my relationship with my daughter.) Where there are problems in relationships, there can be problems of identity. Indeed, people experiencing major problems (a bereavement, for example) will often say: 'I don't know who I am anymore'.

Another important point to recognize about 'people' problems is that one person experiencing a problem can lead to other people experiencing problems. For example, someone who is having personal difficulties may, as a result of the build up of tension, indulge in bullying behaviour. Indeed, it is very commonly the case that someone *causing* problems is also *experiencing* problems. It is therefore important that we do not fall into the trap commonly known as 'the blame game'. Unacceptable behaviour is precisely that – unacceptable, but rather than simply condemning people for such behaviour, it can be far more fruitful (in both the short and long term) to look at why such behaviour is occurring and see whether action can be taken to change the underlying causes. This does not mean that people should not be held responsible for their actions – they certainly should – but, if we want to resolve problematic situations, then we need to go further (and look wider) than simply allocating blame.

People can also cause problems for themselves in terms of how they try to address their problems, in so far as some problems are actually the result of earlier attempted solutions. For example, depression can be understood as a potential way of coping with overwhelming feelings of hurt, anger, frustration, disappointment or grief – an attempted solution that can easily create more problems than it solves. Excessive drinking, the misuse of drugs and violence can also be problems that started off as attempted solutions.

Why is the context important?

The idea that 'all action is interaction' is something I was lucky enough to learn at an early stage in my career. All action is interaction means that we do not operate in a vacuum. What I do is influenced by the actions of others around me, and my actions in turn will influence, to a certain extent at least, the actions of others. We go about our business in a world where people influence each other, where people influence the circumstances in which they live and work and the circumstances influence the people. If we want to develop an adequate understanding of people and their problems, we need to bear in mind that we are dealing with a context of complex interactions, rather than individuals in isolation.

An important concept here is that of 'the person in context'. What this refers to is the need to recognize that, although each of us is a unique individual in our own right, we are all unique individuals in a social context. So, while I am a unique individual, I am also a member of a class group, a gender, an ethnic group and so on. There will be wider sociological factors that have a bearing on who I am and how I go about making my impression upon the world. It is not uncommon for people to forget about the person in context and focus all their attention on the individual, as if he or she lives outside of this context. Sometimes we can make the opposite mistake and see the context and put great emphasis on the significance of wider factors, but lose sight of the actual person at the heart of a situation. The key point to remember here is that we need to bear in mind the person *and* the context and not fall into the trap of looking at either the person or the context.

Another important dimension of this notion that all action is interaction is that problems will actually intertwine – that is, it would be naïve to look at particular problems in isolation. For example, the problem of one person being aggressive may be linked with another problem of someone else being subdued or even depressed. This is not necessarily to say that one problem causes the other, because sometimes they may cause each other or both may be caused by another set of circumstances. But, what it does mean is that we need to look at the big picture. We need to look at how problems may be interacting, perhaps reinforcing each other at times, cancelling each other out at others (although it has to be recognized that the former is much more common than the latter!). Someone who wants to be a skilled problem solver must therefore become accustomed to thinking more widely than seeing just individuals or just individual problems. One of the tools to be discussed in Part Two is that of helicopter vision, and this is a notion closely linked to the point I am making here – the need to get an overview or, as it is often called, 'the big picture'.

A third important point to note in relation to this central idea that all action is interaction is that the helper becomes part of the problem scenario – that is, in engaging with people who are experiencing problems, our input becomes part of the dynamic. This can be positive or negative, in the sense that our input can help, but can also hinder or even make the situation worse. For example, if we do not adopt a facilitative approach, we run the risk of making people dependent and thereby giving them additional problems to contend with and less confidence in dealing with them, thereby 'locking them in' to their problems (see also the discussion of the drama triangle in Part Two).

This third point is particularly important as it puts a lot of responsibility on our shoulders. When we enter a problem situation, it is to be hoped that we are doing so with the genuine intention of making the situation better and, where possible, resolving the problems we encounter. However, it also has to be recognized that our intervention can in some circumstances be detrimental. We can make a bad situation worse.

How do we start?

When we endeavour to tackle people problems, one thing we need to be very clear about is: what precisely is the problem we are tackling (or what are the problems)? A very common mistake is for people to try and come up with solutions before they have carefully worked out what the problem is. Sometimes the pressure of the problem situation leads us to feel that we need to come up with something very quickly. This can be quite dangerous, as we can often suggest or implement actions that are not appropriate. A key problem-solving skill, then, is that of 'problem identification' – the ability to resist the temptation to rush into attempting to provide solutions before we are clear what problem it is that we are dealing with.

Linked to this is the importance of establishing who it is a problem for. The significance of this lies in the fact that a situation could be problematic for different people in different ways. For example, in a situation involving conflict between two people, each of them may see the situation in very different terms and may have very different ideas about the nature, causes and possible solutions to the problem. A situation that can very commonly arise is where something can be a problem to one person, or group of people, but a benefit or a positive development for another person or another group. For example, where a project is cancelled, this may present significant headaches for one group of people, but may be a source of great relief for another group who may have had doubts about their ability to fulfil the requirements of the project.

A further important point to consider in relation to problem identification is the need to take the problem to where the solution is likely to lie. What I mean by this is that there is little point focusing effort and attention on areas of a situation where a solution is not to be found. For example, if the solution to a particular problem relies on the provision of particular resources, then it will be necessary to take that problem to the person, or persons, who control those resources. To understand this further, consider the example of stress in the workplace. The traditional approach to stress is to perceive it as the sign of a weak individual, somebody who is not coping with the demands of their job. However, it is increasingly being recognized that stress is best seen in broader terms in relation to, for example, how the organization is managed. Giving a workload to somebody that he or she cannot cope with is not necessarily the sign of a weak individual, but could just as well be the sign of an organization that is being mismanaged (see the Health and Safety Executive Standards on workplace stress: www.hse.org.uk).

How do we get people motivated?

Problem solving is something we do *with* people rather than *to* them. Therefore, it is important for them to have at least some degree of motivation to bring a resolution to the problems. To be an effective problem solver, we therefore need to have at least a basic understanding of motivation. It is beyond the scope of this book to provide a detailed exposition of what is involved in the complex psychology of motivation. However, what I can more realistically do is concentrate on four sets of issues and refer the interested reader to Part Three of the book where guidance on further learning in this area is provided.

1. *Pain versus pay-off.* Very often the pain or suffering involved in a problem situation is enough to motivate the persons concerned to make the necessary changes. However, it is not always that simple. Sometimes, despite the pain involved, the individual or individuals concerned may be receiving some sort of pay-off or reward from the problem situation and this in itself can sustain it. For example, in a situation where somebody is developing a drink problem, he or she may be aware of the difficulties that this is causing and may wish to solve the problem, but the benefits that are derived from excessive drinking may stand in the way of this (see 'Motivational interviewing' in Part Two). Motivation, then, is not simply a matter of 'you've either got it or you haven't'. It can involve certain conflicts and, in particular, a trade-off between pain and pay-off.

2. *Balancing risks.* People who are not motivated to tackle their problems often say that it is because they lack confidence in doing so. In my experience, lack of confidence can often derive from a person weighing up the risks of taking action and comparing this with what they perceive as the relatively easy option of doing nothing. However, this can be misleading. This is because there are risks involved in doing nothing. A more realistic approach, therefore, is to weigh up the risks involved in taking action compared with the risks involved in not taking action. Very often people become embroiled in a problem situation and can see the risks involved in trying to resolve it, but perhaps are less open to the suggestion that there are significant risks involved in not tackling their problems. A skilled problem solver can therefore often be involved in trying to help people get a more balanced perspective on the risks involved in their situation from the point of view of both taking action and not doing so.

3. *Resistance, change and grief.* It is not uncommon for people to resist tackling their problems because to do so would involve some degree of change. When we enter into a change period in our life, particularly a significant amount of change, this can lead to a grief reaction. This is because even though the change may be very positive, we may lose certain things that we value as part of the change process. This is a point to which we shall return below in the section headed 'Promoting change'.

4. *Problem embedding.* This is a term I use to refer to the process whereby trying to tackle one problem can bring us up against another problem, and trying to solve the second problem can bring us up against a third problem and so on. That is, sometimes problems are embedded within wider problems – in the same way that Russian dolls

are embedded one within the others. Where this 'problem embedding' occurs, it can be a real test of motivation. For example, someone can try very hard to solve the first problem, but when they realize that this leads to a second problem, they may give up. They may regard the situation as irresolvable rather than turn their problem-solving attention to the second problem they encounter. Practice focus 1.1 illustrates this.

PRACTICE FOCUS 1.1

Lin had a lot of experience of helping people solve their problems. She was aware that trying to solve one problem often unearthed another one. She was also aware that coming across a second problem would often lead to people giving up on the first – to adopt a defeatist attitude when they realized that one problem was embedded in another. She was therefore ready for this whenever the situation arose, as she could anticipate that it would be an issue. Her way of dealing with it was to make it clear from the beginning of her work with a particular individual or group that one problem might reveal another and that it would be important to then turn their attention to this second problem rather than give up. This did not guarantee that people would not become defeatist, but it did seem to lessen the chances of that happening, and it also gave her a good platform from which to challenge the defeatism if it did arise.

How do we find the right way forward?

Revans (1998) draws an important distinction between problems and puzzles. He argues that puzzles have a single, definitive solution. For example, in a crossword puzzle, there is only one correct answer (in principle) for each clue. A problem, by contrast, is something that can have many solutions. Each potential solution will have strengths and weaknesses, costs and benefits, advantages and disadvantages. It will rarely be the case that there is a solution that will be entirely positive without some sort of drawback. There are two key issues arising from this. First, there is the question of ownership. We have to remember whose problem it is. There is little point in our trying to impose our own solution on someone unless that person is committed to that particular solution. This is an example of working in partnership which will be discussed in more detail below in the section headed 'Why do we need

PRECISE practice?'. What it involves is working with the individuals concerned, but without taking over – without trying to impose our solution. It is more a case of working together to identify possible solutions, evaluating them and coming up with what is perceived as the best way forward.

Second, this means that different problem solvers will adopt different approaches. It certainly does not mean that it is inappropriate or unacceptable that you are adopting a different approach from that adopted by a colleague, for example. It does mean that all of us involved in people problems can learn from each other and benefit from each other's experiences, but we must avoid coming to the simplistic solution that there is one right answer or one correct approach. Each approach, as noted above, will have its strengths and weaknesses.

How do we promote change?

Problem solving can be seen as a process of moving from an undesirable situation to a more desirable one. Change is therefore essential to that process. When we are talking about problem solving, we are, of course, talking about promoting change. This can be seen to apply at six levels:

1. *Individuals.* The resolution of very many problems involves changing the behaviour or attitudes of one or more individuals. Sometimes the behaviour of one person can cause problems for one or more others – for example, when a key person is behaving in an insensitive way. However, what can also occur is when an individual, through his or her behaviour and attitude, causes problems for him- or herself. An example of this would be somebody who perhaps adopts a confrontational attitude towards other people which results in a far higher level of conflict or even aggression than is necessary. The individual concerned may not realize that it is his or her behaviour that is leading to the problematic reaction being experienced.

2. *Families.* The point was made earlier that individuals need to be understood in context. The family context is a big part of this. Even where an individual lives alone and not apparently as part of a family, it is unlikely that relationships with family members or the influence of family members through upbringing, for example, will not still be a significant part of the situation. The family context is therefore an important part of understanding problems. This is largely because families

develop a set of unwritten rules – their own culture, as it were. Families also tend to have sets of power relations and certain channels of communication. Problems can arise in relation to any of these – that is, culture, power relations and communication. What is also interesting, and important to note, is that problems within families can lead to problems elsewhere – for example, in the workplace. Someone who, within their own family, is in a relatively powerless position may therefore lack confidence in dealing with the exercise of power in the workplace. However, we should be careful not to oversimplify here, as the transfer of problems from one domain (that is, the family) to another (the workplace) is not inevitable.

3. *Groups.*   This can refer to formal groups, such as staff teams, project teams, committees and so on or, more importantly, to gatherings of people who come together for a particular purpose, or just by force of circumstance. A key concept here is that of group dynamics. There is an extensive literature (see Part Three) which addresses the way in which individuals, when combined in a group, can produce complex patterns of interaction. As with families, much of this can relate to cultures based on unwritten rules, power relations and communication.

4. *Communities.*   When an individual is experiencing problems, these can affect not just that individual and his or her immediate family and perhaps colleagues, but also the wider community. For example, somebody experiencing mental health problems can cause distress and concern within a community. However, it is not simply the case that individual problems can become translated into community problems; communities themselves can have problems – for example, as a result of the lack of certain resources or amenities. There may also be tensions or conflicts within a community, perhaps for historical reasons, perhaps linked to social problems like racism or sexism. It is sadly the case that the community level is often one that is neglected by many people in the people professions. It is a very easy mistake to make to concentrate predominantly on individuals, perhaps paying some attention to their family or work context, but without considering the wider community, both in terms of how the individual can be affecting that community and how that community can be affecting the individual.

5. *Organizations.*   I have previously made the point (Thompson, 2011a) that organizations are dangerous places. What I mean by this is that organizations can have a very detrimental effect on us. For example, the organization we work for can have a hugely influential impact on our lives, sometimes in a negative way. Consider, for example, the following scenarios:

(a) An employee is devastated by being made redundant and is extremely worried about how he or she will be able to manage financially without a regular salary to rely on.

(b) A staff member is bullied by a manager to the extent that he or she becomes ill as a result of the stress involved.

(c) An applicant for promotion feels bitter, angry and distressed when his or her application is declined.

(d) A whole group of employees are extremely concerned when they are told that their team is to be disbanded as a result of reorganization.

Of course, these are not the only examples of how organizations can have a negative impact on people within them. Problems often have their roots in the way organizations work and the way they treat people. Although the idea of an organization is traditionally presented in very rational terms, in reality organizations are very emotive places. By this I mean that emotions play a very important role in how business is conducted and how organizational life is experienced by its participants. When the emotional dimension of organizations is neglected or mishandled, significant problems can arise.

6. *Society.* Some problems can be seen to arise from the very workings of our society – that is, they have their roots in complex political and socioeconomic matters way beyond the scope of individuals. While, as problem solvers, we may be in no position (apart from voting every so often) to change the nature of society and its political workings, we can at least take account of them in understanding the complexities of the problems we deal with at the other five levels.

This brief overview of the six levels should be sufficient to paint a picture of just how complex the notion of promoting change is. One key point that I wish to emphasize is that it is important that we move away from the idea that promoting change is exclusively, or even predominantly, about promoting individual change. Very often the need for change lies elsewhere, and it would be foolish for us to ignore that fact.

Part of this complexity is the fact that problem solving can be, and often is, a source of growth and transformation. It is not simply a matter of trying to return to the situation that existed before the problem arose, but rather attempting to capitalize on the situation to learn and develop as a result of the experience. This is especially the case when the problem involves a crisis (see 'Capitalizing on crisis' in Part Two) or grief (see the important work of Schneider (2006) on transformational grief.

Why do we need PRECISE practice?

PRECISE is an acronym for:

Partnership-based
Realistic
Empowering
Creative
Integrated
Systematic and
Effective practice.

This is a framework that I have devised to try and get across the point that good practice in problem solving needs to fit in with these seven areas. Let us look at each of them in turn.

Partnership based

The point was made earlier that there is little point in trying to impose a solution on people, as this is very unlikely to work. There are also ethical considerations about whether we have the right to try and impose a solution on somebody else. This approach is therefore best avoided. What is much more appropriate is an approach based on partnership. What this involves is working closely with the people concerned to:

(a) identify what the problem areas are;
(b) establish possible solutions;
(c) evaluate those solutions and choose the most appropriate way forward; and
(d) implement together, where appropriate, a plan of action.

In some circumstances, our role will be to help people understand how best to move forward and then leave them to implement the plan themselves. But in other circumstances, we will also have a role in working in partnership with them actually to implement the plan itself.

Realistic

This can be seen to apply in two senses. First of all, we need to be realistic in the sense of making sure that our proposed solutions are workable. It can be harmful and counterproductive to generate unrealistic expectations. We therefore have to make sure that our feet are firmly on the ground when it comes to tackling problems. We also need to be realistic in the sense referred to earlier – namely, to avoid the unhelpful extremes of pessimism and negativity on the one hand, and naïve optimism on the other. Realism, in my view, is the healthy balance between these two extremes. It involves recognizing that, in any situation, there will be positives, but there will also be negatives (see 'Promoting realism' in Part Two). The danger with pessimism is that we see the weaknesses, but fail to address the strengths. The problem with optimism is that we see the positives, but do not take adequate account of the negatives, thus leaving ourselves very vulnerable.

Empowering

Literally, the term 'empower' means to give power to. However, we cannot do this in a direct or literal sense. What empowerment is really about is helping people gain greater control over their lives and circumstances. This can involve helping them to recognize obstacles to progress, both within their own mind, where appropriate, and in their wider social circumstances – for example, if they are being discriminated against or disadvantaged in some way by other people. Empowerment also involves helping people solve their own problems rather than making them dependent on us. This is because, in the former case, the power mainly lies with the individual concerned. Once we leave the situation, they are in control of their circumstances to a larger extent than they were before if our attempts at empowerment have worked. However, if we act in such a way that creates dependency, then this sets up a power relationship in which the person we are trying to help is actually less powerful because they are now in a subordinate relationship to ourselves. A key part of effective problem solving, then, is that we make sure that, as far as possible, we empower people to resolve their own difficulties rather than do it for them and, in the process, risk making them dependent on us.

An important part of this is to recognize people's strengths and seek to build on them. It is very easy, when dealing with problems, to lose sight of the strengths dimension and thereby adopt an unduly negative perspective on the situation being dealt with. We all have strengths to draw upon, but it is not unusual for the pressure of certain problem situations to cast a shadow over them, perhaps to the point where we forget to take them into consideration and make full use of them.

Similarly, resilience is a characteristic that can usefully be fostered as part of an ethos of empowerment. Being 'resilient' means being able to bounce back from adversity and, where possible, using the situation as a basis for developing new strengths – 'growing' as a result of the experience. The notion of resilience as part of empowerment helps us to appreciate that people problem solving is not about doing things *to* or *for* people, but rather doing what we can to help them resolve their own difficulties, to draw on their strengths and to use the experience to develop new strengths where possible.

Creative

In the very pressurized work settings in which so many people professionals operate, it is very easy to get into habits and patterns, to get into a rut. This can be very destructive in a number of ways – for example, in the detrimental effect it can have on morale. Another problem that it causes is that such an approach closes off our ability to be creative, to find a range of potential solutions and to explore these together, rather than simply to opt for the first solution that comes to mind.

There is a common stereotype that associates creativity with being artistic. This is misleading as some of the world's greatest scientists have been very creative indeed. Art may indeed involve creativity, but creativity does not need to involve art. Being creative means not getting stuck in ruts and coming up with standard solutions. It involves being able to look carefully at a situation and to be able to generate a number of different outlooks, a number of different ways forward.

Integrated

In many situations, there will be more than one person trying to help. If we are not careful, this can lead to a very fragmented approach, where some people's efforts actually get in the way of, or counteract, the efforts of others. It is therefore important that we adopt an integrated approach – that is, one which takes account of the various issues involved, the various people involved, rather than working in an isolated, fragmented way. This is more easily said than done, but the efforts required to adopt an integrated approach are, none the less, well worth the investment of time and energy involved.

Systematic

Systematic practice is a concept discussed in *People Skills* (Thompson, 2009a). In a nutshell, it refers to the importance of being clear at all times about what we are trying to achieve, how we intend to achieve it and how we will know when we have achieved it. This is very important because, without such a framework, it is very easy for the pressures and demands of the job to push us into a situation where we lose focus, we drift and become prey to a great many distractions. If you are not familiar with the concept of systematic practice, it is highly recommended that you read the relevant chapters in *People Skills*.

Effective

It perhaps goes without saying that there is no point in putting a great deal of time, effort and energy into attempting to resolve problems unless we are to be effective in doing so. The reality of the situation is that some problems, despite our best efforts, cannot be resolved. However, it is vitally important that we 'give it our best shot' and try to make sure that our efforts are as effective as possible. Much of this will come from the accumulation of experience and wisdom. However, there is also much to be gained, even for those of us in the early stages of our people problem-solving careers, to maintain a clear focus on the principles underlying our practice, and make sure that, in being 'PRECISE', we are maximizing the chances of being effective.

What are the challenges involved?

Tackling problems involves coming face to face with certain challenges. Indeed, it could be argued that one of the rewards of being a people problem solver is that there can be great pleasure and satisfaction derived from rising to, and meeting, challenges. In order to understand the complexities of problems and challenges, it can be helpful to divide challenges into three categories: existential, interpersonal and sociopolitical.

Existential challenges

This refers to the type of challenges that we face simply by being human beings, by being in the world and seeking to make sense of it –

our 'spiritual journey', as it were, of finding our way through life and maintaining a thread of meaning through it (Moss, 2005). These involve the challenges of growing up, developing our own identity, finding our place in the world, coping with the anguish or 'angst' involved in transitions and losses, and so on. While these may be experienced differently by different people, they are the sort of challenges that, by and large, we all face as we work our way through life. The emphasis here, then, is on rising to these challenges rather than avoiding them. Existential challenges can generally be seen as crises or turning points in our lives – for example, adolescence. Making the transition from childhood to adulthood may well present us with certain problems, but there are also tremendous gains to be made. Responding to existential challenges, therefore, will often involve trying to make the best of the situation to maximize the positive potential of the crisis (Thompson, 2011b). These are the sort of challenges that we all have to go through at some time or another, and so there is a wealth of wisdom and experience to be drawn on in dealing with these. ,

However, balanced against that, it must be remembered that each of us will experience a crisis in our own personal way. However much we may have in common with others who have experienced similar crises, it still remains our own personal crisis, a unique experience for each of us.

Interpersonal challenges

Based on the theme of 'all action is interaction', as discussed above, we can recognize that many of the challenges we face in life are interpersonal challenges. By this I mean that they arise from our relationships with other people. We live in a social world and this means that other people play an important role in our lives, whether we like it or not. Many problems arise as a result of conflict, and this in turn is frequently due to interpersonal issues. In many cases, helping people to solve their problems involves a large amount of work geared towards managing relationships.

Sociopolitical challenges

These are the types of challenge that arise because of who we are in relation to broader society. They are connected to such matters as 'social location'. This refers to our position in the social hierarchy in terms of power relations connected with, for example, race, class and gender. An example of a sociopolitical challenge would be that of dealing with poverty. We all have the challenge of making ends meet but, for some people, their social circumstances mean that this is a much greater struggle than it is for the majority of other people. Traditional approaches to people and their problems have tended to individualize matters, to focus on what relates to specific unique individuals ('atomism' is the technical term for this tendency to fail to adopt a broader, more holistic approach). And, while recognizing the uniqueness of the individual is clearly important, this also has to be balanced out by recognition that each person is an individual in a social context. We can produce a very distorted perspective on the situation if we ignore the social context, as argued earlier. However, I am not simply reiterating that point here, I am making the related point that often the challenges we encounter are not only experienced in a social context, but *arise from* that context.

PRACTICE FOCUS 1.2

Rachid undertook a project on depression as part of his course. He obtained permission to interview a number of people who attended a mental health day centre and who had been diagnosed as suffering from depression. He felt it would be better in terms of privacy and confidentiality to carry out the interviews in people's own homes rather than at the centre. This proved to be a very significant decision as it meant that Rachid visited the homes of several members of the day centre – and from this he saw for himself the powerful role social circumstances can play in people's problems. He saw evidence of considerable poverty and deprivation, very poor-quality housing, stigma and discrimination, high crime rates and little social cohesion. He began to think that he would be depressed if he lived in circumstances like that. When he discussed the situation with his tutor, the point was emphasized that, in order to understand a person's problems, we need to understand issues relating to the individual *and* to his or her social circumstances, and that we should be careful not to oversimplify by looking at one set of issues without considering the other.

To connect this with another point made earlier, this is another reason why it is important not to adopt a judgemental attitude, as often what are perceived as personal inadequacies on the part of a particular individual may owe more to the social circumstances of that individual than to any personal characteristics.

Is there a problem-solving process?

There is no single, definitive process that should be adhered to rigidly, but this is not to say that there is no common pattern that can be helpful. As I argued earlier, we are dealing with problems, not puzzles, and so there will be a multiplicity of ways in which we can tackle the issues arising and there is no simple right or wrong to this. We are dealing with much more complex issues than that. It is important to emphasize, then, that what I am presenting here is not a dogmatic approach, but rather a set of guidelines based on experience and research which I have found to be useful in my own extensive experience of problem solving and in my equally extensive experience of teaching others how to tackle such problems.

The process I propose can be seen to comprise ten steps. I shall discuss each of them in turn.

1. Information gathering

It is dangerous to try and tackle problems in the dark. We need to have information about key aspects of the situation. We need to gather information about people's perception of the problem(s), their feelings about them and reactions to them, the factors that appear to be significant, and so on. Knowing what information to gather is a skill that takes time to develop. To explore these issues further, a useful starting point would be the chapter on 'Assessment' in *People Skills*.

2. Analysis and problem definition

Gathering information can lead us to a situation where we have a lot of data, but it does not really tell us anything. This is where the analysis comes in. It involves piecing together the relevant bits of information, forming patterns, making sense of what we see. From this, we can then start to engage in the process of problem definition: What precisely is the problem/are the problems? Who is it a problem for? and so on, as discussed earlier. An important pitfall to avoid here is that of drowning in information. This seems to be a characteristic of our modern age – the fact that we have access to so much information. On occasions, problem solvers can cause problems for themselves by gathering so much information that they do not know what to do with it. They fall into the trap of gathering as much information as possible rather than gathering the relevant information they need. Well-developed analytical skills can therefore be seen as an important part of the effective problem solver's repertoire.

3. Identification of strengths and opportunities

It is very easy when dealing with problems to focus predominantly, or even exclusively, on the negatives, to fail to see that situations also involve strengths and opportunities. This is something that will be discussed in more detail in Part Two under the heading of 'SWOT analysis'. However, at this point, it is important to emphasize that we should not allow ourselves to produce an unbalanced assessment of the situation that fails to take account of the positives as well as the negatives.

4. Exploration of possible solutions

Following on from our discussion earlier of the importance of creativity in problem solving, we can note that there is much to be gained from exploring a range of possible solutions, rather than simply opting for the first one that comes to mind. The chances of the first solution that occurs to us being the best one possible are clearly pretty slim. We therefore have to be careful that we do not allow our anxieties to produce a fairly rapid solution to a problem or set of problems and lead us into a situation where we fail to consider other options.

5. Evaluation of possible solutions

Once we have a good understanding of the potential solutions, the next step is to weigh them up, to work out which in the circumstances is likely to be the best way forward (or which combination of solutions is likely to be the most effective). It should be remembered that this evaluation needs to be undertaken in partnership – that is, we need to work together with the people concerned to identify what is likely to work best. It is not simply a matter of our prescribing the cure.

6. Formulation of a plan

Sometimes gathering information about a problem, analysing it, and discussing this with the person concerned, can be enough to free them up to take the initiative and resolve matters. However, this is not always the case and, in many circumstances, what is needed is to formulate a plan of action. Having evaluated the possible solutions, we now need to look at such matters as the timescales involved, who is going to be responsible for what, and so on (this links closely with systematic practice as discussed above). Having a plan is very important because, on the one hand, it helps to maintain a structure and discipline to the work being undertaken – it prevents drift and a lack of focus. On the other hand, it also enables us to monitor progress and to ensure that we are in fact heading in the right direction.

There is no need for the plan to be rigidly adhered to if it is not working, as there is always scope to review the plan. However, at this stage, it is important to map out the route we intend to follow to arrive at the problem resolution. It is unlikely that we will simply arrive there without having first worked out our route plan.

7. Revisiting the information and analysis

Before implementing the plan that we have formulated, we just need to make one further quick check. We need to go back to the information that we gathered and the analysis of it that we performed, partly to reassure ourselves that we have got it right before we start taking important steps forward, and partly to see whether the situation has changed or is changing, as we go through the problem-solving process.

8. Implementing the plan

Once we have reassured ourselves that we have produced the right information and analysis as far as we possibly can in the circumstances, we are now ready to implement the plan, to take the steps identified in that plan in order to work towards our desired outcomes.

9. Monitoring and review

People and circumstances change, and so it is essential that we keep the situation under review. It would be very naïve indeed, and it would also be dangerous, simply to allow situations to move on without keeping a clear focus on whether things are moving in the desired direction. Often, what enables us to be effective problem solvers is that our presence and support can give a sense of confidence and security to the people experiencing the problems. If we fail to monitor and review the situation, then that confidence can be lost. That security can disappear and we can very quickly find ourselves back at square one, having wasted a lot of time, effort and energy. In so doing, we may also have

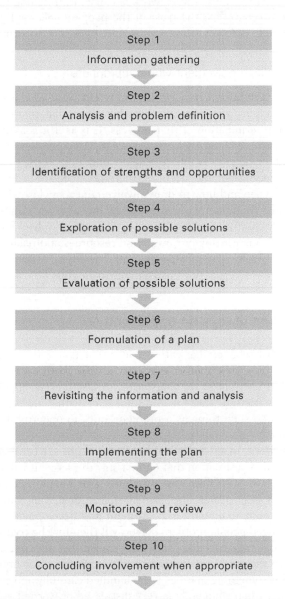

Figure 1.1   Ten steps towards problem solving

'blown it' in terms of any future work because, if, in failing to monitor and review, we have lost the trust of the people concerned, then it is going to be very difficult, if not impossible, to regain that trust.

10. Concluding involvement when appropriate

A very clear trend that I have noticed in works which discuss problem solving or helping processes is that they often fail to mention the conclusion or termination of that process. It is as if it is assumed that work will continue indefinitely. Given our discussions above of empowerment and the need to avoid creating dependency, clearly this is highly problematic. Considerable attention therefore needs to be given to the question of when and how to draw involvement to a close. Timing will be important. We do not wish to withdraw too soon and run the risk of our good work unfurling. Nor do we wish to stay involved longer than is necessary, thus wasting our own time resources and risking creating dependency. How to conclude is also important. There are skills involved in how to bring our involvement to an end.

Is a problem always an opportunity?

You will probably be familiar with the idea that 'there's no such thing as a problem, only an opportunity'. This idea is both inaccurate and dangerous. If we were to say that problems *also* present opportunities, then that is something that I would fully agree with. However, to argue that there is no such thing as a problem, only an opportunity, is naïve in the extreme.

Reference was made earlier to the notion of crisis, a turning point in somebody's life – a situation that cannot stay the same. It will either get better or get worse. Often the problems that people encounter are indeed crises and, as such, they can be quite threatening, but they can also be a gateway to growth, improvement and development. A skilled and experienced people problem solver will therefore be trying to capitalize on problem situations, particularly those that are crises, in order to maximize the positive potential to bring out the silver linings, as it were. This is something that has to be handled carefully and sensitively. For example, when somebody is very distressed or worried about their situation, if we are trying to be positive about the situation in an insensitive, ill-thought through way, we may only serve to alienate that person from us. They may see us as somebody who does not understand what they are going through because we are trying to put a positive gloss on something that they perhaps find acutely painful. We should therefore be wary of tackling these issues in an insensitive way. They call for very careful and sensitive handling.

What is the role of reflective practice?

The final chapter of *People Skills* (Thompson, 2009a) is devoted to the topic of reflective practice. This is an approach to professional practice and management which seeks to avoid the extremes of (i) adopting a mechanistic approach to the use of professional knowledge (research, for example) and (ii) of rejecting the professional knowledge base in favour of a 'common sense' approach. There are two ill-informed and ill-advised schools of thought. There is the school of thought that sees research, theory and professional knowledge more broadly as the source of 'the answers', and adherents of this school are often disappointed because the knowledge base does not tell them precisely what they need to know. It does not give them a clear plan of action to follow. At the other extreme is a school of thought that says 'I prefer to stick to practice', as if research, theory and professional knowledge have got nothing to do with the work they undertake. In between these two dangerous extremes is reflective practice. Reflective practice involves a number of things but for present purposes, I shall concentrate on three in particular; three that are very relevant to this particular book:

1. *Not just using tools mechanistically.* The point was made earlier that the tools provided in Part Two of the book will not do the job for us. They are a means to an end, but they cannot be relied upon to do our work for us. One of the tenets of reflective practice is that we need to act like skilled tailors cutting the cloth of the professional knowledge base to suit the specific measurements and requirements of the garment we are trying to create. That is, we need to draw on the professional knowledge base in such a way that it fits the specific practice realities – the problems we are seeking to solve – as closely as possible.

2. *Art and craft.* Traditional approaches to research and theory have tended to emphasize science and rationality, but the proponents of reflective practice (for example, Schön, 1983) have emphasized the art and craft involved. What this refers to is that the knowledge and

understanding available to us have to be crafted to suit circumstances, just as an artist or a craftsperson has to draw on a set of skills and the benefit of experience in order to produce the desired outcome. But, to return to the point I made earlier, it is important not to confuse the creativity involved with being an actual artist. In parallel fashion, having a degree in science and technology does not make someone into an engineer. It may provide them with much of the core knowledge that they need to be an engineer, but actually achieving the status of an engineer means developing the artistry and the craft skills to be able to use that knowledge in practice. This is very much what reflective practice is about, not simply having the knowledge but having the craft skills to be able to use it appropriately in real-life problem-solving situations, whether we are engineers working with materials and natural substances, or problem solvers in people professions working with people.

3. *Analytical skills.*   The point was made earlier that well-developed analytical skills are an important part of a problem solver's repertoire. This is largely because analysis is a key part of reflective practice. To be a reflective practitioner, we need to be able to make sense of the complex realities we deal with, to be able to cut through the confusion and the indeterminacy, as Schön calls it, of real-life situations. We need to be able to create a picture of what we are dealing with that is sufficiently clear to enable us and the people we are working with to understand the nature of the problems and the possible solutions.

Reflective practice, then, is clearly an important basis for good practice in working with people and their problems.

It is important to recognize that some problems are more difficult than others to solve and that some may not be capable of resolution at all. An important concept to note in this regard is what Clarke and Stewart describe as 'wicked issues':

> Wicked problems ... are those for which there is no obvious or easily found solution. They seem intractable ... . There can be hope that wicked problems will be solved over time, but that requires learning the nature of the problems and of their causes. They require a capacity to derive and design new approaches for their resolution and to learn of their impact. They are likely to be resolved not directly but through an iterative process – learning, trying and learning.
>
> (2003, p. 274)

They go on to comment on how such problems can be addressed:

Tackling wicked issues therefore requires:

- holistic not partial or linear thinking, capable of encompassing the interaction of a wide variety of activities, habits, behaviour and attitudes;
- a capacity to think outside and work across organizational boundaries;
- ways of involving the public in developing responses;
- embracing a willingness to think and work in completely new ways.

While most people will come to this trapped or constrained by conventional organizations, labels and assumptions, what is needed is willingness to entertain the unconventional and pursue the radical.

(p. 275)

The idea of an iterative process plus the notion of being willing to think and work in new ways are both strongly consistent with reflective practice. A reflective approach to the complex, often ingrained problems we so often encounter can therefore be seen as a much better option than a mechanistic approach that seeks to apply a similar formula or that tries to achieve a simple solution. The fact that so many of the 'people problems' we deal with can be seen as 'wicked', in Clarke and Stewart's sense, shows how important it is to adopt an approach premised on reflective practice, especially *critically* reflective practice – that is, practice that does not take situations at face value or fail to see them as part of a wider context (Thompson and Thompson, 2008).

How do we make things happen?

Operacy is a term introduced by Edward de Bono (de Bono, 1983), the writer best known for his work on lateral thinking (1990). He presents it as a term parallel with literacy and numeracy. Literacy refers to the ability to use words to good effect. Numeracy, similarly, refers to the ability to use numbers appropriately. Operacy refers to our actions and is used by de Bono to mean the ability to get things done, to 'make things happen'. While we can never guarantee success in our problem-solving endeavours, we can at least adopt a 'can do' attitude, a positive commitment to achieving the outcomes we seek as far as we reasonably can.

Operacy and a 'can do' attitude are the opposite of the defeatism, cynicism and 'learned helplessness' that is unfortunately far too common in some sectors of the helping professions due to low morale. We are often trying to make progress in very difficult circumstances, perhaps having to struggle by without the resources we need and not receiving the support, appreciation or recognition we deserve, and so it is understandable that there is a tendency to feel cynical and defeatist. However, the fact that it is understandable does not make it acceptable. This is because a negative, defeatist attitude makes it less likely that we will be able to help people solve their problems rather than more. And, as noted above, given that our intervention can actually make people's problems worse in some circumstances, adopting a defeatist attitude is a very dangerous undertaking.

If we are being defeatist or cynical because we are feeling stressed, then I would argue strongly that we are duty bound to take steps to deal with that stress, rather than allow the people we are trying to help lose out because of our own problems.

PRACTICE FOCUS 1.3

Robbie had been in post for just over a year when his enthusiasm started to wane. Within a few months he was at a very low ebb indeed – he had become quite cynical and defeatist. His supervisor should have been in a position to help him tackle the issues, but he too was at a low ebb and they were both part of a culture of cynicism and defeatism that had developed over time. Things came to a head for Robbie when he applied for a post in another department within his office and was not even shortlisted for it. When he sought feedback from the section head in the department he had applied to work in about why he had not been shortlisted, he was told quite clearly and firmly that there was no room in that department for people who were paid to help others with problems, but who appeared to make no attempt to solve their own difficulties.

Conclusion

Part One has covered a wide range of issues, and it could be argued that it has not done justice to any of them. However, my intention here has not been to provide an in-depth exposition of problem solving. That would be far too unrealistic in the space available. Rather, my intention has been to provide an overview which will, it is to be hoped, alert you to some of the complexities involved and give you a framework for developing your studies of problem solving in greater depth and breadth. In this respect, this book parallels *People Skills* (Thompson, 2009a) which provides an introductory overview to a wide range of skills, but does not have the luxury of examining any of them in any great detail. That is a task that must be left to other texts and other occasions.

PART 2

Problem-solving methods

Introduction

This second part of the book contains 88 'tools' – methods or tech niques that can be used to help tackle problems. They are geared towards 'operacy' (see the discussion of this in Part One), Edward de Bono's (1983) notion of 'making things happen'. Achieving our goals often depends on being able to solve problems – for example, removing obstacles to progress. Problem solving, then, is not a peripheral activity – much of what happens in various work settings is about problem solving. So many of these problems are 'people' problems, in the sense that they relate to human factors, such as relationships, emotions and needs. Many of the problems that appear on the surface to be techni cal problems may also have their roots in the 'people' dimension.

No tool is guaranteed to work, but when used skilfully and in the appropriate circumstances, these techniques should significantly increase the chances of success. How you use the tools will be a key factor. To assist you with this, for each of the techniques you should consider the following before putting the ideas into practice:

1. *What are the key ideas?* Are you sure you understand them? It would be dangerous to proceed to using the tool without a proper grasp of the ideas involved. The tools are a means of integrating theory and practice, not a substitute for a good theoretical under standing.
2. *In what circumstances does it apply?* What would make you select this particular item from your toolkit? It is important to match the technique to the circumstances, rather than just rely on trial and error.
3. *In what circumstances would it not apply?* Of course, not all tools will apply in all circumstances. Are there any 'contra-indications' about a particular tool for the issues you are trying to deal with?
4. *What preparation is needed?* Is there anything you need to do or put in place before using this particular method? A good tool used at a bad time could be very problematic. Doing the necessary prepa ration could make all the difference in some cases.

5. *What support is needed?*   Do you have the necessary back up? If you are not very experienced, do you have a more experienced colleague or manager to consult or gain support from? Do not leave yourself unnecessarily vulnerable and unsupported.

6. *What do I need to be wary about?*   Are there any pitfalls to avoid? Forewarned is, of course, forearmed. Avoid getting yourself into difficulties that could have been anticipated (and thus avoided) if you had thought ahead. In using these tools, it is also worth remembering that your role is one of facilitator, in the sense that it is not up to you to solve the problems yourself, but rather to help the people concerned to do so. 'Problem management facilitation' may be a bit of a mouthful, but the reality is that this is what tackling people problems is all about.

It is also worth remembering the role of power and the dangers of discrimination. Whether you are using the tools presented here or any other for that matter, you will need to bear in mind that, whenever we are dealing with people, there is the possibility for discrimination and disadvantage to creep in (see Thompson, 2011a and 2012b for a discussion of these issues). Make sure that, at all times, you are:

- not relying on stereotypes or making assumptions about people;
- not being judgemental;
- looking at the situation from their point of view and not imposing your own;
- taking account of the role of discrimination in people's lives and recognizing that it can be a key factor in the problems people are experiencing;
- valuing difference and diversity – rather than distancing yourself from people because they are in some way different from you; and
- promoting equality by ensuring that everyone is dealt with fairly.

It is likely that, the less experienced you are, the more you will get out of this book, but it is to be hoped that even very experienced practitioners and managers will gain something from it. I anticipate that more experienced readers will gain most benefit when they are feeling 'stuck' with a particular problem. That is, when there is a problem that is exercising their thoughts a great deal, but little or no progress is being made, revisiting the tools here may give fresh insights and offer a way forward.

Each tool has a certain degree of affinity with other tools, and so you will find a link at the end of each description to other tools that have something in common, or an important connection, with the tool concerned.

Important notes

1. Working with children and adolescents

Many of these tools can be used in working with children and adoles-cents – indeed, some of them can be particularly effective when used with children ('Consequences', for example). However, if you work with children and young people, it will be important for you to consider the stage of development of the individual(s) concerned and make a profes-sional judgement about which of these tools are appropriate and in what circumstances. If you are in any doubt, seek the advice of a senior colleague.

2. Caution in using the tools

Owning a saw does not make someone a carpenter. Similarly, knowing about the methods and techniques described here will not necessarily make you competent in using them. They offer helpful insights that can be very useful as a foundation for problem solving, but they will not do the job for us. We will still need to (i) build up our knowledge of the thinking behind the tools (see Part Three); (ii) use the knowledge gained as part of our critically reflective practice; (iii) steadily develop the skills that are needed to be able to use the tools to best effect; (iv) attend relevant training courses where possible; and (v) take the oppor-tunity to learn from others where we can.

Avoiding attribution errors

Avoiding oversimplifying the reasons for people's behaviour

This tool involves recognizing the significance of what are known as 'attribution errors' and showing how they can cause problems rather than help to solve them.

It is important to recognize that, generally speaking, things tend to happen due to a combination of reasons, rather than as a result of one single cause. To use the technical term we would say that events are 'multifactorial'. In other words, it is generally the case that there will be a variety of factors that contribute to a particular outcome, rather than one single, definitive one. Some factors will relate to the person(s) concerned in the situation (known as 'dispositional' factors), while others will relate to the circumstances that are, to a certain extent at least, beyond the control of the individual(s) involved (the situational factors). Examples of dispositional factors would be particular choices or decisions made, the level of commitment to seeking a particular outcome, and so on, while an example of circumstances that contribute to a particular situation would be the actions of other people over which we will have no control and often little influence.

An important concept drawn from the psychological literature is the 'fundamental attribution error'. This refers to the tendency for us to choose one or other set of factors (dispositional or situational), rather than understand their combination and their interaction. That is, instead of recognizing that dispositional and circumstantial factors will interact and together produce a certain outcome, we can have a bias towards one set of factors rather than the other. For example, someone who is likely to focus on personal factors may play down the significance of circumstantial issues, thereby potentially being very unfair to the individual concerned, placing more responsibility on their shoulders than should be the case. This unfairness would perhaps have been avoided if a fuller understanding of the situation had developed which took account of the wider circumstances. However, the error can also go in the opposite direction, in the sense that some people can focus on the circumstantial factors and ignore the personal factors. They can put situations down to just bad luck or just 'one of those things' without recognizing the contribution made by particular actions (or inactions) on the part of a particular person.

What is very common is for the fundamental attribution error to apply differently depending on whether we are talking about ourselves or others. So, for example, it is very easy to play down our own role in a situation and emphasize the circumstantial factors perhaps by saying something like: 'It wasn't my fault; it was because of circumstances beyond my control', whereas we may be more likely to attribute the behaviour of others to causes associated with dispositional factors: 'They didn't try hard enough'; 'They weren't competent'; 'They weren't committed', and so on, without giving full attention to the role of wider circumstances.

The reason it is important to be aware of this issue is that it can have two sets of unwelcome circumstances. First of all, it can mean that people are failing to take ownership. They are failing to recognize what part in a situation is the net result of their own choices, actions or inactions. This can be seen as a form of bad faith where we are denying responsibility for the part we may be playing in a situation. Second, there is also the set of problems relating to the unfairness involved in focusing on someone else's contribution to a situation without taking account of the wider circumstances, in so far as such a narrow focus is likely to be unduly harsh. It is therefore important that, in our understanding of problem situations, we cover both aspects: the person and the situation and do not choose between them. In this way, we can develop a holistic approach, one that sees the big picture and is not distorted by focusing on one aspect of the situation at the expense of other, equally important aspects.

Being aware of the significance of the fundamental attribution error can be a useful way forward in terms of problem solving. It can be used as an explicit tool of analysis, in so far as it can enable us to weigh up both sides. This would involve the worker engaging with the individual(s) concerned to identify which factors were within their control and which were not so, that a more balanced view of the situation is arrived at.

▶ **Challenging cognitive distortions** ▶

Avoiding avoidance
Facing up to our responsibilities

'Avoidance behaviour' is an important concept in the world of tackling people problems. This is because the sorts of problems that people encounter often generate a degree of anxiety, and that anxiety can lead people to try to avoid circumstances they face rather than to tackle them. Avoidance behaviour can take two main forms. First of all, there is direct avoidance behaviour. This is where we know something is problematic for us and we deliberately steer clear of it. In some circumstances that can be a very healthy and helpful way of dealing with the issues. However, in a wide range of other circumstances, this can be problematic because it means that we do not actually engage in problem-solving behaviours, and so the problem persists, perhaps getting worse over time.

The second type of avoidance behaviour is denial. This is where we try to deceive ourselves into thinking that there is no problem. This is sometimes referred to as the ostrich approach – putting our head in the sand and hoping that, if we cannot see the problem, then it cannot exist. Naïve though this approach may be, it is none the less very common. What tends to happen in such circumstances is that the problem situation creates anxiety and we deal with that anxiety by putting some distance between ourselves and whatever it is that is raising the anxiety in the first place. One very sad thing to note about denial is that, ironically, it can lead to situations where people who could have helped us will not help us, because they are, in effect, taken in by our denial. If we deny that there is a problem and somebody who could have helped us to resolve the problem accepts our denial, then we have missed the opportunity of perhaps gaining some very valuable help.

As we shall see later in the discussion of 'Know your enemy', it is helpful to translate generalized anxiety into specific fears, and this can certainly be a good way of 'avoiding avoidance'. However, there are other means of doing so.

One potentially very effective way of tackling avoidance behaviour is through sharing. As anxiety is a significant factor in the root cause of avoidance behaviour, then anxiety can best be tackled jointly. This could apply in terms of joining with the anxious person in a shared endeavour to deal with the issues affecting them. This may give them the confidence to go beyond avoidance. However, this can also be done through developing mutual support systems. For example, we could consider bringing together a number of people who share the same problem, so that they feel more confident in tackling issues together. This is the basis of support groups (see 'Brokerage').

In trying to deal with avoidance behaviour, it is important that we consider it at three levels. First of all, we need to ask, 'Am I doing it?' Being a problem solver does not make us immune to this difficulty. There may be aspects of the work we do that we feel uncomfortable with and that we will avoid if possible. If that is the case, then we need to ask ourselves: 'Is this helping me or is it hindering me?'; 'Is my development being hampered by the fact that I feel uncomfortable about facing up to certain issues?' We may then need to consider adopting a problem-solving approach ourselves to look at what steps we need to take to get over this type of unhelpful avoidance behaviour.

We also need to ask the question, 'Is the person I'm trying to help doing it?' If the answer is yes, then we need to look carefully at what steps we can take to help them avoid falling into this trap. We should handle this very carefully, as avoidance may be acting as a form of crutch and, while it is not healthy to rely on crutches in the long run, taking away somebody's crutch before they feel confident to walk unaided could prove disastrous. They may need to be weaned off it, rather than have it taken away in what could come across as a fairly brutal attack – even if this is certainly not what we intended.

The third question we need to ask is, 'Is the group of people doing it?' As we shall discuss in more detail below, there is an important psychological concept known as 'groupthink' (Janis, 1982). This refers to the tendency of groups of people to develop like-minded thinking to the extent that it becomes strongly established as part of their culture, even though such thinking may at times be unhelpful. For example, one member of a group may be thinking that the course of action that has been agreed is not a good one, but is reluctant to say so because being part of the group is more important than making the right choice of action. In this respect the group bonding, as it were, becomes problematic. People become reluctant to challenge any aspect of the group's thinking or actions for fear of disrupting the group – for fear of being seen as a potential outsider to the group. Groupthink commonly manifests itself as avoidance behaviour. That is, a whole group of people may be avoiding something important and, while certain individuals within the group may recognize the danger of this, they do not raise it because of the power of groupthink.

An important consideration when looking at avoiding avoidance is whether what is being avoided is something that can actually be dealt with. This is an important consideration because, in some circumstances, it is quite appropriate to avoid certain things, because there is nothing we can do about them and if we engage with them, they are likely to do us harm. For example, if we know that going to a certain part of a certain town late at night is likely to lead to violence, then avoiding being there is actually quite wise and is certainly not a problem to be solved. The key question to ask, therefore, is, 'Is that which is being avoided something that can be dealt with?' In other words, are people missing out on potential progress by not being prepared to face up to the problems that they are experiencing?

This is a very important tool because, if we are not careful, we can undermine everything that follows. That is, the other 87 tools presented here will be of little value if avoidance behaviour means that people are not prepared to address the problems they face. If we want to make a success of people problem solving, then we have to become very competent at 'avoiding avoidance'. We need to be very wary of this significant danger of trying to distance ourselves from the issues that are causing harm. We need, over time, to develop fairly in-depth knowledge and a set of skills to help us ensure that avoidance is not part of our own work; is not something that is preventing progress for individuals whom we are trying to help, and is not a characteristic of groups or teams that can cause them major difficulties.

▶ **Consequences** ▶ **Risk assessment** ▶

Brainstorming

Maximizing our range of options

The basic idea behind brainstorming is that, by listening to as many creative solutions as possible, we can break free from our usual constraints and limitations (of thought and habit) when looking for solutions.

It is important to note that there are two myths associated with brainstorming. The first one is that the term itself is not 'politically correct' – see Thompson (2011c) for my views about this misunderstanding. The second myth is a more serious one. It is based on the idea that brainstorming is simply a matter of making a list of potentially workable solutions and then choosing the way forward from that list. In reality, it is much broader than this (and both much more fun and much more effective).

The process does indeed involve listing as many solutions as possible, but it does not matter whether they are workable or otherwise. Participants in this activity should be as fanciful as they like – outrageous even. The idea is that, by coming up with as many solutions as possible without respecting the boundaries of what is feasible, we are able to move beyond the tramlines which can hold us back. In this way, the process may be able to produce, first, directly sensible, feasible ways forward from among the range of possible solutions which will include not so sensible feasible ones; or, second, the process can produce potential solutions which are not in themselves workable, but which trigger off a line of thought that can lead to sensible ideas that could subsequently work.

The approach can be used in three main ways:

1. It could be used by an individual worker to explore the range of ways forward to try and find a breakthrough in a difficult situation where it has so far been impossible to provide any sort of way of progressing the issues concerned.

2. The second way is to involve one or more other persons (including family members), so that the group of people together can work on developing as wide a range of potential solutions as possible.
3. The third possibility is for this technique to be used with a team or group of people. For example, it could use a flip chart to act as the focal point for recording ideas. This is something that can be used occasionally, as part of a team meeting, team development awayday or possibly as part of a training course. It can also be used by workers who are operating on the basis of a group work model, so that the problem-solving methods are not simply based on individual interactions, but also on operating as part of a group process.

The brainstorming process involves five different sections or steps:

1. In working with other people in producing a brainstorming outcome, it is important to begin by explaining the rationale behind the process so that they do not fall foul of the common misassumption that it is simply a matter of listing potentially sensible solutions.
2. List as many potential solutions as possible, allowing the imagination to run wild and having no boundaries in terms of what counts as a way forward and what does not.
3. Once this part has been completed, move on to eliminate the unworkable solutions that have appeared on the list, but not before you have considered whether they could lead to realistic ways forward. In other words, although you may not be adopting the unworkable options, they may give insights that can lead to options which, in themselves, could potentially be useful.
4. Prioritize the remaining potential solutions and consider combining elements of some of them to provide a way forward that was not considered as part of the brainstorming exercise itself, but which has emerged from the analysis of the results of that exercise.
5. From the remaining prioritized list of potential solutions, plan how best to move forward.

When used properly, this can be a very useful way of mapping out the potential solutions to a problematic situation and can help us to break free from the restrictions of our dominant ways of thinking.

▶ **Encouraging creativity** ▶ **Lateral thinking** ▶

Brokerage
Redirecting people to sources of help

A longstanding tradition in the human services is the idea that the greatest tool that any professional worker has available to them is their own self. Hence the notion discussed below of use of self as a tool in its own right (see 'Modelling and use of self'). However, what is important for us to realize is that, beyond ourselves as a resource, we could have access to a vast range of other resources, in principle at least. Just as an insurance broker does not provide insurance services him- or herself, a 'people problems broker' can look for access to a wide range of other services or resources that may be very helpful in dealing with the problems being addressed.

In order to be able to use brokerage to good effect, we have to be able to move away from the assumption that we are responsible for solving other people's problems. We are, as mentioned earlier, 'problem-solving management facilitators'. This means that we share with others the responsibility for solving problems and, at the end of the day, the ultimate responsibility for a problem lies with the person who is experiencing it. We all have our own lives to lead. We must therefore not become precious about the problems we are trying to help people to solve. In many situations, there may well be others who are far better placed to deal with the issues than we are. Our challenge, then, is twofold: first, to be able to recognize those situations where someone else may be better suited to helping; second, to be able to make the necessary referral (with the consent of the individual concerned, of course) or to redirect the individual concerned.

Naturally, in order to be able to do this, we have to have a knowledge of what other resources and possibilities are available. This does not mean that we are expected to have an encyclopaedic knowledge of the possibilities available, but we should at least know the basics and, just as importantly, know how to find out more. Do we know what sources of help are available in our area? Do we know who offers what and do we know how to find out – how to fill the gaps in our knowledge?

Help with problems can come from a variety of sources. Consider, for example, the following:

- *Within the workplace.* Sources of help here would include perhaps employee assistance programmes, occupational health and trade union support.

- *The statutory sector.*   Government bodies such as social services and the health service can provide a range of services that could be very helpful in certain circumstances.
- *The voluntary sector.*   There is a huge network of voluntary organizations ranging quite considerably in size and scope. All, however, have as their basic *raison d'être* a commitment to addressing particular problems.
- *The private sector.*   There are various organizations that offer problem-solving help in one form or another, for a fee.
- *Informal sources of support.*   This would include help from family, friends, colleagues and so on.

A very common obstacle to people using the help that is available to them is the notion of stigma. Often this is misguided. For example, there is a common assumption that someone who receives counselling is in some way mentally disturbed or inadequate. Similarly, some people feel that if they accept help from a voluntary body (Relate, for example), then this somehow makes them a 'charity case'. Part of a brokerage role may therefore be clearing up any misconceptions or stereotypes about the nature of the help that can be offered and what accepting such help would actually mean.

Another important part of brokerage is making sure that, in referring or redirecting someone to another source of help, appropriate information is communicated. For example, I have come across a number of cases where someone has made a referral to a particular helping agency, but has not made it clear how significant or pressing the problem is, only for the agency receiving the referral to put it at the bottom of their priority list, often with disastrous consequences. We cannot blame another agency for not acting appropriately or sufficiently swiftly when we have not given them sufficient information to make it clear what is required in the circumstances.

In the spirit of partnership, as discussed in Part One, it is important that the person we are trying to help is fully aware of what we are proposing and is fully in agreement with it. Initial reluctance or resistance may need to be overcome through further discussion and clarification but, at the end of the day, it is pointless trying to make a referral to another source of help without the commitment of the person concerned, as clearly any such efforts will be doomed to failure if the individual concerned is not committed to making it work.

Another danger to be aware of in undertaking a brokerage role is the pitfall of what could be described as fobbing people off. If we do not take our brokerage role seriously, it can be perceived by the person who has asked for our help as a case of fobbing them off, simply redirecting them to another source of help because we cannot be bothered to deal with the situation ourselves. As you can imagine, this can lead to a great deal of ill-feeling and can cause a number of problems. It is therefore important, when we feel it is appropriate to refer somebody on to another source of support, that we make it perfectly clear what we are doing and why we are doing it, and do not leave that person with the impression that we are deflecting them on to somebody else.

▶ **Educating** ▶ **Giving feedback** ▶

Capitalizing on crisis

Realizing the potential of critical moments in a person's life

Crisis intervention is a longstanding, well-established approach in the caring professions in general, and mental health services in particular. It is based on what is known as crisis theory. The key elements of crisis theory are as follows:

1. A crisis is a turning point in somebody's life. It refers to a situation that may get better or may get worse, but it will not stay the same.
2. At a time of a crisis, the people involved are more likely to take steps that can have a significant impact on their situation. That is, somebody who is not in a crisis may be resistant to change but, when a crisis arises, he or she is likely to be more willing to take steps to alleviate or resolve the situation.
3. Because of (2) above, individuals in crisis can be very vulnerable to external influences and may need protecting from harmful influences – for example, people who may be seeking to exploit them in some way.
4. A crisis can generate a considerable amount of emotional energy. This energy can be positive and constructive or negative and destructive, depending on how it is managed by the individual concerned and the influence of others involved.
5. Where an individual is in crisis, he or she is likely to need help sooner rather than later. This is because the crisis situation is likely to be short term (crises by their very nature are short-term events) and opportunities could be missed to make changes to factors within the problem situation that perhaps gave rise to the crisis.

(based on Thompson, 2011b)

The idea of capitalizing on crisis is based on the fact that people are more willing to make changes to their life and circumstances during the crisis than they might otherwise be. For example, somebody who is not very assertive, and who has experienced significant difficulties in their life because of this lack of assertion, may become more assertive in a crisis as if the emotional energy generated propels them forward. Similarly, somebody who is normally resistant to taking advice from others, perhaps in the arrogant view that no one has anything they can teach them, is likely to be more willing to listen to what others have to say when experiencing a crisis.

A very important issue here is keeping a clear focus on our role as a problem solver. We have to remember that our task is to help the individual, or individuals, concerned to deal with their problems. If we lose this focus, we can very easily exploit the individuals concerned by trying to use the crisis to manoeuvre them into a position that is more convenient or beneficial for us. We have to be very careful that we do not fall into the trap of kicking somebody while they are down. Helping some body in crisis is a matter of trust. If that individual is prepared to accept help, then we have to be very careful to ensure that we do not abuse the trust involved. It takes a lot of courage for somebody to ask for help, and we should be careful to ensure that we do not exploit that courage inappropriately.

The basic idea behind crisis intervention is that we do, indeed, capitalize on the crisis; that we use the energy generated to move in a positive direction to resolve difficulties, make progress and, it is to be hoped, achieve an outcome that is an improvement on the original situation. Practice focus 2.1 illustrates this.

Timing is very important in capitalizing on crisis. By its very nature, a crisis is a temporary event. If an individual is going through a crisis, then it is likely that some sort of resolution will be achieved in a relatively short period of time. However, if we are not careful, that resolution will be a negative outcome rather than a positive one. This is because the tension involved in being in crisis can often lead people to taking inappropriate, unhelpful or counterproductive steps in order to get themselves out of it. This may have the effect of making the situation worse or, at least, perpetuating the problem. A crisis, in itself, will therefore not guarantee a positive outcome. The task of the problem solver is to analyse the situation carefully and look at how the positive energy generated can be used to make progress. If we are too slow to respond to the crisis, we may find that we have, in effect, missed the boat – that the person concerned has already taken perhaps inappropriate steps to resolve the situation.

One final point to note in relation to crisis intervention is that we have to make sure that we receive adequate support ourselves. Sometimes, helping somebody through a major crisis in their life can place immense pressures on us. If we do not have adequate support systems in place, we run the risk of entering a crisis ourselves because the sometimes intense heat of the crisis moment can be too much for us to bear when added to our existing life pressures. Self-care is therefore an important part of capitalizing on crisis.

PRACTICE FOCUS 2.1

Kim had been struggling to deal with the conflicts in her team for some time and was beginning to wonder whether she would ever reach the point of having a team that pulled together instead of pulling apart. When it was announced that there would be a reorganization and her team might be disbanded, the team members were very shocked. To Kim's amazement, team members started to put their differences to one side and began to look at how they could campaign to retain their team identity in the new organizational structure.

Kim was able to capitalize on the crisis by getting the team to pull together to justify their existence in order to safeguard their future. She was delighted to see people who had been 'daggers drawn' previously were now working closely together in response to the crisis situation.

▶ **Finding the growth zone** ▶ **Promoting realism** ▶ **Providing an anchor** ▶

The CBC approach

Putting people at their ease

This stands for 'chat – business – chat', and it a useful basis for communicating with people in a way that maximizes our chances of engaging with them effectively. If interactions are too formal for people to 'connect' as human beings, a significant price can be paid, not least the following:

- *Unnecessary tension.* Being too formal can put everyone on edge and act as a barrier to people communicating openly with one another.
- *Distraction.* If people feel uncomfortable because of the level of formality, then their attention may wander; they will be distracted by this and therefore not get the full benefit of the communication taking place.
- *Mistrust and suspicion.* If there is a high degree of formality, then people may be wondering why that is so, why that is necessary, rather than a more relaxed and friendly approach, and are therefore likely to become suspicious. In this way, too much formality can be a significant barrier to moving forward in partnership.

As a result of these problems, too much formality can get in the way of rapport-building and is therefore a poor basis for partnership (see the **P** of PRECISE practice in Part One).

On the other hand, if interactions are too informal, then there is a danger that they will tend to be too unfocused and descend into an aimless, unfocused chat. This can be problematic for a number of reasons:

- A chat does not achieve what the interaction was intended to achieve and can therefore leave both parties feeling frustrated by the failure to make progress.
- It can also leave people confused and wondering 'What was that all about'?
- It can also create suspicion 'Were they checking up on me'?
- The worker can also 'lose the plot' and end up wasting a great deal of time, which is both ineffective (that is, fails to achieve its goals) and inefficient (resulting in a waste of resources). This reflects the **S** of PRECISE practice – the need to be *systematic* (that is, clear and focused).

The CBC approach is a useful framework for avoiding these problems. It takes the following pattern:

– Chat –

This involves establishing a rapport, connecting person to person, taking an interest and putting people at their ease. It should be just a short period of informal conversation to create a relaxed atmosphere.

– Business –

This entails focusing on the reason for the interaction, getting down to business as it were. It involves clarifying concerns, what needs to change and so on. This is where the main elements of the discussion take place.

– Chat –

This involves rounding off the interaction with more of the informal conversation that helps to cement the working relationship and to build trust. It also adds a pleasant note to the proceedings, which can be helpful to both parties.

Following this pattern can be a very helpful way of avoiding the extremes of too much formality or too much informality. Beginning with chat to create a relaxed atmosphere and begin to build rapport, followed by a business-like focus on the main issues that need to be discussed, and then concluding with a little bit more chat to cement the relationship. This process can offer significant benefits if it is used skilfully and not just in a mechanistic sort of way.

The approach reflects the ideas of Carl Rogers (1960) in terms of, first of all, 'genuineness': if we come across as genuine people with an authentic interest in the person we are communicating with, we are much more likely to form a positive rapport and helpful bond with them than if we just simply stick to business. Rogers' idea of 'unconditional positive regard' is also important here. It means that, regardless of any difficulties that the person may have presented which may lead other people to disapprove of them or their behaviour, by being prepared to be civil and friendly to that person, we create the opportunity to focus on the main issues, enabling us to move forward in terms of being able to address the problems involved.

This approach can work on a one-to-one basis – person to person, that is. It can also be helpful in terms of a working with groups (including families), and is also potentially very beneficial for meetings. Whichever way it is used, it has excellent potential for being a very effective contribution to our problem-solving toolkit.

▶ **Modelling and use of self** ▶ **SOLER** ▶ **Tuning in** ▶

Challenging cognitive distortions

Trying to get a balanced view of the situation

This is an extension of the idea of the fundamental attribution error discussed earlier. It is a tool that helps practitioners to gently challenge distorted understandings, so that a clearer picture of the situation can be established.

What I mean by a cognitive distortion is a type of thinking that leads to situations being poorly understood because there is some process of distortion going on. A particular aspect may be receiving more attention than it deserves, resulting in other aspects being ignored. The net result can be that an unhelpful picture of the situation emerges, and people within the problem scenario can find themselves struggling to move forwards because their understanding of the situation is so unhelpful.

To illustrate this I am going to discuss four particular forms of cognitive distortion that can be helpfully challenged by problem solvers.

Unrealistic expectations

Some people can have expectations of a situation that are highly unlikely to be realized. This can be for a variety of reasons, but the outcome tends to be the same: the sense of disappointment and frustration. One thing that can be very helpful in this regard is the practice of 'setting out our stall' (Thompson, 2009a). This refers to the process of making it clear to people what we can and cannot do so that, if the people we are trying to help do have unrealistic expectations of what we can do to help them, then the opportunity to negotiate around these expectations is created by having a conversation about what can and cannot be achieved in the circumstances.

There can be two aspects to the process of working with unrealistic expectations. One relates to a lack of understanding on the part of the person(s) we are trying to help. For example, somebody may have unrealistic expectations because they have insufficient information on which to build up a picture of what they could realistically expect. In those circumstances, it should be relatively straightforward to use our negotiation skills to clarify what is, and what is not, realistic in the circumstances. The second type of problem associated with unrealistic expectations is when they are used as a deliberate negotiation tactic on somebody's part. For example, if a person expects to receive a particular service at a particular level, then by trying to claim it at a much higher level, they may feel that they are more likely to get what they want through a process of negotiation. This can be more difficult to deal with, but it follows the same pattern in terms of setting out our stall, in the sense that what needs to happen is for clarity to be established about the boundaries of what is possible.

Paranoia

This refers to situations where people have an unduly negative perception of the situation in terms of the threats involved. That is, they are tending to exaggerate the dangers posed to them by a particular set of circumstances. This is often associated with depression and/or low self-esteem. When people are faced with the challenges of depression and the related problems of low self-esteem, then it is not uncommon for a degree of paranoia to be present. Associated with this as well is the fact that people who have been abused at some point in their life are less likely to trust others than people who have not experienced any form of abuse. That level of mistrust can also at times result in a degree of paranoia. There can also be a combination of factors in the sense that abuse can be a source of depression which then, in itself, can, as we have already noted, contribute to paranoia. What is important in such situations is helping people to get some degree of perspective on a situation, to see things in proportion. Simply reassuring somebody that there is nothing to worry about is unlikely to be of much help to them. What is likely to be more useful is to discuss the potential dangers in a situation and put these in a context which enables the person concerned to get a more realistic perspective on the hazards involved.

In terms of paranoia, however, it is important that we should not confuse justified suspicion with paranoia. We need to emphasize the importance of empathy. We have to be able to understand situations from a person's point of view so that what seems to us superficially like irrational paranoia, from that person's point of view may actually be a well-justified degree of suspicion and mistrust. We therefore have to be careful not to be judgemental and regard paranoia as some sort of deficit in a person, rather than understand that often fears will be quite genuine in the circumstances.

Cynicism and defeatism

It is understandable that people who have experienced a number of problems, often of an entrenched nature, over a long period of time may become cynical and defeatist. This is often shown by comments like 'I've tried that' whenever a way forward is suggested, as if they are trying to block any form of progress. This can be a very difficult approach to challenge, but it comes back to the same process of establishing clarity about what is realistic and what is not. This may take time to establish if somebody has an entrenched defeatist attitude. What can sometimes be of use is to get across the point that cynicism tends in itself to be a reflection of a problem or set of problems and, as such, can create a vicious circle. That is, the more cynical a person becomes as a result of their problems, the more they can become locked into those problems.

It is important to differentiate between cynicism on the one hand, and scepticism on the other. Being sceptical involves feeling that a certain amount of confirmation is needed before the person concerned is able to trust whoever is trying to help them sufficiently to enable movement forward. Cynicism, by contrast, is where that healthy degree of scepticism has been overtaken by an undue degree of negativity which is, in effect, not seeking confirmation and trust before being able to move forward, but ruling out the possibility of trust and moving forward. Scepticism says: 'Proceed with caution', whereas cynicism says: 'What's the point of proceeding when it's not going to work anyway?'.

Magical thinking

This is a form of thinking that is normally associated with children. It is characterized by the idea that, if we want something to happen enough, then just wanting it so badly will make it happen. This is clearly an illogical or irrational point of view, but unfortunately it is not uncommon among adults as well as children. It is as if the person concerned is waiting for somebody to solve the problem for them, as if the worker, for example, has some sort of magic wand and will just make the situation better without any effort on that person's part. It reflects the problem identified earlier in relation to attribution errors, namely the unwillingness to take ownership of our actions. It is quite common for people to be desperately unhappy about their situation and to want intensely for the situation to improve, but not actually take any steps to bring that about. It is as if they are paralysed by their anxiety in terms of how they should approach what can, of course, be a very scary situation, which is taking the first steps towards resolving our problems. So, to challenge magical thinking we need to be able to get across the message clearly, but gently and constructively, that steps need to be taken, as simply wanting the situation to improve – however badly we may want that – is not going to be enough on its own.

Challenging cognitive distortions can be demanding work, and there will be different levels of success in the sense that, in some situations, progress can be achieved fairly easily, while in others there may be a long and hard job to persuade someone to give up a distorted view of the situation. Cognitive behavioural therapy is often used as a way of challenging such distortions, but it is not the only way of tackling this problem. The tool of challenging cognitive distortions can therefore be seen as a potentially very helpful one, even if at times it may be difficult to put into practice.

▶ **Avoiding attribution errors** ▶ **Negotiating expectations** ▶

Chunk up or chunk down

Finding the right level of analysis

This rather strange-sounding tool comes from the world of neuro-linguistic programming (NLP). It has similarities with helicopter vision. According to this technique, there are two basic ways of focusing: broad and narrow. To switch from narrow to broad is referred to as chunking up; from broad to narrow as chunking down. To switch from big chunk thinking to small chunk thinking (chunking down), means moving away from the broad issues towards the finer detail. The opposite, chunking up, involves not getting bogged down in detail and trying to see how these details connect together to form a broader mosaic. It is not a question of deciding which is the 'correct' level of analysis, the broader issues versus the finer detail, but rather the ability and flexibility to switch between the two as appropriate.

Things can go wrong and our efforts can fail if we are looking at the wrong level at the wrong time. Part of the skill of high-quality people work is the ability to be able to recognize when it is appropriate to look at the broader issues and when it is appropriate to concentrate on the finer detail. It is not enough to focus on one at the expense of the other – we need the breadth of both. An approach that focuses on the wider issues, without concentrating on the significance of detail, can lead to disaster if one of those details happens to be crucial in determining the outcome of particular actions in a particular direction. Conversely, if we concentrate on details, we may not appreciate the way those details fit together into a significant pattern (as per 'Helicopter vision' below).

The ability to switch between the two levels and, just as importantly, to recognize when it is appropriate to do so, is an essential task of the people worker's repertoire. Sometimes we can be influenced by others in this regard. We may be working with someone, for example, who prefers to stick to the finer detail, who likes to have all the t's crossed and the i's dotted, and this can hold us back from looking at the broader picture. Alternatively, we may be working with somebody who is a big-picture person, as it were, and who is reluctant to focus on precise detail, perhaps because there are particular details that he or she wishes to avoid (because they are painful, for example) or simply because that particular person finds it tedious to look at detail and is eager to remain at a broad level and continue trying to make progress without getting bogged down in detail. The trick, then, is getting the balance between the two. This is something that can be developed, over time, through experience and a focus on reflective practice – that is, analysing carefully how we tend to operate, making sure that we are switching between levels when we should be doing so. In other words, we are making every effort to learn from our experience and develop our skills in this particular area.

As with so many other tools, this one can be used at a number of different levels. For example, it can be used in working with teams. I have come across situations where certain teams tend to focus on the minutiae of particular issues. Particular concerns can dominate at the expense of looking at the overall situation. Sometimes these details are very important but if the team are not careful, they can be very destructive and counterproductive because the detail tends to obscure an understanding of the overall picture. By converse, it is also possible to have teams who, for example, hold meetings where they agree matters in broad outline, but do not discuss the detail of how this is going to be implemented. Consequently, it is quite possible that the agreement will never come to fruition because, although broad agreement was reached, nothing has happened to ensure that it is translated into specific action points that facilitate implementation. Both these problems – a focus on the smaller chunks and a focus on the bigger chunks

– are unfortunately very common. A good people worker can be very helpful in supporting groups of staff in developing the flexibility necessary to switch between levels and not get stuck at either of them.

▶ **Eating an elephant** ▶ **Helicopter vision** ▶ **Mind mapping** ▶

The CIA framework
Managing pressure and stress

This is a tool that is especially helpful in preventing stress from arising, or for helping people get out of difficult situations once stress has already managed to become established in that particular set of circumstances. The CIA framework is an extension of development of the 'Serenity prayer', which suggests that we should change what we can change and accept what we cannot change. The CIA framework is a more sophisticated version of this.

C stands for control, **I** for influence and **A** for acceptance. The basic idea is that, in everything we do, there will be things that we can control, things that we cannot control but we can perhaps influence, and things that we can neither control nor influence and must ultimately accept. The theory behind the CIA framework is that if we do not assign the tasks we face to the appropriate category, then we are likely to experience unnecessary additional pressures that can lead to harmful stress. Let us look at each of the three elements in turn.

There is much in our life that we can control. However, if we do not control what is ultimately within our control, we run the risk of experiencing problems. An interesting and significant point to note here is that often the sphere of what we can control is much greater than people generally realize. People often feel uncomfortable about taking charge of particular issues and say 'I can't', when perhaps what they really mean is: 'I choose not to'. This can be very significant in people work from both sides of the fence, as it were. If the people we are seeking to help adopt this 'I can't' argument for things that they can actually control, then they will be closing off possible avenues of progress. They will be limiting themselves unnecessarily and perhaps thereby sustaining the problems they are experiencing. But for those of us involved in problem-solving work, failure to recognize what we can control can also be very problematic. It, too, can lead to avenues to progress being blocked off unnecessarily. We should therefore not be too hasty in deciding that certain things are beyond our control. If push came to shove, if we were really under pressure, could we actually control that particular thing? If we could control it in extreme circumstances, then why can't we control it in general circumstances? What is stopping us?

There are many things that we cannot control, but we can perhaps influence – other people, for example. Except for very extreme circumstances, one person cannot control the behaviour of another person, but it is a daily occurrence for people's behaviour to be influenced by the actions and attitudes of other people. We therefore need to ask ourselves, of those factors that are beyond my control, is there some way in which I can influence them? Again, there are two sides to this. We can help other people to look at what they can influence to change circumstances they are currently encountering, but we must also make sure that we practise what we preach in terms of looking at how we can influence the situations that we ourselves are part of. The point was made in Part One that there is a danger that problem solvers can become part of a culture of defeatism, cynicism and learned helplessness. Where such a culture exists, or even a tendency in that direction, it can result in things that can be influenced not being influenced because of this attitude of pessimism.

For those things that we cannot control, and we either cannot influence or have chosen not to influence for whatever reason (exhaustion after years of trying, for example), the only option, then, is acceptance. If we cannot control or influence a situation, then clearly we have to accept it. However, it may take time for people to come to terms with this. It can be similar to a process of grieving, to let go of our hopes of resolving a situation and accept that it is not going to change.

Pressure can be increased, perhaps resulting in harmful levels of stress where we are unsuccessful in assigning the challenges we face to the appropriate category of CIA. For example, if there are things that we can control, but fail to do so, then we can experience increased levels of pressure. If I am in control of communicating important information to a particular person, but do not do so, then I must accept the consequences of that, and this may well add to the pressures that I face. If there are things that I could influence, but do not attempt to, then, as indicated earlier, I am unnecessarily limiting myself and cutting off possible solutions. For example, if somebody's behaviour is causing me distress, but they are unaware of this, then my failure to raise the issue tactfully and assertively with them could lead to a vicious circle whereby my distress is increased, resulting in greater reluctance to address the issue, thus resulting in greater distress, and so on.

In terms of acceptance, this too can be problematic when people do not accept what ultimately they have to. Notwithstanding the transition period often required, as mentioned earlier, people can create a great deal of worry, anxiety and ill-feeling by becoming stuck in between, on the one hand, control and influence and, on the other, acceptance. That is, they are neither controlling nor influencing, but nor are they accepting. They may be raging against a particular set of circumstances and this can become a dangerous situation in which they are trapped in a cycle that generates aggression outwardly or turns inwards as depression. Sometimes, these issues can be so complex that particular individuals may need professional help in dealing with them. However, this does not alter the fact that most of us, most of the time, should be able to make sure that we:

- control what we can control;
- influence what we can influence; and
- accept those things that we can neither control nor influence.

Once again, this is a tool that can be used at different levels:

- as an individual, self-awareness, self-help tool;
- as a tool of intervention with others who are experiencing difficulty in managing their pressures; or
- as an exercise with a group.

It can also be used either in a preventative way, to make sure that problems do not arise in future, or in a remedial way to address problems that have already arisen.

The CIA framework was first introduced in my book, *Stress Matters*, in 1999. Since then, I have had many people tell me that adopting this framework has made a huge difference to their lives. By making sure that they control what they can control, this has given them a greater sense of confidence. In turn, that has given them greater confidence to try and influence what they cannot control and they have learned by becoming more skilled and confident at the control and influence levels to recognize what they have to accept.

▶ **Know your enemy** ▶ **Promoting realism** ▶ **Stress audit** ▶ **Worst case, best case** ▶

Circular questioning

Establishing the importance of interrelationships

This is a useful approach to interaction drawn from the family therapy literature which has also been used in organization development (OD) approaches to workplace problems.

A key feature of this technique is the recognition that people are constantly interacting as part of a context of change. It teaches us to understand people's behaviour not in isolation, but as part of a set of interactions and relationships, as dynamic rather than static. As Brown explains:

> instead of asking why someone is depressed, a circular form of questioning would inquire about when someone shows depression and what other people do when this is happening.
>
> (1997, p. 109)

This approach reflects social constructionist thinking which emphasizes the ways in which meanings arise from social interactions (Gergen, 2009). A strong advantage of this type of thinking is that it helps us to adopt a holistic perspective, providing an overview of the situation, rather than making the 'atomistic' mistake of simply looking at the role of individuals.

Circular, or 'recursive' questioning involves trying to establish what Bateson (2000) called 'patterns of connection', trying to clarify how people and other aspects of the situation all interrelate. These patterns will reflect both similarities and differences, with the differences being potentially quite significant. This can include differences with regard to:

- *Relationships.* Do different members of the family, team or organization have different perceptions of the situation? Are there differences in how particular individuals relate to one another? Who is closer to whom? Who (mis)trusts whom?
- *Values.* Are there differences in values that are causing tensions or creating significant dynamics? Who is motivated in what direction and by what values?
- *Time.* Have there been changes over time that are affecting the situation? Do people have different perspectives on what they want the future to be like?

This approach enables people to broaden their view and see the bigger picture. For example, as well as asking: 'How do you feel about this situation?', we can ask: 'How does your wife/colleague/boss feel about this situation?'. In this way we can build up a picture of the interrelationships and interactions.

It can be particularly useful in relation to situations involving conflict. This is because it can help prevent people adopting entrenched positions or encourage them to move out of them if they have already reached that point.

It can also help to improve communication (for example, by helping people see the need for communication as a result of their increased awareness of the wider context and the interrelationships involved). This emphasis on what Hopkins (1986) called 'the space between people' (rather than simply on the individuals themselves) is also helping to prevent blaming and scapegoating (see 'Releasing the scapegoat' below).

Circular questioning is not a set of specific questions; it is more a style of questioning that highlights interactions. Three particular types of question are often used in this technique: descriptive ('Can you describe what is happening when …?'); explanatory ('How would your husband explain your reaction to …?'); and hypothetical ('What if …?'). The approach can be summed up as: 'Don't think of individuals in isolation, think of people interacting and influencing one another'.

This is a tool that can take time to develop, but it is one that can be very effective indeed in moving people forward.

▶ **Helicopter vision** ▶ **Motivational interviewing** ▶ **Transactional analysis** ▶

Confronting without being confrontational

Using assertiveness skills

As practitioners we can sometimes be unconfident about confronting the key issues involved in a situation. The framework of 'confronting without being confrontational' encourages us to do so but without overstepping the mark and becoming confrontational.

It is basically a matter of assertiveness, which involves finding a balance between submission on the one hand and aggression on the other. It involves working towards win–win outcomes in which we do not bully the other party into submission, but nor do we allow them to bully us into behaving in a way that we are not happy or comfortable with. It is an important approach to interactions in general but can be particularly significant in those situations where there are issues that need to be addressed if progress is to be made – that is, issues that need to be confronted. These include the following:

- *Where someone's actions are blocking progress or even making the situation worse.* In such circumstances, it is easy to recognize that, if we do not tackle this matter, then we are not only going to fail to improve the situation, but may also end up bearing witness to a considerable deterioration in it.
- *When there are significant risk factors that people seem unaware of.* In many situations, people are only too aware of the risks involved, and this can lead to a high degree of anxiety. However, there can be other situations where the opposite is the case, where people seem to be complacent about risk factors. It would be very dangerous on our part to fail to bring this situation to their attention, to allow them to continue to put themselves or possibly other people at significant risk because they are not 'tuned in' to the hazards that they face.
- *When people seems to be misunderstanding our role or what we are trying to do.* There can often be situations of mismatch in which someone's expectations are very different from our own. This brings us back to the idea of setting out our stall, being clear about what we can do, what we cannot do, what our role is and so on.

What these examples should teach us is that there are often situations where there are issues that do need to be confronted, but preferably not in a confrontational way. That is, they need to be tackled gently, tactfully and constructively, so that nobody loses face, nobody is embarrassed or humiliated by the experience. This can be accomplished in a number of ways, not least the following:

- *Non-threatening body language.* The significance of nonverbal communication is quite immense in most situations, but especially in this type of situation where we need to confront difficult issues. Making sure that the way we present ourselves bodily as assertive without being threatening is therefore an important approach.

However, we should also not go too far to the other extreme and come across as if we are apologetic for what we are doing, as that will lose us considerable respect and trust.

- *A firm but friendly tone of voice.* This helps to make sure that we are avoiding giving off signs of anxiety or a reluctance on our part to address the issues. This approach to how we speak to people can make a significant positive difference.

- *Choosing our words carefully.* We need to make sure that we do not say anything that unwittingly implies criticism, accusation or blame. If people are expecting to be 'put down' because that has been their experience in other walks of life, then they may be very sensitive to any forms of language that reinforce the message that it's all their fault. We therefore have to be quite cautious in how we put our message across.

- *Emphasizing the importance of clarity, openness and working together.* This refers to two sets of issues: there is what should have preceded the circumstances in which we now find the need to confront issues (that is, by having developed a good rapport based on respect and trust beforehand, then getting to the point where we need to confront sensitive issues is going to be much easier). But there will also be the importance of establishing clarity, openness and a spirit of partnership at the time that we are doing the necessary challenging.

This can be quite a difficult technique to use and requires a certain degree of skill. If you anticipate struggling with it, then it can be wise to practise with it first with a friend or colleague. It is too important not to get it right, and so the more we practise the technique, the safer and stronger a position we will be in.

PRACTICE FOCUS 2.2

Linda was a student on placement as part of her professional studies. She was working with a number of families and found it relatively easy to form a positive rapport with them. However, there was one aspect of her practice that she was struggling with. At times, there were sensitive issues that she needed to address with some of the families, but she felt so uncomfortable about doing so that she generally 'chickened out' and avoided the subject. However, it soon became apparent to her mentor that she was doing this and so it was made clear to her – gently and supportively, but also firmly – that she was likely to fail the placement if she did not manage to get past this barrier. Fortunately her mentor was sufficiently skilled to help her learn the skills (and to develop the confidence) she needed to be able to confront these difficult issues.

▶ **Avoiding avoidance** ▶ **Dealing with objections** ▶ **Elegant challenging**
▶ **Naming the process** ▶ **Negotiating expectations** ▶ **Releasing the scapegoat** ▶

Congruence

Getting on the same wavelength

A recurring theme across many of these tools is the need to 'engage' or connect with people. Unless we are able to do this effectively, it is unlikely we will be able to make a positive difference in relation to the problems they face (and/or they are causing). Congruence is a tool that can be used to help in this regard.

It has its roots in neuro-linguistic programming (NLP), although it can be used in its own right without having to make any commitment to this particular approach to interpersonal relations. The key to the NLP version of congruence, then, is being able to recognize the style of communication a person feels comfortable with and using that style with them, so that they feel more comfortable with us.

In NLP these styles of communication are linked to the senses. Basically there are three types, as follows:

1. *Visual.* A 'visual' person is likely to use language related to sight or vision, such as: 'I see what you mean', 'I get the picture', 'Do you see where I'm coming from?'
2. *Auditory.* An 'auditory' person is likely to use language related to hearing, such as: 'I hear what you're saying', 'That rings a bell', 'Sounds good to me'.
3. *Feeling* (or 'kinaesthetic'). 'I grasped the idea straight away', 'I just couldn't connect with what she was saying', 'It didn't feel right'.

The basic argument is that each of us will feel more comfortable with our 'favourite' style, although we will not be restricted to that style. That is, we may use a mixture of styles at any one time, but we are more likely, it is argued, to favour one style over the others.

To use congruence as a tool with a particular individual, we need to listen carefully to what he or she is saying and see whether we can note what style (visual, auditory or feeling) is featuring most. If we then adopt that particular style, we increase the chances of the individual concerned feeling comfortable with us (thereby increasing the chances of 'engagement' and being able to make progress in tackling whatever problems need our attention).

In my view, the NLP approach places too much emphasis on the sensory dimension of communication styles. While there may well be a case for arguing that sensory preferences play a part in shaping communication patterns, I feel that there are other dimensions of communication style that also need to be considered – for example, formality. Some people like to speak on a fairly formal basis and may feel they are not being taken seriously if we speak to them in too casual a style. Conversely, someone who feels more comfortable with informal styles of speech may feel alienated by formal speech on our part.

In addition to sensory differences, styles of communication can vary in the following ways:

formal	vs.	informal
direct	vs.	indirect
open	vs.	closed
telling	vs.	asking
calm	vs.	aroused
and so on.		

Communication is a very complex topic and it is dangerous to oversimplify it. However, it remains the case that there is much to be gained by developing congruence in our communication by (i) trying to find common ground (in terms of communication styles) with the person(s) we are seeking to help; and (ii) also matching the style of communication to the context in which we are working (for example, informal style in an interview that forms part of a formal investigation may not be appropriate).

To develop congruence as a tool you may find it helpful to think about your own preferred styles of communication and those of others you regularly interact with.

- Can you identify any patterns (sensory or otherwise)?
- Try to get into the habit of listening to other people's styles of communication. Can you recognize any patterns there?
- Who do you regard as a really good communicator? Does he or she use particular styles?
- When you encounter a conflict situation, are the antagonists using different styles of communication?

Over time we can develop a heightened awareness and increased sensitivity to communicative styles and thus be able to develop our skills in working with people in a variety of settings by making good use of congruence. If we work with someone on a short-term basis, it will be a big challenge (but not necessarily an impossible one) to be able to become sufficiently sensitive to their communication styles. However, if we work with someone over a longer period, we are likely to find it easier to identify their communication preferences.

A word of caution should be sounded here, though. Beware of making the mistake of equating congruence with matching. The NLP emphasis on sensory preferences implies that it is best to match the other person's style so that they feel comfortable with us. In many situations this will be highly appropriate. However, in others, a congruent style may actually be one that differs from the other person's. Congruent should be read as 'fitting' rather than 'matching', as in some circumstances, it is fitting to use an opposing style – for example, using an open style in working with someone who is adopting a closed style.

Congruence can be used on a one-to-one basis as an aid to communication – for example, when we are in discussion with a particular person. However, it can also be used in helping people relate to one another. For example, in work involving conflict (whether between two people or within a group), looking at communication styles could be a potentially useful way forward. If it is found that there are conflicting styles of communication, this could become the basis of trying to resolve any difficulties being experienced.

▶ **Responding to feelings** ▶ **SOLER** ▶ **Transactional analysis** ▶ **Tuning in** ▶

Consequences
Exploring options and their likely outcomes

This is a very simple tool that can be very effective in helping people appreciate where their behaviour is likely to lead them to. It can be used in circumstances where someone is behaving in a way that is causing problems, either for themselves or for other people. This can be for a variety of reasons. It may be that the individual concerned is deliberately being destructive (or self-destructive) or it may be that the emotional pressures of the situation have led to this individual behaving in problematic ways (for example, someone feeling stressed and taking it out on other people instead of trying to identify the cause of the stress and deal with it).

The technique involves taking a sheet of paper and drawing a line down the middle to form two columns. The left-hand column should be headed 'Actions' and the right-hand column 'Consequences'. Through discussion with the individual concerned, a number of courses of action can be listed on the left-hand side. These should arise through discussion and should include both courses of action that the person concerned has already undertaken or is likely to undertake plus others, which in your view, may be more appropriate in the circumstances. Both of you can contribute to drawing up the list, but it is best if most if not all of the options are elicited from the person concerned (so that he or she takes maximum ownership of the process and its outcomes).

You may, if you wish, add bizarre or ridiculous courses of action just to add a note of fun and humour. However, I would not recommend that you do this until you have used the technique a few times and feel comfortable and confident with it. Even then, you will need to judge carefully whether humour is appropriate to the situation. Of course, humour can be an excellent tension reliever and a great help in forming good working relationships, but it can also be disastrous if used inappropriately (for example, if it gives the message to the person you are trying to help: 'I am not taking your problems seriously').

The object of the exercise is to identify the likely consequences of each course of action and to weigh up, on the basis of that consideration, which is the best way forward. So, for each course of action listed on the left-hand side of the page, the likely consequences should be discussed and recorded on the right-hand side of the page. This can be done, for example, by asking simple questions like: 'If you were to do this (referring to an item on the left-hand side of the page), what do you think the likely consequences would be?' The response is then recorded on the right-hand side of the page. We would then move on to the next item on the left and ask the same question. In this way, we will build up a list of possible actions (on the left-hand side of the page) and the likely consequences of each (on the right-hand side).

As a practical point, we should make sure that we leave plenty of space between entries in the left-hand column because it is likely that we will need more space on the right-hand side for recording the consequences of the action concerned (although, by using note form, we should be able to overcome any problems here).

What should happen is that the individual concerned will co-operate in identifying likely problematic/harmful consequences of certain courses of action and more positive/constructive consequences of their actions. In other words, it should become apparent which courses of action have desirable consequences and which do not.

This process, then, involves weighing up the pros and cons of each particular course of action. This can be very useful in helping somebody to appreciate how what they have been doing, or what they are likely to do, can be harmful for themselves and/or for others. It is a helpful way of bringing order to what can perhaps be a chaotic, confused and complex situation. Consider the following example:

Action	Consequence
Bite people's heads off.	I feel better in the short term, but worse overall. People like me less and I risk losing friends.
Say nothing and keep my anger to myself.	I don't risk losing friends, but feel worse and I risk letting all the bad feelings bottle up until they all come rushing out at once. Or, I make myself ill by bottling it up.
Tell people calmly why I am not happy.	This would be great, but I'm not sure I could do it.
Avoid the problem in the first place before it builds up.	I would be much happier with this. I would not lose friends and I would stay calm and feel better. But I'm not sure I would know how to do this.

Here we have identified only four actions and sets of consequences, but could have taken this further. However, even with only four options to explore, a clear pattern is emerging: we are able to identify that this person could benefit from help with preventing pressures from building up and in keeping calm when they do. The exercise will also have taught him or her that biting people's heads off is not a helpful reaction and that alternative responses need to be developed.

One important note of caution, though, is that we should be careful not to make this a lesson in moralizing. It is very easy to oversimplify this process and to polarize good actions and bad actions. This can come across to the individual concerned as simplistic and unhelpful. As with any tool, it needs to be used with skill and care. When used appropriately, it can be helpful in identifying problems to be avoided and alternative courses of action. When not used appropriately, it can appear to be a club to beat somebody with. We have to be careful to make sure that we promote the former and avoid the latter.

This approach can be particularly helpful with children but, of course, it will be necessary to take into account their level of development and establish whether or not they will be sufficiently mature to understand the process and its outcomes.

▶ **The CIA framework** ▶ **Cost-benefit analysis** ▶ **Educating** ▶

Cost-benefit analysis

Balancing the pros and cons

Cost-benefit analysis is basically a decision-making tool. It involves taking a sheet of paper, drawing a line down the centre, heading the left-hand column 'costs', and the right-hand column 'benefits'. When trying to make a decision about whether to adopt a particular course of action, this analysis can be very useful in giving us some very strong messages about what problems we might encounter or, indeed, how we might gain advantage by adopting that particular route. What can be particularly useful is to break down the costs into their different types. What types are applicable will depend on the circumstances but these can include:

- financial costs;
- human costs (will anyone suffer in some way if this decision is made?);
- goodwill costs (will this course of action cause ill-feeling?);
- opportunity costs (will we be closing other doors by opening this particular door?);
- reputation costs (will people think less of us if we adopt this plan?); and
- ethical costs (does this course of action compromise our values in any way?).

We can then adopt a similar process in terms of highlighting the benefits. These too can be broken down into their different types along much the same lines as the costs. Some people adopt a very mechanistic approach to cost-benefit analysis by, for example, attaching figures to costs and benefits, adding up the totals and then deciding how to proceed, based on the mathematical result from this. To my mind, this is too rigid an approach. It oversimplifies some very complex issues and is therefore best avoided.

Some people have a very narrow perspective on cost-benefit analysis. They may have used it in its literal sense – that is, at a financial level, to look at what benefits we will get for our money (the cost). However, this technique can be used much more widely and much more creatively to look at any situation because, if we think of costs and benefits in a much wider sense than purely financial, then this can be a useful tool for weighing up advantages and disadvantages, pluses and minuses.

One important consideration when developing a cost-benefit analysis is to look at: for whom is this a cost? And, for whom is it a benefit? If we do not do this, we may miss out on some key issues. For example, there may be conflicts between particular groups that may not come out unless we ask these important questions around this key issue of 'for whom?'. Asking these questions may also indicate why certain people are resistant to change. It may well be that, from where they are sitting, there are lots of costs but few benefits. Other people may be very keen to adopt a particular course of action because, from their point of view, there are few costs but great benefits. We must therefore not oversimplify the issue by looking at cost and benefit in absolute terms but, rather, to make these issues relative to the positions of particular individuals or groups who have an interest in the outcome of the situation we are dealing with (stakeholders).

Cost-benefit analysis can be helpful for individuals to use as a means of weighing up options. It can be something that we can do with other people as a tool of intervention – for example, when somebody is so anxious about a situation that they are paralysed when it comes to decision making. Similarly, it can be used to help people who are rushing into a particular course of action without fully weighing up the consequences and finally, it can be used with groups of people for making joint decisions about particular courses of action. One bonus of using it in this way is that it can identify actual or potential conflicts between different stakeholders within that group.

PRACTICE FOCUS 2.3

Liam was faced with quite a challenge when trying to help Tom resolve his current difficulties. Tom had been through a period of major change and was now 'punch drunk', feeling very confused about what to do next and very anxious that, in this unsettled period in his life, he might make decisions that he might regret later. Liam asked Tom whether he had ever used cost-benefit analysis. Tom replied that he had heard of it but was not entirely sure what was involved in it. Once Liam explained, Tom was keen to pursue this. Liam therefore sat down with him, helped him identify the various options available to him and to weigh up the costs and benefits of each. Tom found this a very helpful process, especially as the structure it provided gave him a sense of security and boundaries, something that had been missing from his life recently because of all the changes he had been through.

▶ **Objectives tree** ▶ **SWOT analysis** ▶

Creative tension

Making sure expectations are realistic

Where the gap between capabilities and desired outcomes is too great, we can become demotivated and feel hopeless and defeated. However, if we can achieve what is known as 'creative tension' by having goals that are realistically close to our current capabilities, we can be motivated to extend ourselves further to achieve them.

Creative tension is an important part of motivation theory. What it boils down to is that, if the gap between where we are and where we want to be is small enough to be manageable, then a positive tension will be created, and that in turn will motivate us to move forward. This is what is meant by a creative tension. It is a positive, constructive tension between where we are now and where we want or need to be – our aspirations in effect.

However, if the gap between where we are and where we desire or need to be is too great, then the net result is a tension that is not creative but, rather, destructive. If the tension is too great it demotivates us, making progress and success much less likely. What this means is that it is important to ensure that we are not asking too much of people, either of ourselves or of others, because if we are setting ourselves or other people up to fail, we are creating a situation that will make such failure more likely by demotivating people. If the task seems too much for us, then we are likely to be daunted by that, but if the task seems perhaps difficult but manageable, then the net result can be motivation, rather than demotivation.

If we do not help people to produce creative tension in relation to their problems, then we are creating a situation in which we are putting them in a position where they are more likely to fail, rather than better equipped to succeed. Creative tension can produce a 'virtuous circle', while its absence can create a vicious circle. What this means is that creative tension can motivate people, thereby making success more likely, and therefore creating a positive situation all round, unlike its opposite, a vicious circle, where things go from bad to worse because people feeling that they cannot succeed makes them feel less confident, which in turn makes them actually less likely to succeed, and therefore in turn less confident again. It is therefore important to make sure that goals are realistic and achievable.

The tool of creative tension can be an unimportant one for us but we have to be clear about what we are doing and how we are doing it. It offers us a great way of making sure that what we are expecting of ourselves and of other people is realistic, so that unrealistic expectations do not get in the way of moving forward.

▶ **Eating an elephant** ▶ **Negotiating expectations** ▶

Critical incident technique
Learning from significant experiences

This is a method that can be used by supervisors in trying to help their supervisees to learn from their experience. It involves the following steps:

1. Identify a particular incident which is significant in some way. It may have particular emotional connotations, or there may be other aspects of the situation that make it stand out from day-to-day practice.
2. Briefly record what happened in the incident. There is no need for a detailed description here, just the key points.
3. Record how you would account for what happened in this incident. In other words, provide a basic explanation for what occurred.
4. What other explanations could there be for what happened? For example, what other conceptual framework could help us to understand this incident?

This can be a very helpful way of encouraging practitioners to think carefully about what happens in their work and how they account for what happens. It can be very useful for linking theory to practice for helping practitioners (and, indeed, managers) to realize that their work is based on a professional knowledge base, even though this may not always be explicit. As I have commented previously: This simple but effective framework provides an excellent basis for discussion and exploration of the linkages between theory and practice in a way which enhances practice and brings theory to life. It is a technique which can be used on a one-to-one basis or as part of a group exercise.

An important point to note, however, in using this technique is that it can often generate strong emotions. Incidents encountered can have a powerful emotional impact and the analysis of the incident can rekindle intense and painful feelings. This has two sets of implications:

1. Facilitators need to be ready and able to work constructively with such feelings as and when they arise, for example by creating a safe environment.
2. It needs to be remembered that theory has a role to play in dealing with the emotional dimension ... . We need to be wary of the

false assumption that theory is 'rational', and therefore incompatible with the 'irrational' world of feelings.

The use of the critical incident technique therefore represents an important and potentially very effective strategy for integrating theory and practice.

(Thompson, 2000, pp. 100–1)

This is a well-established technique that has an associated literature. It can be very helpful in encouraging practitioners to think about their practice and to develop, from this, critically reflective approaches to practice. However, in a revised version, this technique can also be used to help people we are trying to support through problem situations to develop an awareness of their own part in what is happening to them – to develop insight into the situation they face.

This revised version would involve:

1. identifying an incident that has caused concern to the person concerned;
2. clarifying what happened in that incident;
3. seeking their explanation for what happened; and
4. looking at alternative explanations.

Once again, this is a tool that should be used with skill and craft and not simply in a mechanistic, unthinking way. If handled carefully and sensitively, it can help individuals to appreciate that their initial understanding of a situation may be misleading and that there are other explanations for what has happened. If we simply tell somebody that they are wrong and that they have misunderstood a situation, we should not be surprised if we meet resistance. If, however, we help them to explore alternative explanations, then they may well come to the conclusion themselves that their initial view was a partial one and needs to be replaced by an alternative version. This is not to say that people's understanding of their problems will always be misguided or inaccurate or partial, but we have to be realistic and recognize that this is often the case. We should not be surprised by this, as it is often the result of the tensions associated with the problem situation. It is not uncommon for people facing significant problems to find it difficult to think clearly, or to adopt a balanced overview of the situation.

The technique can also be used as a team-building exercise or, indeed, with any group of people who need to look at particular events and explore their understanding of them. This four-step process can give a clear and helpful framework that provides structure and focus for a skilled facilitator to use to enable the group of people concerned to broaden their understanding, deepen their insight and look at positive ways forward.

▶ **The six thinking hats** ▶ **TOTE** ▶ **Using personal constructs** ▶

Culture audit
Making sense of organizational cultures

This involves analysing the culture we work in as part of a plan to change it for the better. It has arisen from my earlier work (Thompson, 2009b) in which I talk about the importance of understanding the significant influences of a culture or set of cultures within an organization.

A culture can be defined as 'the way we do things round here'. It relates to a set of taken for granted assumptions, unwritten rules and shared meanings. It becomes well established as a set of powerful norms that influence not just behaviour, but also the way people think and feel who are part of that culture. Of course, while a culture is powerful, it is not all-powerful, and a culture can be influenced and changed where necessary. So, in situations where an organizational culture appears to be contributing to, or sustaining, one or more problems, then a possible way of tackling such issues is to use a culture audit as a way of first of all getting an overview of what the significant aspects of that culture are so that subsequently a plan for making any necessary changes to that culture can be developed.

A culture audit involves identifying key aspects of a culture and rating them along a continuum from positive to negative. This can be seen to be quite helpful in terms of clarifying that, if a score is close to the negative pole of the rating, then this is giving us a clear message that things need to change. However, where the rating is closer to the more positive pole of the continuum, then this is strongly suggesting that this is an aspect of the culture that needs to be safeguarded and reinforced.

The audit can be divided into nine key sets of parameters. The first one of these is negativity versus positivity, reflecting the overall emphasis of the audit in terms of which is more to the fore. However, in terms of this particular dimension, the focus needs to be on how negative or positive the culture is overall. In terms of negativity, for example, is there a high level of cynicism, defeatism and general negativity or, looking towards the other pole, is the focus more on positive aspects of the situation, with the result that there is a degree of hope, commitment and passion to succeed?

The second criterion is dependency versus independence. This relates to asking ourselves the question: Do the people who work within this culture constantly rely on guidance or even instructions from their managers, or are they more in keeping with the idea of being self-starters and only seek the support of management where it is wise and necessary to do so?

The third dimension I refer to as tramlines versus creativity. What I mean by tramlines is the tendency to rely too heavily on habit and to not explore different options. A team or group of staff which is firmly embedded in a tramlines culture is unlikely to do anything different from week to week, month to month, or even year to year. By contrast where there is an emphasis on creativity, then teams of staff can come together very effectively to help bounce ideas off each other and explore fresh ways of working.

The next parameter is that of problem avoidance versus problem solving. There is no guarantee that any specific problems in an organization can be definitively solved, but there is much to be gained by members of a particular team or staff group pulling together to attempt to deal with the problems that they face. The negative pole of this parameter relates to the idea of not facing up to problems. Problem avoidance means pretending that the problems do not exist, or skilfully navigating around them, perhaps too anxious to meet them head on and try to do something about them.

The next parameter is about change, and the negative pole here is the automatic resisting of change, whatever the change may be. Whether it has the positive potential to be a significant improvement or not, the response becomes an ingrained one of automatically trying to resist anything that brings about change. At the more positive pole, we have the idea of capitalizing on the opportunities presented by change situations, trying to make the best of the situation, so that, even where the change has been imposed from without, and that change is not welcome, there is still the opportunity to think about how the opportunities presented by the change can be used positively, how they can feed into developments that can be helpful and constructive.

Another important parameter is the distinction between unsupport- ive and supportive work cultures. Where there is an unsupportive work culture, then the likelihood is that people plough their own furrow, that they simply get on with their own job and take little time and make little effort to support their colleagues or to create a welcoming, nurturing and productive work atmosphere. At the opposite pole, we have supportive work cultures where people generally recognize that everyone benefits from having an open and supportive atmosphere where it is not considered a sign of weakness to ask for help and, in fact, often there is no need to ask for help, because people will offer that help and support as soon as they get any indication that there is a need for it.

The final parameter is characterized by the idea of closed versus open cultures. A closed culture is one which is quite rigid and dogmatic, very resistant to change or outside influence. This means that it is likely to be a powerful culture, but often powerful in a negative way, leading to problems and difficulties because of the rigidity involved. By contrast, an open culture is one where there is openness to learning, where the idea of doing things differently and exploring alternative ways forward is not only tolerated, but also actually welcomed and encouraged.

It is certainly not the case that these are the only parameters to consider but in my view (and in my experience as a consultant over the years), these are the most important elements. It is also important to recognize that these can interact and reinforce each other, whether positively or negatively, so considering each of these elements in their own right is an important part of a culture audit but so, too, is the idea of considering how they relate to one another as part of a holistic overview of the situation.

The idea of a culture audit is rooted particularly in an organizational context, and is therefore best used in relation to matters relating to teamwork and organizational development. However, there is no reason why, in a modified form, it could not be used to consider how families or any other group of people come to operate after they have developed their 'scripts', their established patterns of thinking, feeling, behaving and interrelating.

This tool has very good potential to be a useful way of making sense of complex situations and providing a foundation from which we can not only develop our understanding of the intricate interactions involved, but also have a basis from which to work towards changing those elements of the culture that are problematic in some way and reinforcing and enhancing those aspects that are positive and productive.

▶ **Chunk up or chunk down** ▶ **Eco maps** ▶ **Force-field analysis** ▶

Dealing with objections

Persuading people to move forward

A characteristic of problem-solving efforts is that, as plans are developing and potential solutions are emerging, some people raise objections. This tool is one that has been developed to encourage us to invite those objections so that they can be dealt with constructively, rather than attempting to suppress them and thereby allow them to fester and cause greater problems over time. It is based on the idea that it is understandable, realistic and potentially quite constructive for people to raise objections to proposed plans of action (see 'Motivational interviewing').

What is also very significant in terms of the idea of dealing with objections is that, as we noted earlier, people can easily become 'locked into' their problems. This can happen in a variety of ways:

- Anxiety can be a key factor. People may be unwilling to move forward to potential solutions because they are operating on the basis of a high level of anxiety which stands in the way of genuinely engaging with potential solutions.
- There can also be difficulties arising from the operation of one or more vicious circles. What I mean by this is that some aspects of a situation can reinforce others in such a way that the negative and destructive tendencies become a downward spiral. When this occurs, people can find it extremely difficult to break out of the problematic situation they find themselves in. For example, somebody who has low self-esteem and therefore a low level of confidence may be reluctant to try particular ways of trying to address their problems and the net result is that they are blocked from making progress. The fact that they do not make progress can then be interpreted as a sign of failure on their part to reinforce their sense that they are not worthy, that they are not important, that they

are not able to address their own problems, needs and issues. This then brings us back to square one and reinforces the intensity of the problem. Another vicious circle is born.

- Interactions with others can also be very significant. For example, family members, colleagues or other people can counteract the help that is given by the worker. Initiatives to bring about change can be undermined by other people perhaps having less faith in them or having their own agenda which can lead them to try and sabotage problem-solving efforts.

- Likewise, interactions with the problem-solving worker can result in people being locked into their problems. For example, a worker may be doing certain things that have the unintentional effect of creating dependency. It may appear to the person seeking help with their problems, for example, that the answer lies with the worker. This is clearly something we should not be encouraging, but it is surprising how often this sort of destructive dynamic can develop.

Where people are locked into their problems in this way, they can respond by demonstrating resistance to changing the situation. What this involves is that change (and I include within this positive change, that is, progress) can be experienced as a frightening aspect of human experience. This can lead people to adopt the stance of 'it's better the devil you know'. They would rather, therefore, stay with their current problematic situations than try and move towards a better outcome for fear that what they may actually end up with is the situation getting even worse. It is not surprising, therefore, that so many people will tend to 'play it safe' and therefore be resistant to change efforts.

What this produces, therefore, is a situation where, very often, people can raise objections to what we are suggesting, possibly because of the above reasons but also possibly to test us out, to see whether we are competent enough to earn their trust or respect. Recognizing that such objections as a form of resistance are not uncommon and widely encountered, we reach the point where we need to consider how we can respond to this situation, how we can, in a sense, get past the objections.

Thomson (1996) identifies the ways in which this can be possible:

1. *How we phrase things is important.* If we are not careful with the words we use, we can reinforce people's objections, but if we are able to carefully, subtly and constructively use more empowering forms of language that open up doors, rather than close them, then we are in a much stronger position to deal with objections. An example that

Thomson uses is: if somebody says 'I don't like blue', this can be translated into a question along the lines of 'What colours do you have other than blue?'

2. *An objection can also reflect a need for further information.* The person concerned could be making a decision against something that we are offering based on limited information. It may well be that, once they have a fuller picture of what is involved, they will be happy to go along with it, but until they have that information, they are understandably not prepared to commit to a particular course of action.

3. *It may be that they really do mean no but find it hard to say so.* Their objections may therefore be put forward as ways of slowing down the process, and hinting at their resistance to move forward when they are not confident or assertive enough to come out and say that they are not happy with a particular aspect of what we are proposing. In such circumstances, it is important to explore why they are objecting, so that we may not be able to remove the objection, because it is, to some extent, a legitimate one, but we may be able to remove the cause of that objection and therefore be able to deal with it in that way.

4. *Testing out can also be a source of objections.* This could be a matter of the need to know enough about what we are proposing. We may be subject to a test that we are competent enough to be trusted in relation to a particular matter or a particular aspect of the situation.

5. *There may be genuine misgivings.* It may well be that there are aspects of the situation where the person objecting understandably does not feel comfortable with what is being suggested. In this case, it is then a matter of once again trying to establish what exactly they are unhappy about and exploring ways of dealing with it.

It is important not to ride roughshod over people's objections and to try to dismiss them. However, it is also important that we do not simply take objections at face value and assume that somebody is not interested, not co-operating or not committed to changing their current circumstances. The reality is far more complex than that, and the idea of dealing with objections helps us to engage with that complexity in ways which will make it easier for us to be able to understand why somebody is objecting and to assess how reasonable those objections are and where they are unreasonable or problematic in some way, to try and work towards addressing the problems that cause it.

▶ **Avoiding attribution errors** ▶ **Motivational interviewing** ▶ **Naming the process** ▶ **SARAH** ▶

Doing the right things versus doing things right

Balancing efficiency and effectiveness

The distinction between doing the right things and doing things right is generally associated with the management thinker, Peter Drucker (see Drucker, 1954). It is broadly similar to the distinction between effectiveness and efficiency (effectiveness = doing the right things, efficiency = doing things right). Being effective means achieving our goals. Being efficient means achieving those goals with the most effective use of the resources available to us – that is, without waste.

Sometimes we can be effective in that we achieve our goals, but it is not necessarily the case that we do so efficiently. That is, while we may well achieve our goals, we may do so in a way that involves greater use of resources than was necessary. Such resources could be physical, financial or human. Ironically, it is possible for us to be efficient without being effective – that is, we may be concentrating on making sure that we do not waste resources and make the best use of the resources available to us, but without necessarily achieving our goals. This can be linked to the discussion of systematic practice in Part One of the book, where it was emphasized that it is important to keep a clear focus on what we are trying to achieve. It is sadly the case that the history of organizational life is littered with examples of teams of staff, or even whole organizations, who have devoted considerable time and effort to making sure that they were operating efficiently, but without making sure that they were actually achieving their goals. This results in a bizarre situation where efforts to save time and money through efficiency end up being perhaps a total waste of time and money, because all the resources invested in that effort do not achieve the goals that they are intended to. This can happen for a variety of reasons. One very common one is that people get engrossed in 'office politics' and lose sight of the reasons for their organization's existence or the specific aims it is trying to achieve.

The worst case scenario is when our efforts are neither effective nor efficient. That is, we fail to achieve what we set out to do and use up a great deal of resources in the process. Sadly, this is not uncommon. We could devote a whole book to the possible reasons for this but, for present purposes, suffice it to say that the complex organizational and interpersonal dynamics involved in people work can often result in this worst case outcome.

The best case scenario is, of course, the direct opposite of the above. This is where we are both effective and efficient. That is, we both achieve our aims and do so with the best use of the resources available to us. While it would certainly be idealistic to expect to achieve this every time, we should be working towards achieving this best case scenario as frequently as we possibly can.

An important way of doing this is to keep a clear focus on both aspects – the efficiency and the effectiveness. That is, to make sure that we are doing the right things and that we are doing them right. A necessary prerequisite for this is reflective practice, as discussed in Part One. It is important that we allow ourselves the space to be able to review what we are doing and to plan ahead. If we allow ourselves to fall into the trap of rushing around trying to achieve too much, then the danger is that we may achieve very little and waste a lot of time, effort, energy and money (not to mention the good will of others) in the process.

Systematic practice can help us to make sure that we are doing the right things, that we have a clear picture of our objectives and how we are intending to meet them (and, of course, how we will know when we have met them). To this we need to add the dimension of efficiency to make sure that we are 'doing things right'. This can be achieved by exploring the various options available to us and not simply relying on the first thing that comes to mind. This is because, while the first thing that comes to mind may well work (although even that is not guaranteed), it may well be the case that there are other methods that could be equally successful, if not more so, but which involve less use of valuable resources.

To sum up, what this important technique involves is:

- being clear about what we are trying to achieve (as per systematic practice – the **S** of PRECISE practice);
- exploring different options for achieving those ends;
- seeking to ensure that the option we have chosen is, where appropriate, the most efficient as well as most effective; and
- ensuring that we do not allow a narrow-minded focus on efficiency to mean that we are not being effective, thus leading to a significant waste of resources. We should make every effort to ensure that this 'fool's efficiency' is not allowed to hijack our efforts to achieve effectiveness.

▶ **Gantt charts** ▶ **Not tolerating vagueness** ▶ **Objectives tree** ▶ **Visioning** ▶

The drama triangle
Avoiding being drawn into being a 'rescuer'

This is a framework associated with transactional analysis. It warns of the dangers of getting drawn inappropriately into conflict situations. It can be a useful tool to clarify our own thinking and also help others (individuals or groups) to understand the problems they are experiencing.

In the drama triangle, there are three players. First, we have an individual who feels that someone else is giving him or her a hard time. This is the person known as the victim. The person in the 'victim' role is someone who feels that another person is acting unfairly or is even deliberately 'gunning for' him or her. The role of victim can be real or imagined. That is, the victim's perception may be based in objective reality or not, but if the person occupying the victim role perceives him- or herself as a victim, then he or she will act accordingly. We therefore have to take this seriously, even if there is no objective basis to that perception.

The second player in the drama triangle is the person referred to as the persecutor. The person occupying this role may not perceive him- or herself as a persecutor but, if perceived as such by the 'victim', then the unhealthy dynamic between victim and persecutor can, none the less, commence. In many situations the dynamic can be reciprocated – that is, one person perceives the other as a persecutor, while that person perceives the so-called victim as a persecutor – each feels that the other is being difficult. This is a common occurrence in negotiation situations or, indeed, in conflict situations more broadly. It is a very unhelpful dynamic, whether one-way or reciprocal, because what it tends to do is to 'lock' each person into that particular role, to encourage them to become entrenched in their respective views. He or she then fails to see the broader picture and tends to see the situation only from that specific role definition, whether it is accurate or not.

If the perception of role is accurate, it can be a significant problem, as the individual concerned will tend to adopt a narrow perspective and is likely to fail to see the big picture (see the discussion of 'Helicopter vision' below). Where the perception is inaccurate, for whatever reason, then this can make the situation even worse, as it means that this particular individual is adopting a distorted perception. One of the things that the drama triangle teaches us is that one person's distorted perception can lead to distorted perceptions on the part of others. It can be a destructive dynamic in this respect. For example, a victim's attitude towards their alleged persecutor can lead the persecutor to feel guilty, even though he or she may have done nothing wrong.

The third player in the drama triangle is known as the rescuer. Professional helpers can often be cast in the role of rescuer. People involved in the destructive victim–persecutor dynamic, especially the person occupying the victim role, can put great pressure on problem solvers to adopt the rescuer role, to come to their aid in removing them from the situation of being persecuted. Being drawn into the rescuer role is a very dangerous move for a problem solver. A very easy mistake to make is to be seduced by the victim's claims of being persecuted to the point where we fall into the trap of seeking to rescue the victim from the 'evil' persecutor. Where this happens we have, in effect, been seduced into taking sides in a conflict situation and/or played a part in reinforcing an individual's distorted perception of how they are being treated by another person or persons. This can be disastrous. We can find that our efforts to help have actually made the situation worse (see Practice focus 2.4). What can be particularly destructive about the drama triangle when we get drawn into it is that it can prevent us from adhering to the principles of good practice. For example, it can lead us to miss out the assessment stage and move straight into trying to resolve a problem without first looking at the precise nature of the problem, the factors relevant to it, and so on.

An important stance to take when faced with the situation that could lead us into the drama triangle is to remember to remain neutral. These situations are often based on conflicts and, in any conflict situation, it can be dangerous to take one side against the other without first carefully weighing up the situation and considering our role within it. Before we act on one person's perception of the situation, we need to check out the perceptions of others involved, so that we can get an overview and make up our own mind about how best to intervene (if at all).

What makes a drama triangle particularly dangerous is that people involved in people problem solving are often highly motivated to resolve difficulties and to assist people in distress. The plea of the victim can therefore be very seductive and draw us into this destructive three-way interaction by bypassing our normal practices such as assessment, gaining an overview of the situation, checking our perceptions with others, and so on. That is, problem solvers are particularly prone to being drawn into this triangle. We therefore have to be very wary of it.

PRACTICE FOCUS 2.4

Diane had been aware of conflicts between Paul and Graham for some time. However, she was very surprised when Paul came to her and claimed that Graham had been bullying him. Paul was quite distressed and was making strong allegations against Graham. Diane was very supportive of Paul and promised that she would help him deal with Graham's inappropriate behaviour, if necessary through disciplinary proceedings. After Paul left, she was quite annoyed at Graham and she felt that, although he and Paul had never got on, he had gone too far this time. She decided she would need to take a firm line in dealing with him.

She was therefore very surprised indeed when, later that afternoon, Graham came to see her to seek her support in making a complaint about Paul's behaviour. He claimed that Paul had been intimidating him and had threatened to 'get him into trouble'. Diane was taken aback by this and had to review her understanding of the situation. Who was the victim here and who was the persecutor? She realised that it wasn't that simple and that she had made the mistake of forming a view of the situation having heard only one side of the story. She didn't know who to believe but she did know that she had made a mistake in allowing herself to be drawn into a drama triangle situation and that she would need to assess the situation more carefully before deciding what to do about it.

▶ **Challenging cognitive distortions** ▶ **Negotiating expectations** ▶ **The RED approach** ▶ **Releasing the scapegoat** ▶

Eating an elephant

Being realistic about what we can achieve

This refers to the old but important question of 'How do you eat an elephant?' and the equally important reply of 'One mouthful at a time'. What this tool is about is ensuring that we do not bite off more than we can chew. What it is concerned with can be summed up in one short phrase: reasonable ambition. This is to be contrasted with the two unhelpful extremes of:

1. A lack of ambition where people are defeatist and render themselves helpless and powerless, perhaps unnecessarily so. This lack of confidence and ambition can be a major drawback in trying to deal with many problems.
2. At the other extreme, we can have too much ambition. Being over-ambitious can, in certain circumstances, be disastrous. It can lead to lots of effort and energy being wasted when our efforts have collapsed as a result of our taking too much on and then finding that we cannot cope with the pressures.

In between these two extremes of lack of ambition and overambition, is the healthy balance of realistic ambition, as I like to call it. Realistic or reasonable ambition is about being sensible about how much we can reasonably take on. An important issue here is self-awareness. Think for a moment about your own tendencies (or ask somebody who knows you well). Which is more likely if you are going to get it wrong? Are you likely to be not ambitious enough (not fulfilling your potential) or too ambitious (taking on more than you can cope with)? The answer to this question will give us a strong clue as to how to proceed in terms of making sure we achieve the balance of being realistically ambitious. If you have a tendency to lack ambition, then this raises issues of confidence. If you have the opposite tendency, namely to be overambitious, then this is giving you a warning shot across the bows, as it were, and telling you that you need to focus on being realistic.

Whichever direction we tend to go in (if either), the tool of eating an elephant can be very helpful. The basic message of 'How do you eat an elephant?' is that it is important to break large projects down into manageable chunks or 'bite-size pieces'. Taking on a large project can be a significant undertaking. People who tend to be not ambitious enough can find it so daunting that they may choose not to get involved at all, and thus miss some valuable opportunities for progress and development. People who are overambitious may try to tackle things too hastily. In either case, breaking the project down into its component parts can be a very valuable and worthwhile exercise. In fact, it is often essential for success.

An important way of doing this is to get the overview of the project, the big picture, as it were (see the discussion of 'Helicopter vision' below). By having such an overview, we should be able to break it down into its main sections. If those sections are manageable as they stand, then this should be sufficient. However, depending on the size of the project, these sections may also need to be divided into subsections. This can be achieved by drawing a tree diagram – see the discussion below of using 'Objectives trees'.

The 'eating an elephant' technique can be used in two ways. First, we can use it ourselves as a guide to managing your own projects. It can be very helpful in making sure that we do not get ourselves into difficulties in terms of large projects. Second, it can also be used as a tool for helping others, those we are seeking to help (whether individuals or groups). We can help other people to become more proficient in managing their projects by supporting them in achieving the reasonable ambition that is part and parcel of the notion of 'eating an elephant'. For example, managers can help the staff they supervise to make sure that they are operating according to this principle, while staff in the caring professions may find that the people they are seeking to help are having difficulties because they are either biting off more than they can chew or not having the confidence to tackle the issues they can tackle because they perceive the overall challenge ahead of them as being too big.

▶ **Creative tension** ▶ **Negotiating expectations** ▶ **Stress audit** ▶ **Stop trying** ▶

Eco maps

Mapping out relationships across groups of people

An eco map is a tool deriving from an 'ecological' approach to working with people – that is, one that emphasizes the relationship between the individual and his or her environment. It is helpful in moving away from individualistic models that focus too narrowly on individuals and do not take sufficient account of wider factors in the individual's environment that may also be significant.

Different people draw eco maps in different ways, and so there is no standardized way of doing so. Figure 2.1 provides an example of one way of producing such a map. What they will tend to have in common is a means of mapping relationships between an individual and key aspects of his or her environment, including people and organizations.

Eco maps can be used in different ways: as a means of clarifying our own thinking about a particular situation; as a tool for helping people understand their own situation; or as a method of helping members of a group or team to understand and, where necessary, change group dynamics. Let us consider each of these in turn.

In trying to help someone without falling into the trap of failing to take account of important environmental or contextual factors, we can make good use of an eco map. We place the individual concerned at the centre of the map, then consider the significant people, organizations or factors that are impinging on the situation we are dealing with and represent these on the map. Next we can draw the connections or relationships between the individual and the contextual factors as a set of lines. We can use different types of lines (or different colours) to indicate different types of relationship. Commonly used are:

- *Weak vs. strong (or distant vs. close)*.   This gives us an indication of how significant the relationship is.
- *Positive vs. negative*.   Is it a helpful or a problematic relationship?
- *Formal vs. informal*.   For example, formal line management vs. informal mentoring relationship.
- *Direction of power*.   This maps out power relationships.

However, these are not the only ones that can be used. Indeed, we are free to use whatever suits our particular purpose at the time.

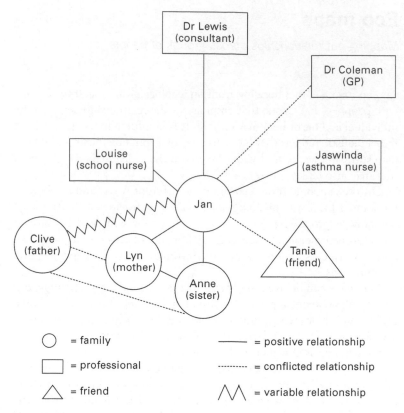

Figure 2.1   An eco map

Once we have completed the map, we can then look at it closely to see if anything significant strikes us about the set of relationships we have identified. It is interesting how important patterns can emerge that may not have occurred to us otherwise – indeed, this is the major strength of an eco map as a tool for clarifying our thinking about a situation. Note, though, that the use of an eco map for clarifying our own thinking should not lead us into adopting a course of action without first consulting and involving the person we are trying to help (see the discussion of partnership in Part One).

We can go through the same process of drawing up an eco map jointly with the person we are trying to help, so that they have an important input into the process. Their perception of the situation may be very different from our own – and this may tell us a lot about the circumstances we are dealing with. Even where their perception matches ours closely, the exercise can be a very useful one in presenting a picture of the relationships involved. It can then give us a good starting point for identifying any changes that may be needed in order to solve or alleviate problems.

A variation on this theme is to ask the person concerned to produce their own eco map (after we have given them suitable instructions or guidance on how to go about this). If we are working with a group of people or a team, each person can be asked to produce a map of their own. These can then be collated (perhaps by an independent facilitator) to see what patterns emerge. This process will generally produce two sets of factors to consider:

- *Areas of consensus.* This can be very significant – to establish clearly what group or team members seem to agree on (for example, that a relationship with a particular external stakeholder is problematic).
- *Areas of conflict.* There can be areas of disagreement that emerge which will need to be tackled if progress is to be made. Often conflicts remain beneath the surface and have a very detrimental effect unless and until they are brought out into the open and dealt with -- the eco map process can facilitate that happening.

In undertaking this exercise it is important that we promise (and deliver) confidentiality. For example, people are unlikely to be truthful about what they perceive as a problematic relationship if they believe that there may be repercussions from doing so. The whole process needs to be handled carefully and sensitively to ensure that it does not cause any unnecessary complications.

A team or group of people could also be asked to develop an eco map as a group exercise. That is, rather than collating individual maps from team members, our role could be to facilitate a group or team eco map – on a sheet of flip chart paper, for example.

Congress (2002) argues that eco maps do not take enough account of cultural diversity. She proposes a 'culturagram' as an alternative to, or development of, an eco map. However, my view is that a separate approach is not needed. If we are taking equality and diversity issues seriously, then we should be incorporating such issues into all our actions and should not need a separate tool for doing so. The 'environment' should be interpreted widely to include contextual factors of a sociological as well as psychological nature, including class, gender, race and culture.

Eco maps offer useful insights into complex interrelationships. By mapping out how the individual relates to aspects of his or her environment (and showing how aspects of the environment can relate to each other), we can develop useful pictures that help to deepen our understanding and provide a basis for planning and implementing change.

▶ **Circular questioning** ▶ **Mind mapping** ▶ **Transactional analysis** ▶

Educating

Problem solving through helping people learn

It is very often the case that people are experiencing difficulties because they lack knowledge or understanding of the circumstances they are in and/or the skills to be able to respond effectively to the challenges involved. This can result in a vicious circle in which people lose confidence and therefore make it less likely that they will be able to learn and become suitably equipped to cope with the problems they face.

Education is not simply a matter of getting people together in a classroom setting. It can be understood more broadly to refer to any process that helps people learn. In this sense, many of the techniques discussed in this book are educational techniques or have an educational component to them. However, we can also help people by explicitly identifying answers to the following questions:

1. What knowledge is needed to counter the difficulties currently being experienced? What gaps are there in their understanding that are holding them back from resolving their problems?
2. What improvements in their level of skill(s) could equip them to address their difficulties more effectively?
3. What can we do to help them develop the knowledge and/or skills needed to make all the difference?

Examples of relevant knowledge and skills would be:

- *Expressing feelings constructively.*   Often problems arise because of emotional tensions which are in part caused, or at least exacerbated, by either emotions not being expressed at all or being expressed in destructive ways (through violence, for example).

- *Managing conflict.* Some degree of conflict is inevitable in family life, in organizations and in communities. However, if people lack an understanding of conflict or the skills to 'nip it in the bud', it can escalate and become very problematic.
- *Managing pressures.* Some people can lack the skills to manage their pressures and can get themselves into considerable difficulties. This can produce another vicious circle in which their pressures overwhelm them and make them even less well-equipped to deal with the demands their situation makes of them.

There are various ways in which we can help people learn. This can include providing one-to-one coaching, arranging groupwork sessions or referring people to appropriate groupwork services, teaming up individuals with a peer mentor and, where appropriate, bibliotherapy (recommending or providing appropriate reading materials).

One important point to bear in mind is that our focus is on *education*, rather than simply providing instructions for people to follow. Genuine education is a form of empowerment, helping people to gain greater control over their lives and circumstances by helping them to develop (i) knowledge and understanding; (ii) skills; and (iii) confidence in using the knowledge, understanding and skills gained.

It has to be borne in mind that some people we are trying to help will have had very negative experiences of education in their school-days and may therefore be very resistant to efforts to help them learn. We should therefore not assume that everyone will welcome the opportunity to learn and move forward. We may have to manage some degree of resistance to the idea (see 'Motivational interviewing').

▶ Circular questioning ▶ Giving feedback ▶ Using personal constructs ▶

Elegant challenging

Being constructive in challenging unacceptable behaviour or language

The problems we encounter as people workers are often characterized by conflict. Sometimes that conflict arises because a particular person is behaving or speaking in a way that others object to. For example,

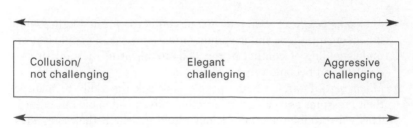

Figure 2.2 Elegant challenging

somebody may be prone to making racist or sexist comments. This can create a lot of tension and ill feeling. Unfortunately, such situations are often not handled very well. This is because, as Figure 2.2 shows, individuals can go to one unhelpful extreme or the other, and often do not find the healthy balance in between.

One unhelpful extreme is simply to ignore what has been said or done, to pretend that it has not been noticed. This can be very problematic because, in effect, it colludes with the racism, sexism or whatever form of discrimination that is being expressed. People who make such comments are likely to be encouraged to continue making them if no one raises any objections. He or she could understandably assume that it is acceptable to make such comments, given that no protest is expressed. At the other extreme, which can be equally harmful, we can have a very strong, even aggressive reaction. This is often problematic because, for one thing, it tends to increase tensions, rather than decrease them and, for another, it creates a situation where the individual who has behaved inappropriately becomes defensive. In such circumstances, he or she is likely to see the problem as being the overreaction of the other party, rather than the inappropriateness of their own behaviour or language. This strong reaction therefore gives the individual concerned a way out of the situation. It enables him or her to reframe the situation as one of overreaction rather than inappropriate action on their part.

In between these two extremes is what is known as elegant challenging. Elegant means sophisticated, and so an elegant challenge is one that is not crude or ill-thought through. It is where the person doing the challenging raises the issue in a helpful way, rather than in an aggressive or attacking way. This can involve using assertiveness skills: finding ways of making it clear to the person concerned that their actions are not acceptable, but doing so in a subtle and constructive way, rather than a personal attack. This is built on the assertiveness principle that, if we are reasonable, it puts pressure on the other party to be equally reasonable. However, if our response is excessive, then we are not encouraging the other party to be reasonable, but rather reinforcing an ethos of unreasonableness.

This tool can be used in the workplace – for example, where you may have a colleague whose behaviour is causing problems and needs to be tackled carefully and sensitively. However, it can also be used as a tool of intervention in helping people solve their problems. If, for example, one individual is behaving in a way that causes problems for others, we may find that other people's response is at one of the destructive extremes. That is, they may not acknowledge that it is a problem and so it continues to fester, as it were, or they may go to the other extreme and up the tension by reacting in an aggressive manner, thus causing problems of interpersonal relations. Helping people to challenge elegantly, to find ways of broaching difficult subjects in constructive and supportive ways, can be a very important way forward.

This can be a useful tool in a management setting – for example, in tackling a difficult appraisal issue where it is necessary to give somebody negative feedback about their performance (see the discussion of 'Giving feedback' below). There are ways and means of presenting issues of poor performance in a constructive and helpful light – in effect, an elegant challenge to seek to end the poor performance. This should, as indicated, avoid the destructive extremes of either not mentioning the issue (thus playing a part in perpetuating poor performance) or presenting the issue in a threatening or over the top way, which is likely to produce a defensive, and thus unhelpful reaction.

Elegant challenging is a very skilful technique. However, with practice, it can be honed to a state where it can be a very valuable tool indeed in our toolbox. It can be of immense benefit if used skilfully in the appropriate circumstances.

PRACTICE FOCUS 2.5

Laura was very anxious about taking up her job as a clerical assistant. It was her first job after leaving school and she was eager to make a good impression. On the first day she arrived smartly dressed and looking very attractive. Not long after she arrived in the office, she was spotted by a man who had a deserved reputation for making sexist remarks. When he saw her, he said: 'Oh look at that! I wouldn't mind getting her into bed.' When Laura heard this, she was very distressed. She was already feeling anxious and insecure and she had never been treated in this way by anyone before. She just wanted the floor to open up and swallow her, such was her embarrassment and distress. The staff who were present were furious with him for this and were tempted to 'go for the jugular'. However, instead, one of them, Sue, said to him: 'Oh come on, you can't say that. How would you feel if you had a teenage daughter and, on her first day in a new job, when she's very nervous and very keen to make a good impression, she had a middle-aged man leching over her and talking about getting her into bed? Would you think that was OK?' As it turned out, he did have a teenage daughter and, while this elegant challenge did not change his sexist attitudes overnight, it did make him think. Sue recognized that it certainly had a lot more impact than an angry response would have done, as this would simply have reinforced his view that the women in the office 'couldn't take a joke' without getting upset.

▶ **Confronting without being confrontational** ▶ **Dealing with objections** ▶ **Giving feedback** ▶ **Naming the process** ▶ **Negotiating expectations** ▶ **Releasing the scapegoat** ▶

Embedded whys

Establishing reasons for our actions

In Part One I made reference to 'problem embedding' and likened it to Russian dolls where one is embedded in another. The same logic can be applied to the question, 'Why?' That is, often when we ask, 'Why?' we do not get a satisfactory answer and we then have to ask 'Why?' again, and perhaps another time or two as well. Larrick and Klayman capture this point well when they argue that:

> Workers at Toyota learned to ask 'Why?' five times before they generated hypotheses to solve a problem. When they did so, they were more likely to find a root cause rather than a superficial one. For example: (1) Why did the machine stop? Because the fuse blew due to an overload. (2) Why was there an overload? Because the bearing lubrication was inadequate. (3) Why was the bearing lubrication inadequate? Because the lubrication pump was not functioning properly ... and so on.
>
> (1998, p. 33)

The example given here is a mechanical one, but it should not take too much imagination to see how this technique can be applied to people and people problem solving.

But why should we want to ask, 'Why?' anyway? Well, basically, because asking 'Why?' can help us to understand the underlying reasons for problems. Sometimes we do not need to know the cause of a problem in order to solve it or at least alleviate it. For example, if somebody is starving, the problem can be solved by giving them food. We do not have to know why they were starving to offer them food. However, more often than not, it does pay to understand where a problem is coming from, as that is likely to give us a better indication of how to deal with it.

A common example of this is how we deal with stress. Some managers, when noticing that one of their staff is showing signs of stress, may suggest that they take a holiday. However, if the stress is being caused by having an excessive workload, being away from work on a holiday could actually make the problem worse. It can therefore sometimes be dangerous to try to solve problems without knowing more about what lies beneath them. This is where 'Why?' comes in, especially 'embedded whys'. Larrick and Klayman again offer apt comment when they argue that:

> In general, when individuals ask 'why' the first time, they are likely to develop answers that invoke some recent event. Subsequent 'whys' are likely to cause individuals to think more deeply about underlying problems that may recur.
>
> (1998, p. 33)

The use of embedded whys can therefore help us get beneath the surface and start to see underlying factors that may need to be addressed in order to solve the problems we are trying to tackle.

Many people will have been taught, in counselling training, for example, that they should not ask 'Why?', but rather ask 'How?' The reason given for this proposed switch is normally that 'how?' is a less threatening question than 'why?' This may well be the case, but it is also a very different question from 'why?' – it will elicit a different response, and not necessarily the one we want in order to make progress. Rather than abandon asking 'why?' because some people may find it threatening, I believe it is far better to make sure that our use of this tool does not come across as threatening. The following pointers can be helpful in this regard:

- *Set out your stall.* At the beginning of your working relationship make it clear that part of what you will do to try and be helpful will be to ask questions and often those questions will begin with 'Why?' Establish that you are doing this in order to develop a good understanding of the situation and that you are not trying to catch anyone out.
- *Ask it often.* If you ask 'Why?' only occasionally, then it may come across as much more of an issue than if you are asking it on a fairly regular basis. If the people you are working with come to expect that you will ask why, they will be less bothered by this.
- *Use appropriate tone and body language.* When asking why, make sure your tone of voice does not come across as threatening or intrusive. Similarly, your body language should be giving a very clear non-threatening message. You may find it helpful to practise saying 'why' in different tones and noting how different the impact could be. You may also find it helpful to think about (or, better still, practise) what non-threatening body language would look like.
- *Use sentences.* Often 'Why?' on its own can be quite stark, but is far less harsh when part of a sentence. Consider, for example, a situation where someone says: 'I was so wound up that I felt I would want to kill the next person who annoyed me'. If the response is a simple 'Why?', that may come across as harsh and unsympathetic, but a full sentence, such as: 'Why did you feel like that?' comes across as far more responsive and supportive.
- *Encourage others to use 'Why'.* Make it clear that it cuts both ways, that you welcome other people asking you 'Why?'

There is no guarantee that people will always feel comfortable with being asked 'Why?', even when it is done with great skill and empathy. However, there are two important points to note here. First, by asking 'why?' skilfully and sensitively, rather than mechanistically, we are significantly increasing the chances of being able to help this person tackle their problems. Second, if they do find being asked 'why?' (in a skilful and sensitive manner) threatening, then that may well tell us something significant about their situation – for example, about their level of anxiety.

▶ **Avoiding avoidance** ▶ **Challenging cognitive distortions** ▶ **Dealing with objections** ▶ **Helicopter vision** ▶ **Using dissonance** ▶

The empty chair

Exploring the influence of an absent person

The empty chair technique is one that has long been used in family therapy, but can also be used to very good effect outside that context. Indeed, it has the potential to be used in a wide range of contexts or settings. It is used to try and understand somebody else's perspective and how particular people feel about that perspective. It can be especially useful in creating an atmosphere where people feel able to talk openly without fear of causing conflict or ill feeling.

The technique can be used in one of two basic ways, literally or metaphorically. When it is used literally, it involves having an empty chair physically present in the room. If somebody who is present is very angry towards someone who is not there, they can be asked to express their anger towards the empty chair, as if the person they are angry with were sitting in it. This may seem a bit silly, but it is surprising how effective it can be and how quickly people can adjust to talking to an empty chair. People may be more willing to say things to an empty chair that they feel too inhibited to say directly to the person concerned.

It is not only expressing anger that can be part of this process. Indeed, it can be used to express any feelings at all, and as such is a very good way of helping people vent what otherwise might remain as pent-up feelings. In this respect, it can be a very useful tool for encouraging people to talk openly about their feelings so that they can then be helped to deal with them (and/or deal with the situation that is causing them). For example, they can be helped to explore ways of communicating their feelings in a constructive way.

After someone has spoken to the empty chair, they can be asked 'What would he or she say in response if they were sitting in that chair?' This can help to develop a discussion further, again to identify issues that need to be addressed. The use of the technique can also involve asking 'Why haven't you said this to him or her before? What has prevented you?' This can identify obstacles to communication, and it may well be an important part of helping this person to look at ways of removing or bypassing such obstacles. It can also help the person concerned to make the effort to try and understand the other person's point of view – to see both sides of the situation.

While literally using an empty chair can be a very powerful and effective use of symbolism, there is the downside that, as I suggested above, some people may feel it is a bit silly and may therefore feel too uncomfortable to benefit from it (or indeed, an inexperienced helper may not feel confident enough to carry it through). In such cases the alternative is to use the technique in a metaphorical way, rather than literally to have an empty chair present. This involves, asking questions like: 'If Tom were here now and asked you to speak openly about how you felt, what would you say to him?' or 'You are clearly feeling let down about how Lyn has treated you. Imagine I'm Lyn sitting here right now. What would you want to say to me? Don't hold back, just speak your mind.'

The examples I have given so far have involved using this technique with an individual. However, it can also be used in groups – for example, if there is a group of staff who are dissatisfied with a manager and there is some sort of investigation into the situation (perhaps the manager has been suspended as a result of allegations of bullying).

Of course, this technique has to be handled very carefully, as it can be very powerful and therefore potentially destructive if not handled appropriately. This is not one to be used lightly or without careful consideration of whether these circumstances are appropriate. If you are not an experienced people worker, but you feel this technique would be appropriate in a particular context, it may be worth considering whether it is worth enlisting the support of one or more experienced colleagues to undertake this work with you until you are more experienced and feel comfortable in using this powerful tool.

An important aspect of this technique to consider is its role in 'catharsis' (see the discussion of 'Recognizing grief' below). The technique can free up feelings that have been 'locked in' for some considerable time. This, in itself, can have positive benefits, but it can also be of considerable use in helping to identify positive ways forward. We need to be prepared for this, as the emotional outpourings can be quite significant. We may also want to make sure that the person going through this cathartic experience has somebody they know and trust to offer them emotional support in the immediate aftermath. They may feel the need to talk things through and you may not be available. In particularly emotionally charged circumstances, you may wish to make sure that the person you are working with has this moral support in place before you make use of the empty chair technique. It would also be wise to make sure that you have suitable support in place too, as an intensive outpouring of emotion can at times leave you feeling in need of an understanding person with a good listening ear.

▶ **Holding**   ▶ **The magic wand**   ▶ **Reframing** ▶

Encouraging creativity

Avoiding getting stuck in ruts

Habit is a very powerful force (see 'The three Hs'). We often do things before we have had the chance to think about them or explore other options, purely because they are things that we are used to doing, things that we have grown accustomed to over a period of time. What this can result in, therefore, is the tendency to stay within our comfort zones where we feel safe and secure and out of harm's way. That can be an appealing place to be, but we pay a significant price for this, not least in the following ways:

1. *Other potentially more effective options are excluded.* We are, in a sense, restricting ourselves to our very limited range of ways of dealing with the challenges that we face in our work and in our lives. In that way, we cut ourselves off from new opportunities to develop even better ways of dealing with what we have to encounter.
2. *Our job satisfaction is reduced.* If we are not taking on new challenges or finding new ways of dealing with existing challenges, then our working life is likely to be quite boring and unstimulating. There will be few opportunities for a sense of achievement and, therefore, overall lower levels of motivation and satisfaction.
3. *We fail to learn, grow and develop.* If we are restricting ourselves to what we feel comfortable with, then new opportunities to learn, to develop our knowledge, our skills and our confidence will be wasted. We will be, in effect, keeping ourselves within a very closed framework of operation that will therefore give us very few opportunities to learn over time.
4. *We miss opportunities to earn respect and credibility and form good working relationships.* In other words, partnership is adversely affected by a tendency to stay within our comfort zone. If we come across to the people we are trying to help as people who play it safe and who have a very limited range of ways of tackling situations, then we are highly unlikely to inspire any sense of confidence.

It is therefore important to pursue creativity for ourselves in order to be able to avoid these problems. There are various techniques we can use to do this, many of which are to be found in this very book. Supervision and team support can also be very helpful in assisting us in having a broader perspective which enables us to explore a wider range of options.

However, it is also important to encourage creativity in others. This involves supporting them in moving out of their comfort zones and out of the tramlines that can prevent them from moving forward in dealing with their problems. This can be especially applicable in situations where their own behaviour, thinking or emotional responses are 'locking them in' to their problems. For example, if someone is in a situation where they tend to get angry because there are many aspects of those circumstances which annoy, irritate or frustrate them, then the frequent expression of anger can result in the situation becoming worse, perhaps cutting off sources of support for them, because other people back off from someone who comes across as frequently irate. If that person can be helped to respond to irritation and frustration more creatively – that is, in ways that are more constructive and geared towards problem solving, rather than just simply expressing anger but not doing anything about the problems that are causing the anger, then creativity can be very helpful.

Many people may need a lot of nurturing to be able to do this, and that nurturing may come from ourselves as problem solvers or may have to come from other significant people in their life. The reason that this nurturing needs to take place is that, as already noted, habit is a very powerful force, and being more creative involves conquering that force, overcoming it so that we have a more open approach to the range of potential solutions available to us, and are not hemmed in by the tendency to follow habit unthinkingly.

It is important, however, to sound a note of caution in recognizing that, while creativity is a useful tool in itself, it needs to be linked in with the concept of innovation. What I mean by this is that creativity is the process of thinking more broadly, more imaginatively, about a situation. Innovation is the process of putting that thinking into practice. Creativity for its own sake is not much use if it does not result in different forms of action taken. The reason I am emphasizing this is that I have come across many practitioners over the years who think quite creatively, but who do not put their ideas into practice – perhaps because they are anxious about the possibility of things going wrong or because they fear being labelled as somebody who is unorthodox in some way. However, when that is the case, it is important to think carefully about what is being lost by not translating more imaginative thinking into more innovative and more effective approaches to problem solving.

Exchange is no robbery
The importance of reciprocity

This technique explores the idea that people respond well to being given responsibility and the opportunity to contribute rather than simply being expected to passively receive help or services. A key concept here is that of reciprocity. This refers to the idea that we can gain as much, if not more, from giving as we do from receiving. This is for at least two main reasons. The first one relates to self-esteem. Where a person is being helped, but has no opportunity to offer anything in return, then they may feel that they are less worthy than somebody who has something to offer other people. We therefore have to be careful that, in trying to help people, we do not deny them opportunities for reciprocity, as this will, in effect, endanger their self-esteem. A second reason for promoting reciprocity is the spiritual notion of 'connectedness'. This refers to the fact that we gain so much of our sense of identity, our sense of how we fit into the wider world, through our connections with other people. If those connections are one way only – that is, we receive but we do not have the opportunity to give in return, then that can lead to a diminished sense of identity and to a compromised sense of being connected to other people, and therefore a sense of spiritual impoverishment.

It is unfortunately the case that some groups of people are regularly denied opportunities to give. For example, people who are very dependent on others as the result of disability or infirmity in old age can find that they are denied the opportunity to make a contribution. For other people, they may have opportunities to contribute in their everyday lives, but there may be particular times when this ceases to apply – for example, when someone is ill or is experiencing personal or family difficulties and others are helping or trying to help.

Consequently, one important thing that we need to bear in mind is that when people need help from us, this is when they are least likely to have opportunities to reciprocate and, as we have seen, the consequences of being denied such opportunities can be very significant in terms of self-esteem and spiritual connectedness. In order to promote a better understanding of reciprocity and a higher likelihood of being able to facilitate this, there are various things we can do. These include the following:

- There are simple practical means by which people can be enabled to contribute. For example, if someone offers us a cup of tea or coffee, then we may be tempted to decline, so that we can focus on getting down to business but, for many people, having the opportunity, even in just such a simple practical way, to reciprocate can be very important indeed. Refusing that cup of tea could have significant consequences in terms of reciprocity.
- We also have the use of language. We can talk to people either in ways that undermine their reciprocity and emphasize that they are in some way dependent on us for help, or we can use forms of language that emphasize the two-way nature of the relationship. It is possible, for example, to use language which gets across the message that we are getting pleasure and job satisfaction from helping, that we are enjoying that person's company, and so on.
- There can also be the potential for organizing, facilitating or suggesting pathways to fuller forms of giving, for example, by exploring opportunities for someone to serve as a volunteer.

Our own motivations to help, to be useful and to serve a positive purpose can ironically be counterproductive in certain circumstances, in so far as we may be denying other people the opportunity to give, to be useful and to feel valued. The idea of reciprocity is therefore one that we should hold firmly in mind when we engage in problem-solving activities. Not only is exchange not robbery, but it can also be a sound foundation for self-esteem, connectedness and partnership in working towards shared goals.

▶ Congruence ▶ Modelling and use of self ▶

Finding the growth zone

Finding the balance between comfort and fear

The growth zone is a positive area for learning and progress and it is to be found in between the unhelpful extremes of our comfort zone (complacency) and the danger zone (where we do not learn because of fear) – see Figure 2.3.

The idea is based on what has come to be known as the Yerkes-Dodson law of adult learning (Thompson, 2006). What is involved in finding the growth zone is trying to establish the balance between the comfort zone and the danger zone. It involves identifying where people are in relation to those zones. If someone is, for example, firmly rooted in their comfort zone and unwilling to move out of it because they are fearful of what might happen, then we can identify from this that we need to be effective in offering reassurance in boosting confidence to the point where they feel it is safe to move forward into the growth zone. What can be helpful is to explain to people that the growth zone actually exists, because, for many people, the situation is that they see only two zones: comfort and danger. They therefore feel that if they step out of their comfort zone they will immediately be in danger, without recognizing that there is a balance in between the two extremes where

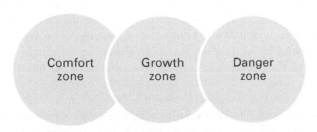

Figure 2.3   Finding the growth zone

learning, growth and development are not only possible, but actually become more likely the more time we spend in that intermediate zone between comfort and danger.

People can also locate themselves in the danger zone, in the sense that they may be in a state of panic or high anxiety that is preventing them from concentrating on the situation that is perhaps holding them back from getting a more holistic perspective which would enable them to see the overall picture. This in turn can lead to the cognitive distortions that I mentioned earlier. What we therefore need to do with people who are in that danger zone is to help to calm them down, to help get them to a point where they have achieved a stronger sense of perspective, where they can see the situation in proportion. We can then lead them, as it were, into the growth zone where they are better equipped to recognize what they need to do in order to tackle their problems. They are then in a position to learn and to benefit from having moved out of the danger zone.

It is also important to recognize from the diagram that there are interconnections. That is, these are not three separate zones of operation; there will be places where two zones overlap, and so perhaps our first step is to get people to move into the appropriate overlapping area and then from that to gently ease them and support them into the balanced, more positive, central area of the growth zone.

Many people will need considerable support in moving out of either the comfort zone or the danger zone, so that they are in a stronger position to learn and make progress. It is therefore important not to expect that we can always achieve quick results in terms of leading people into the growth zone (although at times it is very possible for rapid progress to be made). However, we should also recognize that we may need to think about being in the growth zone ourselves. In terms of our own practice, we may at times find ourselves in the comfort zone where we are being complacent and we are not prepared to try and think in new ways and to be creative, as discussed earlier. However, at times we may also find ourselves in the danger zone where we may feel under too much pressure, where we are being stressed by our circumstances, and there is a risk that we may act rashly. In those circumstances we then need to seek the appropriate support to enable us to get into the positive growth zone.

In effect, finding the growth zone is a form of empowerment. It is about trying to make ourselves redundant, as it were, as problem solvers where people are no longer in a comfort zone of complacency and unwilling to make the changes necessary to address their problems, and are also not in a danger zone where the level of anxiety is such that they are struggling to get a balanced view of the situation that will enable them to take the steps they need to engage with in order to solve or at least alleviate their problems.

▶ **Educating** ▶ **Know your enemy** ▶

Fishbone analysis

A visual aid to problem solving

This is an approach to problem solving that involves developing a diagram in the shape of a fishbone (hence the term) that can provide a helpful overview of a particular situation. It focuses on the possible causes or contributory factors to a problem, so that people trying to tackle particular problems or sets of problems can have a clear overview of what is contributing to the difficulties so that plans can be drawn up to tackle the issues identified.

The technique involves drawing a box on the right-hand side of a page of paper and putting the name of the particular problem in that box. From this, a line is drawn out to the left of the page with lines being drawn transecting that main fishbone (see the example below in Figure 2.4).

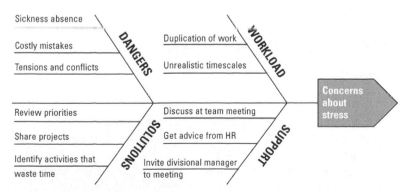

Figure 2.4 Example of a fishbone analysis

Having this type of diagram drawn up helps to make sure that we are not neglecting important aspects of the situation. It gives us a basis for identifying patterns and themes, and is therefore a good platform for setting priorities. When using the diagram, what is involved is adding causes or causal factors to the bones of the fish, as it were, so that each of the main bones coming off the main axis can represent an area relevant to the problem situation, and then possible contributory factors can be linked into that particular 'bone'.

Developing a fishbone analysis enables a collective approach. A team, group or family can be helped to work together to come up with this important overview of the factors that are contributing to the current situation. What can be a useful bonus from this is that, because it is carried out on a collective basis, it can help identify actual or potential differences of perspective which could possibly stand in the way of progress being made when it comes to trying to address the problems concerned.

It can be helpful to practise this technique before trying it for real in a problem situation. It has the potential to be a very useful tool for identifying issues that perhaps otherwise would not have emerged from straightforward linear thinking. It is very adaptable and can be widely applicable in all manner of situations. If you have not used the fishbone analysis before, you may find it helpful to ask around among your colleagues to see if you can find one or more people who have used this technique before and see what you can learn from their experience.

▶ **Force-field analysis** ▶ **Gantt chart** ▶ **Mind mapping** ▶

Fishing for red herrings

Not allowing ourselves to be distracted

This tool involves identifying those aspects of a situation that may be distracting us from the key issues and therefore standing in the way of making progress.

Some issues take up more time, effort and resources than they deserve. They can dominate a situation, even though their significance does not justify this. It is therefore wise to develop an understanding of which aspects of the situation are particularly important and worthy of our attention and which ones are attracting more attention than they really should. This is what is meant by a red herring – the sort of aspect of a situation which can draw resources into it without much by way of positive results.

To use this tool, what we need to do is to develop a list of those factors which are having a bearing on the problem situation, and then categorizing these in terms of which are key issues that need to be addressed and which are red herrings that will waste a lot of time and energy by sidetracking us. Examples of such red herrings would be an underlying conflict which results in people distracting attention from the main issues or, what I like to refer to as 'ego stroking', and what I mean by that is situations where people are demanding attention because it boosts their self-esteem. It makes them feel good about themselves, but does not necessarily take us any further forward in terms of addressing the problems identified.

Sometimes it can be helpful to discuss these distractions openly and try to get a consensus about keeping them out of the picture, but it is not always wise to do so if there are certain sensitivities involved. In such situations it may be necessary to work on red herrings in other ways to prevent them doing damage to our problem-solving efforts.

Fishing for red herring can be extremely helpful in two main ways:

1. *Making progress.* Particularly in situations that are complex and multi-dimensional, there can be significant benefits that arise from identifying red herring and therefore being in a position to ensure that they do not take up more time, attention and resources than they deserve, leaving us with greater time and energy to invest in the aspects of the situation that are much more important and which are much more likely to lead to positive outcomes.
2. *Gaining trust, respect and credibility.* This tool enables us to identify those aspects of a situation which are distracting (and which may therefore be a source of irritation for some people). In this way we can convince people of our effectiveness and underline the important contribution we can make to such situations. As a result of this we can gain a higher level of trust, and the credibility that goes with this can be very worthwhile in terms of influencing the situations that we are dealing with.

Fishing for red herrings may lead to conflict, in the sense that people may have different perspectives on what is to be seen as a red herring and what is not, but this in itself can be a useful thing, in so far as identifying such differences of perspective can help us to work towards a consensus, rather than allowing such underlying differences not to emerge, and yet still to have the effect of slowing down movement towards the desired goals.

▶ **Making the most of meetings** ▶ **Naming the process** ▶ **Working backwards** ▶

Force-field analysis

Managing change

It is often said that the only thing that is constant is that we live and work in constantly changing circumstances. Change is said to be the norm. Force-field analysis is a very well established technique, dating back to Kurt Lewin's work in 1947, that can be used as a useful way of looking at change. It can be used in a variety of ways, not least the following:

1. as a planning or preparation tool (to be used before change in order to try and influence it or channel it in a particular direction – or indeed to attempt to prevent it, if it is an unwelcome change);
2. as a problem-solving tool to work out why change is not working (to be used during a change process); or
3. to evaluate how change happened (after the change has occurred).

Given that so much of problem solving involves either promoting change or reacting to it, a tool geared towards managing change can be a very useful one in the problem solver's repertoire.

Force-field analysis involves identifying two sets of factors or 'forces'. These can include people, events, tendencies (aspects of a culture, for example) or anything else that can influence change (either by promoting it or by inhibiting it):

• *Driving forces.* Those factors that destabilise the status quo and make change more likely – in other words, those aspects of the situation that push in the direction of change.

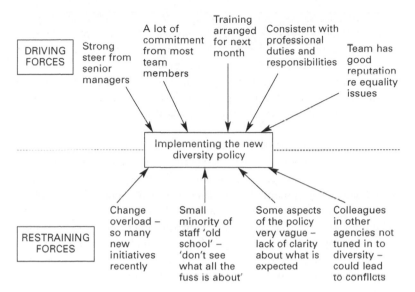

Figure 2.5 Force-field analysis

- *Restraining forces.* These are 'inhibitory' forces, the factors that make change less likely. They are issues that will need to be overcome or bypassed if change is to take place.

This can be done in diagrammatic form, as indicated in Figure 2.5.

The technique can be used as a 'thinking tool'. That is, we can use it to clarify our own thinking. This can be of particular value in times of change (or where change is due to take place). Similarly, we can help others to clarify their thinking in times of change and uncertainty. In this way, it can be used to reduce anxiety and remove or reduce confusion – something that can be very useful in our problem-solving endeavours. And, of course, it can be used in group or team situations as a way of trying to prepare for change, handle it to best effect while it is happening and make sense of it and/or evaluate it after the event.

In addition to these three contexts (self, self and others and group/team), there are three sets of activities the tool can be used to support:

- *To promote change where it is needed.* This would apply in situations where change is desirable – for example, where there is an unacceptable level of risk.

- *To maximize the positive potential of change.*   This relates to situations where change is happening anyway, but we are seeking to channel it in a particular direction so that we get the most benefit we can from the changing circumstances.
- *To prevent change.*   It will often be the case that our problem-solving efforts are geared towards preventing deterioration in a situation and/or guarding against the harmful or destructive effects of change.

Some people seem to have a very rosy view of change and can become overzealous in promoting it. They seem to assume that change is necessarily progress or improvement and take little or no account of the costs of change and its potentially destructive impact. Force-field analysis can be useful in countering that naïve tendency.

Change is a central part of human experience, and so, as 'people workers' trying to solve human problems, we have to be very tuned in to change – its causes, its effects, its benefits and its costs. Force-field analysis does not do all that for us, but it does give us a very useful tool for moving in the right direction.

PRACTICE FOCUS 2.6

Following a major reorganization Moira's team was faced with a very different set of duties. The range of changes was quite extensive and Moira was concerned that what had been a good team could be seriously undermined by the impact of the changes. She had seen this happen in a previous organization she had worked for. She sought advice from a fellow team manager who told her about force-field analysis. He had worked in an organization where a consultant had been brought in who used this tool to help the organization cope with a major change. Moira was quite taken by the idea and so, at the next team meeting, she arranged for the team to use the technique to develop a fuller understanding of what was happening. This did not solve all the team's problems but it made a very constructive contribution to coping with what was proving to be a very difficult situation.

▶ **The CIA framework** ▶ **Cost-benefit analysis** ▶ **PCS analysis** ▶ **SWOT analysis** ▶

Gantt charts

Visual aids for project management

This a very helpful visual tool to act as a basis for project management. It can be used very effectively to underpin our problem-solving efforts. It is named after their inventor, Henry Laurence Gantt who developed the idea in the early part of the twentieth century.

A Gantt chart provides a visual record that can act as a schedule for a project. It is now widely used in a variety of occupational settings, and is generally regarded as a helpful way of getting a clear focus on what needs to be done in what order and to what timescale.

As a problem-solving tool, a Gantt chart can be particularly useful for clearly defined problems that can be broken down into different steps or stages. Such a chart allows people to:

1. Establish a clear, agreed focus with a view to developing a project plan for taking the necessary steps to address the problem in hand;
2. Map out the steps to be taken, in what order and to what timescales. This is the way in which it can be a useful scheduling too. This can help to prevent drift and the momentum for change being lost. It is therefore consistent with the **S** of PRECISE practice (see Part One) which refers to systematic practice.

It is also a good basis for working in partnership (reflecting the **P** of PRECISE practice). This is because a visual tool like this can be developed in partnership by those people involved in the problem-solving project, but also, even if there are people not directly involved in drawing it up, its use as a focal point helps to draw people together to give a clear shared view of what needs to be done and when.

A Gantt chart can also be empowering by giving the people involved a shared sense of purpose and some degree of confidence and security as a result of this. Figure 2.6 gives us a clear picture of how a Gantt

Task	Duration	Week 1	Week 2	Week 3	Week 4	Week 5	Week 6

Figure 2.6   Layout for a basic Gantt chart

chart can work, although there are different variations on this theme. It is also important to note that there is software available that can be used to produce Gantt charts for those people who intend to use them on a regular basis.

▶ **Ecomaps** ▶ **Fishbone analysis** ▶ **Mind mapping** ▶

Giving feedback

Letting people know where they stand

When people are experiencing difficulties they can become very engrossed in what is going on around them and perhaps lose sight of their own part in the situation. To help with promoting problem solving we will often be called upon to give feedback to another person about their own behaviour or attitudes – and sometimes they will not necessarily want to hear what we have to say. For example, someone may be making their problems worse in how they are reacting to them. To make progress in dealing with the problems, it may be necessary to give the person concerned feedback about how they are dealing with the situation. This is a skilful and challenging job, as some people can react quite badly to being given feedback, even when it is done constructively and supportively as part of an attempt to help them deal with their problems.

Managers and supervisors in particular are likely to find that giving feedback – positive and negative – is an important part of their role.

However, all of us involved in people work, whether managers or not, are likely to be required to give feedback at some time. It is therefore important to consider how best to do this in order to lay the foundations for developing good practice.

The skills involved in giving feedback can be developed to quite a high level but, for present purposes, we will need to be less ambitious and settle for covering the basics. The following pointers (taken from Thompson and Gilbert, 2011) should give you a good start in developing your skills in this area:

- *Be clear about what you are saying – don't fudge the issue.* It is important that we should not allow our own anxiety to lead us into making a mess of giving feedback. If we are not clear about what we are trying to say, we will not communicate clearly and, if we do not communicate clearly, we run the risk of making the situation more tense and difficult than it needs to be. Therefore, it is essential that we (i) plan what we are going to say before we say it; and (ii) say it clearly. Fudging the issue will only make people nervous, and that can be a significant obstacle to progress.
- *Give balanced feedback – positives and negatives.* Some people feel comfortable giving positive feedback (see the discussion of 'Positive strokes' below), but uncomfortable giving negative feedback, while for others it may be the reverse (some people feel they are being patronizing when they give positive feedback). Yet other people feel uncomfortable with both types of feedback, positive and negative! It is therefore important to develop your knowledge and skills over time to the point where you can feel reasonably comfortable with, and competent in, both sides of the feedback coin – positive and negative.
- *Raise concerns but don't make accusations.* In trying to help people solve problems, you are entitled to give them feedback as you see fit, if this is geared towards making progress. However, if they feel they are being criticized, they might feel that you are accusing them of wrongdoing or incompetence. We should therefore be very careful to make sure that we do not say anything that could be interpreted as accusatory. This reinforces the point made above about being clear about what we are going to say before we say it.
- *Be prepared to listen – you may have got it wrong.* We live and work in complex circumstances. It is very easy for things to be misunderstood, distorted or misrepresented, so we should not assume that the opinion we have formed is necessarily correct. We may have been

misinformed or may have misinterpreted the situation (perhaps because of a key bit of information we were not aware of at the time). Listening is always a good idea in people work, but it is particularly important in giving feedback.

- *Keep a written record.* People can resent being given feedback if they perceive it as criticism (even if you have bent over backwards to make it constructive and supportive) and may make a complaint. Having a record of what was said is therefore an important self-protection measure. It is, of course, also good practice to have a written record of important work you do.
- *Above all, be constructive.* If you are giving negative feedback, it pays to help to develop ways forward, so that even criticism can be helpful if it is geared towards improvement and problem solving. If you are giving positive feedback, you can also look at how the situation can get even better.

A common approach to giving feedback that can be very helpful is what is known as the 'sandwich approach'. This involves beginning with positive feedback: 'I can see that you have made a lot of progress here in a number of areas', followed by any negative feedback that is needed: 'But, I do feel we need to look at those areas where progress has not been so good and consider why that might be', and finishing with positive feedback again: 'So, it is good to see that we have been able to identify areas of progress where you have done well and we've explored ways of sorting out those areas where progress is slow. I think this has been very constructive and I hope you agree.'

The dangers to avoid are the two unhelpful extremes of avoiding or fudging the issue on the one hand, and taking too hard a line on the other – see Figure 2.7. The healthy balance in between these two destructive extremes is a balanced, constructive approach based on

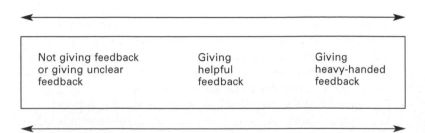

Figure 2.7 Giving feedback

principles of assertiveness (producing 'win–win' outcomes). In transactional analysis terms (see below), it is based on adult–adult interactions rather than parent–child.

Giving feedback does not have to be a difficult or anxiety-provoking activity. In fact, it can be an enjoyable and rewarding part of our work once we build up the confidence and skills to rise to the challenges involved.

► **Challenging cognitive distortions** ► **Circular questioning** ► **Elegant challenging** ► **Negotiating expectations** ►

Grief audit

Getting an overview of people's experiences of grief

As we shall discuss in more detail later (when I explain the tool of 'Recognizing the significance of loss and grief'), the prevalence and significance of grief can often go largely unrecognized. This important tool can help people to identify the range of losses which may be affecting them, either directly or indirectly. A grief audit is, in a way, a further tool for addressing the implications arising from a major loss or a set of losses.

A grief audit needs to be done skilfully through a process of interaction and not mechanistically filling in a form or going through a process simply for the sake of it. A grief audit is a way of getting an overview of the loss issues that are affecting one or more people, whether these are currently live loss issues (in the sense that they relate to matters that have arisen in the recent past) or whether we are dealing with the historical legacy of earlier losses which can be just as significant in many situations. The grief audit tool involves identifying three sets of factors:

1. *Bereavement.* This aspect involves drawing up a list of the key people that the person or persons concerned have lost and, in particular, identifying multiple losses (that is, situations where more than one person was lost at the time) or cumulative losses (that is losses which occur in sequence over a period of time, adding up to a significant set of losses).
2. *Major changes.* These can be divided into two subcategories: there can be: (i) anticipated developmental changes – for example,

adolescence, retirement and so on; but there will also be (ii) situational changes – that is, changes that occur because of the specific circumstances of a particular situation. These changes, whether anticipated or not, can have the effect of producing a significant loss reaction – a form of grieving that is in most ways identical to the grief experience that accompanies a bereavement. It is important to note that the changes we are talking about are not necessarily negative ones. It is quite possible for people to have a grief reaction to what is experienced as a positive change. For example, somebody may be promoted and delighted about the fact, but still experience a grief reaction because they move on from their current circumstances to a new, less secure, set of circumstances and pine for aspects of their previous pre-promotion life.

3. *Traumatic experiences.* There is a wide range of ways in which people can be traumatized by life events. This includes being a victim of abuse, violence or crime, being involved in terrorism or the threat of terrorism and witnessing something horrific. All of these have the potential to produce a psychological (or psychosocial) reaction which amounts to a form of wound (*trauma* is the Greek word for wound).

For each of these three sets of factors, it is important to consider how the person concerned reacted to the loss and dealt with the grief that arose from it and also what support they received. In this way, we can develop a picture which will tell us a great deal about the experiences of loss they have encountered and also, just as importantly, the impact of those losses on their life.

This can be a useful tool in a wide range of circumstances. It can be helpful where it is obvious that there are loss factors to the fore, but it can also apply in situations where people do not immediately anticipate loss or grief being significant factors. For example, where somebody is depressed and there is no immediate suggestion that loss is a factor, a grief audit may reveal significant implications for the person concerned in terms of the losses they have encountered in their life.

In addition, there is now a growing body of theory and research which links mental health problems in adulthood with experiences of abuse, loss and trauma in childhood and early life (Anda et al., 2007). This means that a grief audit may be beneficial for a wide range of people who are encountering mental health difficulties.

▶ **Holding** ▶ **Providing an anchor** ▶ **Recognizing grief** ▶ **Responding to feelings** ▶

Helicopter vision

Obtaining an overview

The advantage of having access to a helicopter is that we can rise above a situation, get an overview, or 'the big picture', as it is often called, and then descend to the appropriate place where we can be of most help, where our intervention can have greatest impact. If we do not get this overview to begin with, then there is a danger that we will not know where and when to intervene. We may be drawn into intervening where the pressures or demands are greatest, but this will not necessarily be the place to achieve the greatest change or the best progress. Before tackling one part of a problem situation, it is wise to have at least some idea of how the different parts of that situation connect together and form the whole.

Sometimes we have to intervene rapidly in a situation where there is some sort of emergency, where there is risk to life and limb, for example. In such cases we may not have the relative luxury of being able to form an overview. We may have to respond there and then. However, in the grand scheme of things, such situations are relatively rare. The vast majority of situations where we are involved in trying to help people deal with their problems do give us at least some opportunity to get the feel of the situation and develop some sense of overview.

If we do not take advantage of the benefits of helicopter vision, we run the risk of allowing our intervention to rely too much on random factors. For example, we may choose to focus on a particular area because, from our particular standpoint, that seems to make sense. But from a different standpoint – the other side of the fence as it were – the situation may look very different. Helicopter vision would allow us to see both sides of the fence and the surrounding environment before deciding on the most appropriate place to focus our actions to try and be of help.

Helicopter vision can be of value at any stage in our intervention. It can be useful at the beginning to get an initial overview. It can be equally useful further down the line, once we have become involved in the situation we are trying to influence, to see whether our involvement has made any difference. This particular use of helicopter vision can be very beneficial, because sometimes we are focusing so much on our own part of the proceedings, as it were, that we do not realize what impact this may have made elsewhere in the situation – how, for example, our intervention may have had a domino effect, changing other aspects of the situation, perhaps without our immediate knowledge of it.

It can also be used when we are considering ending our involvement, as a sort of checking mechanism to see whether we feel it is safe to bring our involvement to a close or whether there are other things that need our attention before we can finally withdraw. Similarly, it can also be used when our intervention has finished, in order to evaluate our input to see what has worked (and whether it could have worked better), what did not work (how we could have done it differently), and what we have learned from the experience for future reference.

The technique of helicopter vision can be used as a guide to our own actions as described above. However, it can also be used as a tool of intervention in helping others. If the people we are trying to help have a tendency to focus narrowly on one aspect of their situation and not see how this relates to the bigger picture, then helping them to develop the skills of adopting helicopter vision can be a very beneficial way forward. For example, somebody who is depressed or anxious may see only the negative, worrying aspects of a situation and may need to be helped to develop a broader picture.

Helicopter vision also has application in working with groups or teams. It can be particularly helpful in situations characterized by conflict and disagreement. It can enable people to see how their perspective fits into the overall picture, thus highlighting where people are in agreement and where differences of perspective exist. This in itself will not resolve the difficulties, but it will provide a platform from which we can build on the areas of agreement and explore ways of dealing with the areas of conflict.

One very simple way to achieve helicopter vision is as follows:

- List the key people involved in the situation (those people who are significant in the development of the problem and possible solutions to it).
- Consider the situation from each person's point of view in turn.

- Next, consider the wider contextual factors. Is there anything significant about the context? Any power struggles, for example? Or hidden agendas?
- Finally, can you identify any common themes or linking threads? Anything that pulls the situation together and helps you make sense of it?

Do not worry if you find this process difficult at first. It can take some time to build up the skills of thinking holistically, which is, after all, what helicopter vision is all about.

▶ **Mind mapping/SWOT analysis** ▶

Holding

Helping to provide emotional security

This is a term that is drawn from the psychodynamic theory base that involves helping people to feel secure in distressing circumstances by metaphorically holding them. Just as physical touch and being held can be immensely reassuring and calming at times of difficulty or of distress, so too can a metaphorical form of holding.

Touch can be understood as a form of language, an important basis of nonverbal communication. In this way it can be very helpful in situations where actually holding somebody would be regarded as inappropriate and perhaps intrusive. This is especially the case in situations involving professional problem solvers where making physical contact with a client or patient, for example, may be regarded as a step too far when it comes to rapport building.

However, there are other ways of holding in a more metaphorical sense that are worth exploring, not least the following:

- *Acknowledging.* This is an important step in terms of holding people to acknowledge their feelings, to acknowledge their presence, their value, their dignity and so on, with a view to helping people to feel validated or affirmed by the way a person reacts to them in a way which acknowledges them as fellow human beings. This can be on a one-to-one basis where it is just a single individual who is doing the acknowledging, or it can be a collective matter where perhaps a family or a team of staff or any other group of people are giving the strong message of affirmation and validation. This can be exceptionally powerful and supportive.

- *What we say.* This refers to the use of empathic language, talking to somebody in terms which recognize the importance and impact of their feelings, finding ways of relating to people that are 'emotionally intelligent'. This is an important contribution to the process of holding.

- *How we say it.* The technical term for this is 'paralanguage', and it refers to such matters as tone of voice, the speed at which we speak, pitch and so on. Making sure that we get this right in terms of giving a comforting and reassuring message is an important part of being successful when it comes to holding. For example, a high pitch can imply anxiety, and so someone hearing us talk to them in a high pitch may actually add to any anxiety they may already be feeling, rather than reduce it, whereas a lower pitch can be more reassuring. It offers a degree of confidence. Of course, it is important to do this skilfully, rather than to try and do it mechanistically and come across as if we are just playing games with people. Getting this right can therefore depend on building up skills over a period of time, and so it may well be a worthwhile use of your time to try practising this with somebody you can trust to give you helpful and supportive feedback.

- *What our body says.* Although physically holding somebody may be out of bounds in the types of situation we are talking about here, there are still ways in which our body language can be supportive. This will include such things as the gestures we make, the use of eye contact and so on. Again, this is something that can be practised over time, and we can also learn from watching how other people convey reassurance through their body language.

- *What our behaviour says.* Acting in ways that show that we are interested and concerned, that we are not just going through the motions because we are paid to, that we are genuinely committed to helping someone. If our behaviour can give such positive, affirming messages, then that in itself can be a significant form of holding.

What all these add up to basically is giving a clear and consistent message of support. That in itself can, in certain circumstances, be all that is needed to enable somebody to cope with the pressures they face and to tackle the problems that are causing them concern at that time.

In other circumstances, of course, it will not be enough on its own to give such a positive message of support, but it can make the overall task of helping that much easier if we are able to create this firm foundation of support.

In many situations there will be nothing that we can do to help people. For example, in circumstances where somebody is grieving, we will not be able to take their pain away (Thompson, 2012a). However, giving people messages of support can be immensely helpful in enabling them to work through some difficult and painful experiences, even if we are not able to help them to find actual solutions to the underlying problems.

▶ **Recognising abuse** ▶ **Recognizing grief** ▶ **Responding to feelings** ▶

Inviting innocent questions

Getting a perspective from outside the situation you are dealing with

Naïve or innocent questions about a difficult situation can sometimes give useful insights about possible ways forward. It can be useful to talk to somebody outside a situation that we are dealing with and to give them simply the gist of the situation without going into detail. We can then ask them to comment on what they think about the situation, how it comes across to them. They will then come up with what I would call 'innocent' questions – for example, such questions as: How did this happen? What can be done about it? Who else is involved in the situation? Some of these questions will perhaps be obvious to us, but what we have to recognize is that different people will ask different questions and this gives us two advantages. The first advantage is that it gives us a broader perspective so, by asking more than one person, we can get a range of responses and that will give us some degree of breadth in terms of the differences, but also some degree of depth in terms of the recurring themes that will come across from asking different people to comment on the same situation. The second advantage is that, because different people see situations in different ways, somebody else may come up with a point of view which had not occurred to us, and so their innocent question may be one that is very worthwhile asking and seeking to answer.

What this is based on is the idea that a fresh perspective can produce fresh insights. It can move us away from our usual patterns of thinking, and it can therefore help us to be more creative about a situation. It is very easy for professional problem solvers to get very close to a situation and, in effect, not see the wood for the trees. In this way, we can be helped to get a more holistic picture of the situation by inviting innocent questions.

One potential way of doing this is through supervision. In a supervision session, it may be appropriate to ask the supervisor for his or her perspective on a particular situation. We can then tune into the ways in which their perspective is similar to our own and in what ways it differs. Both of these aspects can then potentially give us some useful insights when it comes to developing a fuller understanding of the situation, so that we are better equipped to deal with it.

One key point to remember in terms of inviting innocent questions is the importance of confidentiality. We have to make sure that we are not betraying any confidences in asking other people about the situation we are trying to resolve. This means that we have to be careful, first of all about whom we ask and, second, what information we give them in terms of relaying to them the gist of that situation. We have to be very careful that we do not give them enough information to enable them to be able to identify the individuals concerned. However, despite this limitation, inviting innocent questions can be a very useful way of developing a fuller picture of a complex situation.

▶ **Encouraging creativity** ▶ **Stop trying** ▶

Know your enemy

Coping with anxiety

Something that is very commonly encountered in people work is anxiety. This can apply in a number of ways. We can feel anxious ourselves in facing the challenges of helping people solve their problems. In many circumstances, anxiety will be a major part of the cause of the problems experienced by the people we are seeking to help, and even when anxiety is not in itself a cause or factor, it will often be present as a result of the problems – often exacerbating them. Anxiety can also exist at a wider level – for example, anxiety (and thus defensiveness) can be part of an organizational culture and can thus have a very significant impact on the work undertaken in that organization. For example, we may have a team of staff who are very limited and unadventurous in their approach because they have become 'risk averse', as a result of a defensive culture built on a degree of anxiety.

A major problem with anxiety is that it can become self-perpetuating. This is because a common response to anxiety is avoidance. That is, if something is making us anxious, we are likely to seek to avoid it. While that is a perfectly understandable reaction, it is not always a helpful one. 'Avoidance behaviour', as psychologists call it, can be a significant barrier to progress. What it refers to is the tendency for people to, in effect, run away from their problems rather than face up to them and try and deal with them. There are two major problems with this. First, it can lead to a vicious circle. That is, the more we avoid our problems, the more anxious we can become in certain circumstances at least, and thus the more anxious we become, the more we avoid our problems, and so it goes on. Second, avoidance behaviour can lead to other problems. For example, if I am anxious about dealing with person X and therefore avoid doing so, I may subsequently face the situation of having a complaint made against me by person X because of my failure to undertake my duties in respect of him or her.

Another significant aspect of anxiety and avoidance behaviour is that the situation can change without our recognizing it, thus leaving us in a position of avoidance when in fact there is nothing left to avoid. For example, consider a situation where I avoid dealing with an aggressive man because his aggressive behaviour makes me anxious. It may well be the case that this man was being aggressive because of something that was bothering him. However, the situation may have now changed whereby he is no longer feeling distressed and is no longer responding in an aggressive way. However, if my tactic for dealing with the anxiety he generated in me was to avoid him, then I may well continue avoiding him for some considerable time after he has ceased to be aggressive.

One very useful way of dealing with anxiety is to translate it into fear. This is because anxiety tends to be generalized (when we are anxious we tend to have an overall feeling of uneasiness), whereas fear tends to be specific – fear of something. By making our generalized feeling of anxiety more specific, we can get a better picture of what is bothering us and what we need to do to deal with it. In this way, we are able to 'know our enemy', to be clear about precisely what is causing us problems. We are then much better equipped to deal with whatever it is that is causing concern. The following dialogue should help to illustrate this:

ANWEN: You seem to be very anxious. What's troubling you?

PAT: I don't know, I just feel very uneasy about the way things are at the moment.

ANWEN: Is there anything in particular that you can put your finger on?

PAT: Well, I hadn't really thought about it until now, but I suppose I'm mainly worried about all the uncertainty that's around.

ANWEN: Yes, uncertainty can be very unsettling. But is there anything in particular that you dread? Anything that you are afraid might happen?

PAT: Erm … well, I suppose it all comes down to wondering whether I will be able to cope with it all.

ANWEN: You're frightened it will be too much for you?

PAT: Yes.

ANWEN: In what way?

PAT: There's an awful lot expected of me just now, and I'm not sure I've got what it takes to come up with the goods. I suppose I'm having a crisis of confidence.

ANWEN: You're frightened that you will be seen to fail?

PAT: Yes, exactly. Yes, you've hit the nail on the head.

ANWEN: So, would it help for us to look at what exactly is being expected of you and how you might cope with that?

PAT: Yes, I think it would. Thank you, I've started to feel better about it already.

ANWEN: That's good. I think it's always better to be clear about what's worrying us, rather than let general feelings of anxiety undermine us.

This provides a clear example of how 'knowing your enemy' puts us at an advantage compared with the generally unsettling feeling of anxiety. Sometimes helping people realize precisely what is bothering them is all that they need – they can now tackle those issues themselves once they have had our help in pinpointing them. However, in other situations, identifying what the fears are is only the beginning of a longer, more detailed piece of work in terms of working out how best to deal with them. None the less, in either case, the use of this technique will have taken us a significant step forward.

The example given in the dialogue above is on a one-to-one basis. However, the same technique can also be used with groups of people (families or teams, for example) and, of course, we can also use it to help ourselves when we are feeling anxious – helping people deal with problems does not make us immune from them ourselves!

▶ **Avoiding avoidance** ▶ **Holding** ▶ **Providing an anchor** ▶

Lateral thinking

Finding new ways to think about problems and solutions

Edward de Bono's (1990) ideas on lateral thinking can be very useful in encouraging creative approaches to problem solving.

De Bono argues convincingly that we are brought up to think logically. This is especially the case in western societies where we are taught to think 'in straight lines', and there are clear benefits to this sort of rational approach to thinking, but there are also limitations of course. By thinking in such straight lines, we can get stuck in what de Bono refers to as clichéd patterns of thinking or what is often referred to as 'tramlines'. We become entrenched in particular ways of viewing situations and therefore potentially limiting ourselves in terms of the range of potential solutions that could be made available.

Western thinking in particular is based on the idea that rational argument should be used to arrive at the 'The Truth'. We therefore see a strong competitive element emerging which focuses on the idea of winning the argument, of being the one(s) to establish the truth. What this can do is have the effect of blinding us to the wider picture. In a sense, it oversimplifies our perception by trying to narrow things down too closely to 'The Truth'. De Bono refers to this type of thinking as vertical thinking. It has the effect of narrowing down our perspective, which is often a useful thing, to enable us to deal with the wide range of conceptual information that is received by our senses at any one time. Lateral thinking, by contrast, widens out our perspective. It is intended to allow us to see aspects of the situation that we would normally filter out.

Lateral thinking involves breaking out of the restrictive ways of thinking that we are brought up to adopt as part of our everyday approach to the world. Lateral thinking literally means 'thinking sideways' and is therefore a matter of coming at situations from a new angle and thereby gaining fresh insights. De Bono talks in terms of the need to break out of 'the concept prisons' of old and established ideas.

Lateral thinking can be particularly helpful in relation to particular types of problem situation:

- Where we have the information we require but it needs rearranging, what de Bono calls 'insight restructuring'. This refers to situations where we do not mean to look for further information, but rather look more closely and more creatively at the information that we have, so that, by organizing it in different ways, we get new insights that otherwise we would not have been able to see before (see 'Gantt chart'). A chart does not necessarily provide us with any new information, but it helps us to organize the information we have in ways that can help us to spot links, patterns and other aspects of the situation which would not otherwise have been apparent to us.
- Where people settle for the current arrangements they do not explore how things could be better. De Bono refers to this as 'the problem of no problem'. This is about people feeling settled in their comfort zone and not being prepared to try any new ideas, and so what is happening is that people are being denied the opportunity to improve their circumstances. They are therefore denying themselves, potentially at least, a number of positives, because they simply settle for the current situation as defined by their traditional logical thinking, rather than using lateral thinking to look at the situation differently and see what opportunities there are for making a good situation even better.

Lateral thinking involves reviewing our assumptions to see how our understanding of the situation changes if we suspend one or more of those assumptions. This means that, if we analyse a situation in terms of identifying what patterns of thinking we are relying on there (the clichéd pattern that de Bono writes about), we can change one or more of these assumptions and then see whether it improve the situation and, if so, we can ask ourselves: What does that tell us about how we may be able to move forward? It is a matter of experimenting with different aspects of our understanding of the situation to see whether looking at it differently can in any way produce fresh insights that can lead us forward.

Lateral thinking also involves 'reviewing labels'. In focusing on a particular situation, we can ask: What labels have been used and why? Do we need them? What happens if we change them? This, then, is a process of exploring language. The way we use language to define and identify (or label) things is a significant process in its own right, but, again, it can put us into a set of tramlines in terms of how those labels can predefine situations for us. Therefore, if we remove or play with those labels, what difference does that make? Does it give us any ideas about what can be contributing to the problems encountered and does that give us some fresh ideas about how we may be able to find ways forward?

This tool can be useful as a specific approach in certain defined circumstances but it can also have considerable value as a general way of promoting more creative approaches to problem solving.

PRACTICE FOCUS 2.7

Moira's team had worked together effectively for some time, but they were really struggling with their new project following the reorganization. Morale was starting to go down as there seemed to be so many obstacles to progress. Moira, the team manager was worried about how this was affecting the team and was therefore determined to find a productive way forward. One night when she was relaxing at home, an insight occurred to her. The next day she gathered the team together and told them that she thought they were victims of their own success. She told them that it had dawned on her that the reason they were struggling was that their methods of work had always been very effective in the past, but the new project, with different challenges meant that they would have to find a different approach. The situation had changed, but their approach hadn't. She said that they would need to think laterally about the situation and find new ways forward, rather than keep trying to fit the square peg of their well-established methods into the round hole of the new project.

▶ **Encouraging creativity** ▶ **Role reversal** ▶ **The six thinking hats** ▶

The magic wand

Getting as close to the ideal as possible

This is similar to the miracle question in solution-focused approaches (Myers, 2007; see also Part One). It enables us to identify the ideal outcomes and then plan how to get as close to them as possible. It can be used in (at least) three main ways, as follows:

1. *Clarifying our thinking.* By adopting this approach, we can try to identify the steps that need to be taken to get as close to the ideal situation as we can.
2. *Working directly with an individual, couple or family.* This is an extension of the same idea, but instead of simply thinking things through in our own mind to get some degree of clarity, we can involve the people we are trying to help in the process of identifying ways forward.
3. *Working with a group.* The same technique can help groups of people to focus on what the ideal outcome would be and how potentially they can work towards it. Such groups include teams of staff.

What is involved in the actual process is identifying:

(i) If you, the worker, had a magic wand, how would you use it to change the situation in a positive direction?
(ii) How might this possibly backfire? In other words, how could the situation go wrong if, in trying to improve the situation, you experience what the textbooks call a counterfinality (that is, a result that is the opposite of what you intended)?
(iii) What can we learn about the situation from (i) and (ii)? What insights are there to be gained from this consideration of the situation in this light?

(iv)   What would the other person(s) do if they had a magic wand?
(v)   How might that backfire?
(vi)   What can we learn from considering (iv) and (v)?
(vii)   What are the common themes across the worker's perspective and the perspective of others involved?
(viii)   What are the key differences between our own perspective and that of the people we are working with?
(ix)   What can we learn from (vii) and (viii).
(x)   How can we use the insights gained to get us close to the magic wand ideal as we possibly can?

This tool is, in effect, an exercise in (a) creative thinking and (b) negotiation skills. As far as creative thinking is concerned, it is based on looking holistically at the situation and trying to imagine how far away we are from the ideal and what we need to do to get closer to it. In terms of negotiation skills, what is important here is being able to develop the skills we need to help the people we are supporting to expect to make progress, but probably not to be able to reach the ideal situation. It is therefore an exercise in using negotiation skills to ensure that we have realistic expectations, realistic in the sense that people are not expecting too much of what can be achieved, but also not expecting too little by being cynical or defeatist about the situation (and therefore being demotivated as a result of low aspirations).

In working with some groups of people – for example, young children or people with learning disabilities – it will be important to make it clear that we do not really have a magic wand, that this is just a tool for trying to create a vision of where we want to aim for in order to tackle the problems that are currently being experienced.

▶ **Encouraging creativity** ▶ **Motivational interviewing** ▶ **Visioning** ▶
Working backwards ▶

Making the most of meetings

Avoiding time and energy being wasted

Meetings can be vitally important events that play a key role in solving problems, securing progress and pulling people together towards a common goal. Unfortunately, though, they can also be a complete waste of time. Poor meetings can be very wasteful because:

- the time costs are multiplied (ten people attending a two-hour meeting that produces no benefits means that a total of 20 hours has been wasted – almost the equivalent of three full days);
- the time involved in the meeting itself is not all that is wasted – there will be arrangement time (getting the meeting set up), preparation time (participants reading documents and so on) and travelling time (the total time wasted for an unproductive meeting could therefore actually add up to the equivalent of a full week of an individual's time);
- in addition to the time costs, there will be financial costs in terms of heating, lighting, travel expenses plus possibly venue hire and refreshment costs;
- the opportunity costs are significant – not only is time wasted, but opportunities to make significant progress can also be lost;
- they can create a lot of bad feeling and demotivate people, thus contributing further to waste of time, as demotivated people will be less productive.

An unproductive meeting can therefore be very wasteful indeed. Meetings can be unproductive for a number of reasons, not least the following:

- *The wrong people are present.* Sometimes people who do not need to be at a meeting are invited, perhaps because the person doing the inviting did not think the issues through well enough (or was ill-informed about the purpose or focus of the meeting) or perhaps because some people attend certain meetings out of habit or a misplaced sense of duty, even when they have little to contribute to or gain from that particular meeting.
- *The right people are absent.* That is, people who should have been there are not. If a certain person's input to a meeting is crucial, but he or she cannot be there, a lot of time can be wasted.
- *The timing is wrong.* This can apply in two senses. First, it can relate to situations where it would have been better to discuss the subject matter of the meeting after a related decision has been made (the meeting is premature) or to situations where events have already overtaken the agenda (the meeting is too late). Second, it can relate to poorly scheduled meetings – for example, a meeting to

useful, partly because it provides a helpful overview of the range of issues we are dealing with and how they are connected, and partly because the process itself can be useful in its own right – it can help to give a sense of control and confidence in dealing with a set of difficult issues.

Mind maps can be used in various ways. They can be used to clarify our own thinking, to help other people clarify their thinking, or as a group exercise. I have found them particularly useful when people are under stress because they have too many plates spinning – that is, they feel that their life is overcomplicated. Producing a mind map can give an overview of the situation and show how the different elements interrelate. That in itself can be a useful form of intervention.

To draw a mind map we will need a sheet of A4 paper or similar. First, turn it on its side so that it is 'landscape' layout. At the centre of the page write the focus of the map – for example, if the focus for this particular mind map is a current project you are involved with, then write the name of the project at the centre. Alternatively, you may wish to come up with some sort of drawing or visual symbol to represent the project. From this central point, you will need to draw thick lines outwards, one each for the various themes that characterize the project. For example, if one set of projects is around reviewing activities, then write 'reviewing activities' along that particular line. These themes emerging from the central point should be written in capital letters. The lines should be roughly the same length as the words written on them, although this is not crucial.

Once you have identified these main themes, go through each of them systematically and, for each of them, draw lines outwards from the end of the thick line and, on each of these lines, write the particular issues or projects. Continue this process with each of the themes until you have an overview of the situation you are now addressing. What you should end up with is something like Figure 2.8, with a central core concept from which the main themes radiate, each with its sub-themes branching out.

Mind mapping is based on the idea that the brain does not think in straight lines, that our thinking, in other words, is not linear. We tend to jump from one issue to another, and this tends to be not in a random way but, rather, across a connection of interlocking themes and issues. The mind map is intended to be a visual representation of that set of interconnected themes and issues. This non-linear representation can be very useful for at least two reasons. First, it enables us to jump from one part of the map to another as we see fit. This can encourage

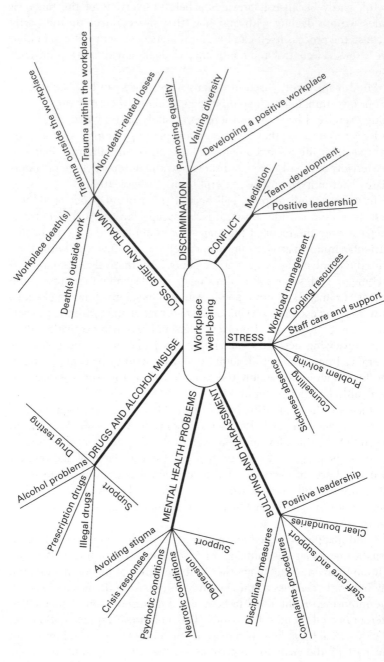

Figure 2.8 Example of a mind map

creativity and a more imaginative approach. Second, it can enable us to see connections that we may perhaps not have previously noticed. For example, I once did a mind map with somebody who was depressed. It was only through producing this mind map that he realized how frequently financial matters cropped up in it. This helped him to realize that a significant part of his problem was financial worries. However, he had been so depressed that he was not thinking clearly and had not been able to work this out, even though, once we saw the mind map, it was perfectly clear that finances were a very significant part of his worries.

Mind maps are generally seen as a good way of helping people to develop their thinking skills. However, in my experience, they also have implications in terms of the other two aspects of 'Think–feel–do' (discussed below), namely emotions and actions. I have experience of using mind maps with people who are anxious, with the result being that they become less anxious. I also have experience of using mind maps with people who were perhaps being overconfident (see the discussion above of 'Doing the right things vs. doing things right') and the technique has been helpful in enabling them to develop a more realistic picture – for example, by showing just how many different strands there may be involved in a particular project they are planning to undertake.

Some people like to be quite artistic in their use of mind maps – for example, using drawings or symbols instead of words. If this is something that you feel comfortable with, then this is to be encouraged, as the idea of the mind map is that it is a tool to help you – it is not a set of rules to restrict you. However, if you do not feel comfortable with drawings, symbols and so on, then by all means stick to words. This will not cause any problems. It is simply a case of finding the approach that suits us or, if we are helping other people to do mind maps, the approach that suits them.

Mind maps can be very powerful tools, and many people use them extensively. If you feel that mind mapping is something that appeals to you and that you are likely to draw upon in your future work, then you are strongly encouraged to read *The Mind Map Book* (Buzan and Buzan, 2003), as this book provides detailed but relatively simple guidance on how to develop our skills in mind mapping. It also provides lots of useful examples of mind maps that can help to give a clearer picture of what is involved and how it can be used.

▶ **Ecomaps** ▶ **Helicopter vision** ▶ **Fishbone analysis** ▶ **Gantt chart** ▶

Modelling and use of self

Using yourself as a tool to help others

The idea of apprenticeship has a long history, especially in trade and craft occupations. Much of the learning involved in apprenticeship is based on the idea of the apprentice watching the 'master' in action and, to a certain extent, copying what he or she is doing. In the people professions, simply copying what somebody else does can be dangerous. This is because the particular style adopted by that person may be something that is based on years of experience and the knowledge and skills that have developed during that time. Someone without that knowledge and those skills could get into serious difficulties by simply copying what a more experienced worker does.

However, this is not to say that there is no room at all for a modelling approach. There is indeed much to be gained by watching a skilful people worker in action. The point is that we must then take that basic learning and adapt it to suit our own circumstances, our own strengths and our own areas for development. Simply copying is not enough.

Modelling as a tool can be very helpful in helping others to sort their problems out. For example, where somebody is experiencing difficulty in managing a range of pressures they face, it can be helpful for someone to sit down with them and help them set priorities. What is important to note, however, is that issues of modelling should not be allowed to become simply doing something for someone. Helping somebody to set their priorities is not the same as setting their priorities for them. However, by going through the process together, a skilled worker can not only achieve the desired result, but also teach the individual concerned some skills so that he or she will be in a stronger position to achieve that result on their own next time.

There is quite an art in doing things with people rather than for them, but it is an important art to develop. This is because doing something for someone may actually hinder their development. We may make them more dependent and less self-sufficient, and therefore in a weaker position to deal with their problems, rather than in a stronger one.

Modelling can also be used in team or group settings. For example, if we have a group member who is especially good at a particular skill, then he or she can be asked to demonstrate that skill to others, so that they have the opportunity to learn from it. This can have the added bonus of encouraging teamwork, as it discourages a competitive approach and supports the idea of people learning from one another. Group members can see others within the group as collaborators rather than competitors.

Linked to modelling is the idea of 'use of self'. In modelling, we are using our own skills and experience to help others. Use of self means going beyond this to help people learn from our knowledge and skills and experience in other ways. A simple example of this would be: in a situation where someone is feeling guilty and disheartened because they have failed at a particular task, it may be helpful for the helper to explain that he or she also failed at that task at some time in the past, but learned from the experience and none the less made progress. This approach can be very helpful, but there are two caveats. First, it is important not to overdo this – for example, by revealing too much personal detail about oneself, as this can undermine our professional credibility.

Second, it is important to be genuine in use of self. I have come across examples of people who have made up stories in order to mimic the use of self. For example, to return to my earlier example, someone may claim to have failed at the same thing without actually having done so. This is a very risky strategy because, if it subsequently emerges that this was a lie, any trust developed with that person could easily be destroyed and the chances of rebuilding such trust would be minimal indeed. There are also, of course, ethical issues about lying to some body we are trying to help.

To help in the development of use of self, it can be beneficial to think of the different areas we are likely to be dealing with in our work as people problem solvers, perhaps listing these on a sheet of paper or drawing a mind map. Once you have done this, you can then look back over your life experience and think of situations where you faced problems similar, in some respect at least, to the ones that we are likely to be called upon to deal with. For example, if your work is likely to bring you into contact with people who are experiencing a lot of anxiety, what anxious situations have you encountered in your life? How did you deal with them? How did you manage to conquer them and move forward?

Of course, it is important to realize that this is not simply a matter of advising people to follow our lead, to take the steps we took (or to avoid the mistakes that we made), as it is unlikely that the parallels between their situation and ours will be quite that simple. However, with careful consideration, you should be able to find at least some links between your experience and theirs. This can also have the added benefit of increasing trust and providing a solid foundation for a positive working relationship.

In using the technique of use of self, be careful not to go to extremes. If we give many examples of mistakes we have made, we may come across as somebody who is constantly making mistakes, and this could undermine our credibility in the eyes of the people we are working with. At the other extreme, if we are constantly giving examples of how we have managed to do well in certain situations, then we may come across as arrogant and unconnected with the reality of the problems being faced. These are both clearly situations to avoid.

Modelling and use of self both indicate that, while each person's circumstances and challenges will be unique in some ways, there are also likely to be common dimensions. There are likely to be places within the problem situation where that individual's experience can connect with other people's experience, thus giving them some degree of a sense of sharing and common endeavour. In trying to help somebody resolve their difficulties, this can be a very valuable asset.

▶ The CBC approach ▶ Holding ▶ SOLER ▶

Motivational interviewing

Using ambivalence to help bring about change

This is an approach commonly used in the drug and alcohol field, but which is more widely applicable to any area where people need help to change behaviour that is causing them (and/or other people) significant problems. It is based on a process of helping people to identify significant discrepancies between what their lives are like now and what they would want them to be like in the future. Recognizing the differences between the two can help to motivate the individuals concerned to narrow the gap between where their life is and where they want it to be. Motivation is the key issue here, as, without it, change is not going to take place.

The technique is based on the concept of ambivalence which arises from having conflicting desires (wanting to drink while also wanting to stay sober, for example). The process on which it is based can be understood to have four elements which need to be incorporated into the interactions between the helper and the person being helped:

1. Forming a rapport based on empathy. It is unlikely that we will be able to help people change their behaviour if they feel there is no rapport. We therefore need to work hard to establish a basis of trust (and develop the skills involved in doing so). It can take a long time to develop a deep relationship, but a skilled practitioner can potentially form a rapport of basic trust fairly quickly (for example, through the appropriate use of nonverbal communication to put people at their ease).
2. Identifying the key discrepancies – for example, between what life is like with the tensions and personal and family costs involved in inflicting domestic violence on one's partner and what it could be like without feeling the need to rely on violent responses. These need to be meaningful to the person concerned, otherwise they will not be a source of motivation. This reinforces the need for empathy – the ability to be able to see the situation from the other person's point of view rather than expect them to 'see it our way'.
3. What Miller and Rollnick (2002) refer to as 'rolling with resistance'. This means learning to recognize that it is understandable that people will express resistance. It should not be seen as a sign that there is something wrong with them – it is a reasonable human response and therefore only to be expected and not a deficit or pathology. Some degree of resistance is to be expected and we need to learn how to deal with it sensitively and constructively.
4. Focusing on empowerment. This entails helping people to take ownership of their problems and the need to do something about them if they are to bridge the gap between where they are now and where they want to be.

Success in using this technique requires very good interpersonal skills as well as the ability to resist the temptation to persuade people to move in the direction we feel they ought to go and, instead, help them to work out for themselves what they must do to resolve the ambivalence that they are currently trapped in.

► **Dealing with objections** ► **Congruence** ► **Tuning in** ►

Motivation audit

Getting an overview of key motivational factors

This is a tool that involves identifying motivating factors, demotivating factors and what are known as 'hygiene' factors to enable motivation to be maximized by, in effect, manipulating these variables.

It is important to recognize the significance of motivation as a key factor in bringing about change. As we have seen, people can become locked into their problems (as a result of vicious circles, for example) and this can act as a serious barrier to progress. It is also important to recognize the significance of motivation in terms of partnership and empowerment. If people are not motivated, then partnership working becomes much more difficult and, by the same token, where we can achieve good partnership working, this can act as a spur in terms of motivation. Empowerment is also significant in the sense that someone who is not motivated is not likely to be empowered – they are not likely to take ownership of their circumstances and therefore take the opportunity to gain the greater control that arises from the process of empowerment.

A motivation audit involves identifying three sets of factors and then considering how these can be developed in a positive direction:

Motivating factors

There are certain things that will motivate us, things that will spur us on in effect. What we need to do is to draw up a list of what those motivating factors are, so that we then have an explicit recognition of what they are. This will enable us to build on the ones that currently exist to try and get them to their level of maximum effectiveness. But, what we can also do is identify any important motivating factors that are absent from the situation and try to establish why. For example, if somebody was previously highly motivated in a particular direction, but they are no longer, then we can try and work out what has changed to undermine that high level of motivation and see whether anything can be done to reintroduce the earlier level of motivation.

Demotivating factors

These are also known as drag factors. They are the things that prevent us from being highly motivated. They are the hassles and the frustrations that can get in the way of our feeling motivated. We can identify what the key demotivating factors are in the current situation, and then we can begin to focus on which ones could possibly be removed, which ones could be perhaps not removed but sidestepped, and which ones can neither be removed nor sidestepped, but perhaps their impact could be reduced in some ways. What this exercise can do is to help the person concerned to put the demotivating factors into a better perspective – for example, helping people to realize how much they dislike something can be costing them in terms of how being demotivated is preventing them from addressing what is bothering them. It is also important to look at what are known as 'opportunity' costs. This refers not to direct costs *per se*, but the opportunities that are lost by being demotivated in a particular way. In other words, there are potential gains for more highly motivated people that less highly motivated people will miss out on.

Hygiene factors

This term refers to the things in a person's life or in a particular situation which will not in themselves produce motivation but their absence will be demotivating. An example of this would be having the necessary facilities to do our work. Having what we need (a desk, a phone or a particular piece of equipment, for example) is not likely to motivate people, but if those things are absent, then the very fact of their absence can be a source of frustration and therefore demotivation. What should happen, then, in terms of a motivation audit is that we will need to, first of all, identify if there are any hygiene factors that are affecting the situation. From that we can look at what is present that is not motivating and help people to appreciate what they have, to put it in context and in perspective, as it were. But, we can also try to do something about those things that are missing, the absence of which is a source of irritation and/or dissatisfaction. In this way, we can help to improve the situation vis-à-vis motivation by removing a range of factors that can add to, and reinforce, the demotivating factors that are already present in the current set of circumstances.

By getting a picture of these three sets of factors and how we can influence them in a positive direction, we are in a very strong position to help build up levels of motivation. It can be a very useful tool when people just need a bit of help to get going, to overcome inertia, as it were, and then they will be ready to be self-propelled. In this way, by helping them to be more motivated, we are enabling them to become *self*-motivated and then continue to move forward under their own steam. This is an important basis of empowerment, of course.

However, we have to be very wary of the dangers of creating dependency. If, for example, it becomes the case that it is only our presence or input that is motivating somebody, then we are potentially in a difficult situation, as the motivation level is likely to drop significantly if we try to withdraw from the situation. To try and avoid this type of dependency we therefore need to focus, wherever we can, on self-motivation and do what we need to do to make the people we are trying to help less dependent on us and more self-propelled.

▶ **Dealing with objections** ▶ **Positive strokes** ▶ **The three Hs** ▶ **Visioning** ▶

Naming the process
Bringing hidden agendas out into the open

Sometimes there are destructive or harmful processes going on in inter-actions between people, but they are going on at a submerged level – that is, they are happening 'beneath the table' rather than 'on the table', as it were, like a hidden agenda at a meeting. Sometimes the use of such processes is deliberate – for example, when somebody is trying to sabotage a particular event or process because it is not in their interests for it to succeed. Very often, though, the underlying harmful process is not deliberate, it is the historical result of various factors that have come together to produce this outcome. For example, the fears of vari-ous individuals may combine to produce a situation in which particular topics become taboo because no one feels comfortable in raising or tackling them. This is not necessarily a deliberate plan, but arises through very complex and subtle processes of interaction between indi-viduals and across groups. We shall first of all consider how naming the process can be used to deal with the deliberate use of destructive processes by one or more people and then move on to consider how the technique can be used to counter less deliberate, but what can be equally damaging processes.

An example of a deliberate, underlying, harmful process would be where somebody chooses to avoid a particular topic by changing the subject whenever this topic arises. It is in circumstances like these that the technique of naming the process can be very useful. For example, if we become aware that somebody is changing the subject whenever we raise an important issue, we may make this visible by 'naming the process' – that is, we may expressly say 'I've noticed that whenever I raise the matter of X, you change the subject. Why is that?' We may then want to follow this up with a comment such as: 'Is there a prob-lem there I can help you with?' (see also the discussion above of 'Avoiding avoidance').

An example of a less deliberate use of destructive processes would be a situation known as 'groupthink'. This is a term used by Janis (1982) to refer to the tendency for groups of people (including teams) to fail to challenge assumptions about the group and what it is doing – the desire not to spoil a nice team atmosphere, for example, can mean that important, but potentially conflictual, issues are not raised. Practice focus 2.8 shows how this can work.

PRACTICE FOCUS 2.8

Over the years the company Tom worked for had developed a very distinctive way of working. They had their own way of dealing with the various tasks they undertook. They were proud of doing everything 'their way'. However, when Tom started attending his part-time Diploma course, he began to realize that there were other ways of doing things. He became aware that there were ways in which things could be improved at work. However, when he raised this with his colleagues, they basically ignored him. He tried time and time again and got nowhere, becoming more and more frustrated as time went by. In the end he decided to raise this in supervision. He again met resistance and, feeling even more frustrated, asked directly: 'Why does this company seem to have such a closed mind when it comes to looking at new ideas? Every time I suggest something new, it gets pushed aside.' His supervisor was a bit taken aback by this, but it did open the door for discussing the company's attitude to outside influences and whether or not there was a problem in this respect. Tom was delighted that he was starting to get somewhere at last.

Other examples of how harmful processes can arise without any deliberate intention can be found in relation to various forms of discrimination. For example, institutional racism refers to forms of racial discrimination that are not direct and deliberate (personal racism), but rather which have arisen over time due to discriminatory practices or assumptions that have become part of working practices and organizational culture. Indeed, this is what makes institutional racism difficult to eradicate – it is not simply a matter of disciplining an individual perpetrator, it is a much more difficult job of changing institutionalized practices.

Although institutionalized racism has received a great deal of media attention, it is not the only form of institutionalized discrimination. For example, institutionalized sexism is also very prevalent – where women are treated in a patronizing way, not as part of a deliberate attempt to cause offence, but out of a naïve lack of awareness of gender equality issues. Older and/or disabled people also face such problems. Naming the process can play an important role in tackling such issues.

In using this technique, it is very important to recognize just how powerful it is. If we are to use the analogy of tools (comparing the techniques in this book with tools used in a physical sense), then naming the process is the equivalent of a chainsaw – that is, it is extremely powerful and therefore very dangerous if used inappropriately. It should not be used lightly. It is best used in circumstances where:

1. we have a good working relationship with the person concerned;
2. the situation is sufficiently important to warrant taking the risk;
3. we feel sufficiently confident in the circumstances that we can deal with the reaction to our use of the tool.

Of course, in using any tool or technique, there is always a risk that the situation will backfire, but in using this particularly powerful technique, the risk is greater and the harm that can be done is also greater. It should therefore be used with great caution. Just imagine, for example, how you might react if somebody used this technique with you.

None the less, despite these notes of caution, this is a very helpful tool when used appropriately and can make for a situation where great progress is achieved in a short period of time. It can cut through issues that could otherwise stand in the way of progress.

▶ **Confronting without being confrontational** ▶ **Elegant challenging** ▶

Negotiating expectations

Being clear about what we can expect from each other

As discussed in one of my earlier works (Thompson, 2009b), this is a matter of 'setting out our stall', to make sure that expectations are realistic and thus manageable. It is very easy for a mismatch of expectations to develop and to result in a range of what could potentially turn out to be considerable difficulties. It is therefore important to clarify expectations, and that is precisely what is meant by the idea of 'setting out our stall'.

There are two sides to this tool. The first one involves making it clear what our role is and this involves making it clear what we can do, what we may be able to do, but cannot guarantee, and what we cannot do. This can be understood by reference to a traffic lights analogy. If we recognize that there are some things that we should have no difficulty in doing, then that is the equivalent of a green light. There will be things that we may be able to do, but cannot promise. These are represented by the amber light. But, there will also be things that we are not able to do, and that is, of course, the red light. If we are not clear about these things in our own minds and we are not communicating that clarity to the people we are working with, then we may be fuelling unrealistic expectations on their part which can then lead to disappointment, resentment, ill-feeling and potentially even complaints.

It is also important to be able to clarify timescales, as expectations of these can diverge significantly. For example, there may be something that we are able to do, but it may take us a certain amount of time to be able to do it – weeks or months in some cases. If, however, the person concerned is anxious that the difficulty should be resolved as soon as possible, they may be under the impression that the changes can be made more or less immediately. If we are not skilful in clarifying the timescales and we are not able to do a good job of giving a clear picture of what is involved then, again, bad feeling and related difficulties can ensue because of differing perspectives and therefore differing expectations in terms of what is to be seen as a reasonable timescale.

It is also important to invite others to clarify their expectations. So, on the one hand, we need to put forward our own view of what is realistic and what is not, but, by giving others the opportunity to say what they expect, we then have a basis for negotiation. This will then also serve as an important and solid basis for partnership. It will give us a foundation for the trust and credibility that are needed for effective partnership working. Underpinning this is the premise that if people know where they stand, then they are likely to feel much more secure. What this means is that somebody who knows what to expect, even if this is less than they would have hoped for, is likely to feel happier than somebody who does not know what to expect and is therefore unsettled by this lack of clarity. Feelings of being unsettled can often manifest themselves as unreasonable demands, and these can then be significant obstacles to clarifying and negotiating expectations.

What is also important to recognize is that, by inviting others to express their expectations, we are creating a foundation for empowerment. This is because it gives us the opportunity to both avoid dependency (if someone's expectations are that we will do the work for them and take away their difficulties without any effort on their part) and provide signposting (that is, guiding people to more appropriate sources of help where we are unable to be the primary source of assistance).

Doing this can be quite a skilful undertaking, but the time and effort required to invest in such development tends to be very worthwhile. People who are skilful at negotiating expectations are likely to get a higher level of respect, trust and credibility and less hassle as a result of that. People who struggle to negotiate expectations can be adding to a sense of feeling insecure and unsettled, and that can potentially lead to a vicious circle where increased tensions result in increased demands, which then result in even more unrealistic expectations, making the job of negotiating expectations all the harder. It should therefore be very clear that it is important for problem solvers to develop the skills needed for the effective negotiation of expectations.

▶ **Brokerage** ▶ **Objectives tree** ▶ **Principled negotiation** ▶ **Visioning** ▶

Not tolerating vagueness

Avoiding the dangers of being too vague

In some circumstances, it is essential to be very precise indeed. For example, in some engineering situations it is necessary to provide measurements within very fine fractions of whatever unit is being measured. Life in general does not normally require that degree of precision, however, and it is perhaps inevitable that a degree of vagueness creeps in. But, when we are working with people and their problems, it can sometimes be disastrous to allow vagueness to become a feature of our work. In my view, an important principle of problem solving is to be clear about precisely what we are dealing with. Any indecision can lead to our heading off in the wrong direction or adopting the wrong approach. Consider, for example, the discussion of systematic practice in Part One of this book. If we were to be vague about what we are trying to achieve, how we are going to achieve it or how we will know when we have achieved it, then the whole process could be undermined. This does not mean that we have to be precise to a scientific degree on all occasions, but it does mean that there is a danger in allowing vagueness to undermine what we are doing.

PRACTICE FOCUS 2.9

Jan told her line manager that she was concerned about Peter because he could be demanding and this made her feel uncomfortable. Her line manager told her this was part of the job and only to be expected. He told her she would have to get used to it. The next day Jan went to visit Peter to discuss his plans. He became more and more agitated until he became so worked up that he assaulted her.

When Jan's line manager found out what had happened, he was very supportive. He asked her if she had had any indication Peter might become violent, to which she replied that she had already told him that she was concerned about Peter. 'Yes, but you didn't mention any threat of violence, did you?' to which she replied: 'I told you I wasn't happy working with him and you said I had to get used to it.'

Jan had been vague in expressing her concerns to her line manager and had not spelled out her concerns about the risk of violence and her line manager had not pressed her to be more precise about what she meant by 'demanding' and 'uncomfortable' – he had tolerated her vagueness and thus missed an important opportunity to help her, and save her from harm.

Practice focus 2.9 illustrates clearly how we can create problems rather than solve them by being vague. As I have argued previously, the people we are trying to help:

> are often in a state of confusion by virtue of the particular problems they face. If we are not careful, we can add to this state of confusion by being vague and unfocused. In situations characterized by confusion and a lack of direction, the people worker's role is often that of an 'anchor', providing a degree of stability, security and clarity. An unfocused approach can therefore not only fail to fulfil this important role, but also add to the confusion and instability.
>
> (2009a, p. 205)

Note, however, that the title of this particular tool is not simply 'Not being vague', but rather 'Not tolerating vagueness'. This adds an extra dimension. While we may put a lot of effort into ensuring our own actions and communications are not plagued with vagueness, in addition we need to go a step further in trying to make sure that those communications we receive, and the actions of other people, are also not plagued with vagueness. This means that we need to have fairly well-developed interpersonal skills to be able to challenge vagueness in a constructive way that will not alienate others. If we simply say to somebody, 'That's very vague, please be more precise', this can easily be interpreted as a direct criticism and can result in unnecessary tensions and obstacles to making progress. We therefore have to become very skilled in asking the appropriate questions in the appropriate ways.

Sometimes people will be deliberately vague – that is, they will be doing this because they have something to hide or there is something they feel uncomfortable discussing. However, it is often the case that people are being vague because they have not thought through the issues, or it is a characteristic mode of communication. It is therefore important not to assume that someone who is being vague is definitely concealing something deliberately. That is quite a big assumption to make and sometimes a dangerous one.

However, where there are grounds to suspect that somebody is being deliberately vague, we have to handle the situation very carefully. A useful principle to adopt here is that of finding the balance between, on the one hand, simply allowing them to continue to be vague and, on the other, pushing them so hard that we risk 'getting their back up'.

Dealing with somebody in such circumstances can easily lead us into a situation that is quite characteristic of this notion of not tolerating vagueness – namely the situation where we have to be gently persistent by continuing to pursue the issue. For example, someone may be quite vague in response to a question, and so our next question pursues the matter further, at which point the person concerned may reveal a little more information, but not much. We will therefore need to probe a little further and continue probing until it becomes clear to the person we are dealing with that we are maintaining that constructive balance between simply letting it go and alienating him or her. This has much in common with the notion of 'assertiveness'. Basically, what it involves is trying to find a win–win solution; a situation where the person we are communicating with does not feel harassed, but where we are not left feeling that we have failed to get the important information that we need to help him or her.

Not tolerating vagueness is not a technique to be used at specific times but, rather, a general tool to be used whenever we are dealing with other people. There may well be particular times (for example, when somebody is being deliberately vague) where we need to use our skills in this area to the full, but my argument would be that we need to be practising these skills at all times. In any interaction with other people there is the danger that we will allow vagueness to creep in, and thus cause problems in our attempts to resolve the difficulties being experienced. Vagueness, then, is clearly an enemy of effective problem solving and we should do everything we reasonably can to make sure that it is not allowed to sabotage the work we undertake.

▶ **Avoiding avoidance** ▶ **Confronting without being confrontational** ▶ **Fishing for red herrings** ▶

O

Objectives tree

A framework for helping to develop plans

In Part One of the book, the importance of keeping a clear focus on what we are trying to achieve was emphasized. One way of doing this is to make use of what is known as an objectives tree. This involves drawing a diagram. Figure 2.9 provides a worked example of this.

At the top of the page we put a box in which we write our overall aim – that is, the particular outcome that we are seeking to bring about. From this box we have lines connecting to other boxes which contain the main elements that will contribute to the achievement of the objective in the top box. For example, if our desired outcome is better communication, then in the boxes on the second tier of the objectives tree we would have those elements that contribute to better communication (clear systems, well-chaired meetings, a culture based on collaboration and so on).

There is no rule about how many boxes there should be. This will vary from situation to situation and group to group. It could be anything between two and twelve or perhaps even more in some circumstances. We should be careful not to rush into deciding what these second-tier 'boxes' should be. The tool should be used to encourage careful reflection on what it is we are trying to achieve (the overall aim in the first-tier box).

From each of these second-tier boxes we then need to draw out a list of the actions that need to be taken to bring about what is written in the particular box. When we have completed this list for each of the second-tier boxes, we will then have in effect a road map from bottom to top. That is, if we look at the steps to be taken that have been identified deriving from each of the second-tier boxes, these should then lead us to success in terms of achieving the desired outcome at the second level which, in turn, will contribute to achieving the overall aim in the main box at the top of the page.

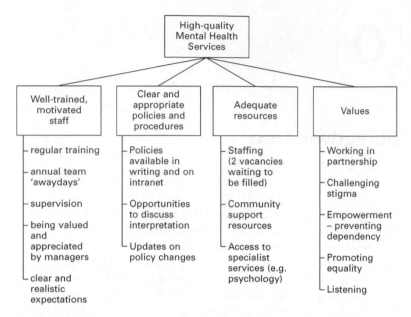

Figure 2.9 Objective tree for a multidisciplinary mental health team

This is a very simple form of objectives tree and, to begin with, it helps to keep it simple until you are familiar with the technique. However, it can also be used in a more advanced form so that, for example, we can have third-tier boxes that feed into the second-tier boxes and, from each of the three-tier boxes, we then have a list of steps that need to be taken. Such steps can then be broken down into further substeps. The whole objectives tree can then become very complex. Some people choose to use a white board, for example, to draw such a complex and large objectives tree. Using a white board or equivalent also gives the flexibility of being able to amend the diagram without having to start from scratch with a fresh piece of paper.

This technique can be used at a number of different levels. It can be used by an individual worker or manager as a tool for focusing one's thinking. It can help to clarify in our own mind where we are going and how we intend to get there. In this respect, it is a useful tool for promoting systematic practice as discussed in Part One.

It can also be used as a supervision or mentoring tool. It can be used to help an individual in the workplace to focus on, for example, their career goals or what they are trying to achieve in relation to a particular project. It can also be used as a tool of intervention in working with somebody experiencing a particular problem. It could well be the case that they have lost any sense of direction in their life, that they have become confused, disorientated and may be acting in ways that are contrary to their own interests. Helping somebody to develop an objectives tree can be very helpful in giving a sense of structure and direction which in turn can give reassurance and boost confidence. This can be of particular value to people experiencing either confusion or depression or anxiety or a combination of the three.

The tool can also be used as a team development technique. That is, on a teambuilding day, a staff team can be divided into sub-groups, each given a sheet of flipchart paper and asked to undertake the task of developing an objectives tree for the team. This can be followed by a feedback session where the team members look at each other's objectives tree diagrams on the flipcharts displayed on the wall and then have what can be a fruitful discussion about similarities and differences. Ideally, this could lead them to developing a unified objectives tree based on the combination of factors arising from the separate objectives trees produced by the sub-groups. I have undertaken this exercise myself with a number of teams and it has proven very valuable in identifying:

1. common ground and consensus that can be built on; and
2. areas of conflict that need further exploration and resolution.

This is a technique that you may find difficult at first. However, I would recommend that you practise using it, and it is then likely that you will become increasingly skilled and confident over time. The more confident and skilful you are in using the technique, the more confidence others will have in you when you help them to develop their own objectives trees.

▶ **Mind mapping** ▶ **Visioning** ▶ **Working backwards** ▶

Paint the toilets

Making a fresh start

Some problems emerge very quickly in a short period of time. However, very many more problems are the result of perhaps years of slow and steady development (or deterioration). The problem situation we are asked to deal with today may have begun to develop many years ago. Often we are dealing with entrenched problems, issues that have perhaps become part of the culture of an organization or group of people. Problems can have long histories and deep roots. In such circumstances, developing solutions can take a great deal of time – implementing those solutions perhaps even longer. A set of problems that have developed over a period of years may equally take years to resolve.

While patience is clearly a virtue, it is not always present in great abundance in circumstances where people have been encountering problems for a considerable time, where their frustration level is high and their tolerance level is low. When we are faced with the challenge of trying to resolve deeply ingrained long-term problems, we may find that patience runs very thin for some people and that we are facing considerable pressure to produce significant results in a short period of time. Often these expectations will be unrealistic and unreasonable, but borne of the frustration experienced by the people concerned over an extended period of time. It is important to resist the temptation to promise to meet such unrealistic demands, but it is also important in order to ensure that the situation does not boil over and that we do not lose the good will and co-operation of the people concerned, that we make a quick and notable contribution to alleviating the situation. This is referred to as the 'paint the toilets' technique because sometimes it can be literally by making such a small but significant and noticeable change that a clear message is put forward – namely that change has begun, that the 'beginning of the end' of the problems has been reached. In an organization it gives a clear message of 'Under new management'. Of course, this is not enough in itself, but it can be a very useful start to make a small but significant change.

The technique involves identifying a small change that can have a big impact, something that can be done quickly and effectively, but which could have a significant result in terms of giving a very clear message – we are taking this situation seriously and we are doing our best to put it right. The goodwill that can be generated by this can buy us time and help to generate an atmosphere where patience is more likely to be the order of the day, rather than frustration and a sense that nothing is happening.

In using this technique, it is vitally important not to allow it to become seen as tokenistic. If we literally or metaphorically just paint the toilets and then do nothing further, then the whole process can prove counterproductive. It can mean that any negativity that has developed over the years will be reinforced rather than broken down. It is therefore important that we make sure that the 'paint the toilets' technique is used appropriately – namely as a technique for making a short-term, significant impact to buy a little bit of time and patience to make the other changes that are necessary. It is, of course, not an alternative to making those changes. In fact, it can be very counterproductive to get off to a good start and then not follow this up. We can easily end up in a worse situation than where we started.

The tool can be used in working with individuals – where we could perhaps identify something that would ease their problems, that could be implemented relatively swiftly and effectively (without causing other problems) and make this happen. In this way we can help to establish a relationship of trust and, where necessary, challenge any feelings of helplessness and hopelessness (such feelings are not uncommon where people have been experiencing apparently insoluble problems over a period of time).

The tool can also be used in working with families, groups or teams on pretty much the same basis – that is, finding something that can make a positive difference very quickly, with a view to creating a positive impact, trying to generate a sense of hope.

Of course, there is no guarantee that this technique will work. Some people will be so immersed in a sense of defeatism that they will not be impressed by even a very positive change. However, even in these circumstances, the tool is likely to be worth using because such attitudes may take a long time to change, but at least we have made a step in the right direction – and that can be very important in laying the foundations for progress at a later date. In dealing with families, groups or teams, we may encounter a mixed response. That is, some people may respond positively while others remain cynical. Where this occurs it gives us the opportunity to try and build on the positives and try and tilt the balance in that direction.

▶ **Capitalizing on crisis** ▶ **Finding the growth zone** ▶

The paradoxical approach
Reducing behaviours by encouraging them

This is a well-establish device for encouraging behaviour change based on supporting people to do the opposite of what we want them to do. I have already commented on the importance of recognizing the power of habit. We can end up behaving in ways that are at best fruitless and at worst counterproductive, simply because we have established a set of 'tramlines', as it were, that we have become stuck in as a result of this force of habit. Sometimes we are driven to do things as the result of anxiety, and we can then lock ourselves into powerful dynamics that sustain that behaviour – even if it is behaviour that is causing us and/or other people problems.

In many situations, therefore, there is a need to change particular forms of behaviour which are proving problematic or even dangerous. Consequently, the emphasis is on eliminating or, to use the technical term, 'extinguishing' certain behaviours. The paradoxical approach involves encouraging people to do the things they are trying to stop doing. A paradox is something that superficially appears to be contradictory, but when looked at more closely, there is actually a logic to it that makes sense at a deeper level. What happens in terms of the use of the paradoxical approach as a tool for problem solving is that we identify particular behaviours that need to change and then focus on trying to encourage those behaviours. This is what gives the approach its title because, superficially, that sounds as though we are going in entirely the wrong direction. The irony of the situation, though – and this is what makes it a paradox – is that, in getting people to focus on those behaviours, it is often the case that those very behaviours decrease or even stop altogether. An example of this would be with children who display temper tantrums. When a child starts to become annoyed or frustrated and we see the beginnings potentially of a temper tantrum, then skilled therapists working with children can encourage the child to have a tantrum. Once the focus is on having the tantrum, it takes away the power of the child to gain attention from doing so, and this can be sufficient to prevent a tantrum from developing.

The technique can also be used with adults, but it is important to make sure that it is not done in such a way that it comes across as patronizing. It is important to explain, for example, what we are doing when we use this technique and why we are doing so, so that it does not come across as manipulative, as if we are playing some sort of power game. It is also important to manage this method very carefully, as there are risks involved, of course. There is a danger that encouraging somebody to engage in a particular behaviour will result in precisely that behaviour. There is therefore a need for close monitoring. It can be dangerous to start the process and then leave people to it and possibly face a worsening of the situation.

This is a tool that is not to be used lightly. It requires careful and sensitive handling, and we need to be able to identify carefully in which situations it will be applicable, so that it is not misused. However, where it is used properly, the results can be quite significant in a positive direction.

▶ **Role reversal** ▶ **Using dissonance** ▶

PCS analysis

Understanding different levels of discrimination

This is a framework that I have discussed at length in my other work (Thompson, 1995; 2011a; 2012b), specifically in relation to issues associated with discrimination. However, it can also be used more broadly as a means of understanding the important interrelationships across different levels of analysis – the different levels or dimensions of human experience.

PCS analysis is based on the idea that there are three interconnected levels that need to be taken into consideration if we are to develop an adequate understanding of discrimination in particular and human experience in general. PCS is shorthand for 'personal, cultural and structural':

1. *Personal.* This refers to the level of the individual and reminds us that we must not lose sight of the perspective, interests and needs of the individuals we are seeking to help. People's behaviour will, of course, depend largely on how they perceive the world, on what their experiences mean to them. In problem solving it is therefore a significant mistake to neglect the personal dimension.
2. *Cultural.* While the personal dimension is clearly important, we should not limit ourselves to considering matters from an individualistic point of view. Although each of us is indeed a unique individual, we are also part of wider cultural patterns and formations – we will have been brought up in a particular cultural context (and thus have been heavily influenced by it) and will now be operating currently within a cultural context. Our current cultural influences may complement or conflict with the cultural context of our upbringing, but either way it will be a significant influence on our behaviour and our understanding of the world. In trying to understand the people we are seeking to help, it would therefore be a major mistake to fail to take account of cultural issues – the shared meanings and 'unwritten rules' that play such an important role in shaping our experiences and thus our lives.
3. *Structural.* The society in which we live and work is not a level playing field. It is divided up into 'sub-groups' that form a structured network. Who we are, how we perceive the world and so on will depend upon not only our personal circumstances, not only on the cultural formations that we were brought up in and now live in, but also on where we fit into the structure of society based on class, gender, race and so on. Power and opportunities in life are not distributed evenly across society, and this uneven distribution will have a significant bearing on an individual's identity and broader social circumstances. For example, it is clear that someone born into poverty will have a very different upbringing from someone born into great wealth.

The basis of PCS analysis is that, if we want to develop an adequate understanding of the people we are trying to help, we need to take account of all three dimensions: their personal perspective and life experiences to date, the cultural influences that continue to shape those life experiences (and our reactions to them) and the structural context of an uneven distribution of power and opportunities.

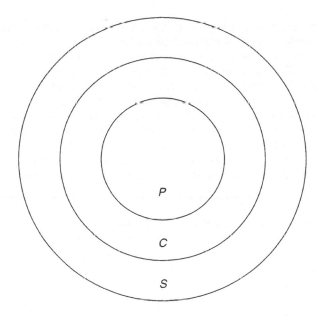

Figure 2.10 PCS analysis (Thompson, 2012b)

PCS analysis is a dynamic model – that is, it is based on an interaction of the three levels (a moving picture rather than a snapshot). An individual's sense of self (personal) will be influenced by culture and structure, but culture and structure are also influenced by the cumulative effect of individual actions over time. Similarly, cultural ideas influence and are influenced by structural factors.

This approach can be used in working with individuals, groups, families or even whole organizations or communities. It is an analytical tool for making sure that we do not adopt too narrow a focus on the individual without considering the wider cultural and structural context.

PRACTICE FOCUS 2.10

Jonathan enjoyed the course on equality and diversity and was particularly interested in the presentation about PCS analysis, as this gave him a much broader perspective than he had previously had. He started to consider his workload in terms of the three dimensions – personal, cultural and structural – instead of concentrating only on the individual level as he had done before. At first he felt a little daunted when he realized how complex situations became when viewed in terms of three dimensions instead of just one. However, once he realized how it deepened his understanding of the situations he faced, he recognized that it would be a useful tool for making sure he did not adopt too narrow a perspective.

By seeing many of the situations he encountered in his work as having three dimensions rather than just one, he began to appreciate how, in the past, he had tended to oversimplify issues, especially those relating to discrimination. He had tended to see discrimination as primarily, if not solely, a matter of personal prejudice. Being introduced to PCS analysis had enabled him to develop a much more sophisticated understanding of these issues.

In terms of problem solving by promoting change, it has to be recognized that we have a decreasing level of influence from personal to cultural to structural levels. That is, influencing a culture is more difficult than influencing an individual, and influencing a structure is likely to be an even more difficult undertaking. We therefore have to be realistic in acknowledging that we may not be in a position to change cultural or structural factors (except on a long-term, collective basis); appreciating how these wider levels have an impact on the personal level will help us develop a fuller picture of the circumstances we are dealing with (see the discussion of sociopolitical challenges in Part One).

▶ **Helicopter vision** ▶

Peacemaking circles

Drawing on Native American wisdom

This is an approach that has come to be associated with what is known as 'restorative justice', which involves focusing on reparation and healing rather than revenge and punishment. The basic idea is that traditional approaches to crime and justice are based on the idea of an eye for an eye which, of course, can in certain circumstances simply create more resentment, more ill-feeling and hatred and potentially, therefore, more crime. This approach, by contrast, is intended to tackle the problems from a very different angle, focusing on creating positives out of negative situations, rather than adopting a negative approach that can amplify the difficulties in certain situations. It is also potentially useful as a conflict management tool and as an approach to problem solving more broadly.

The techniques derive from Native North American traditions (McCaslin, 2005; Pranis, Stuart and Wedge, 2003). The process involves bringing together a group of people to enable them to look at what has gone wrong and to consider how reparation can be made, how the people involved can be helped to 'heal' as a result of the hurt done by crime, conflict or other problems.

It involves creating a 'sacred space' that all participants are expected to respect. This creates a positive and constructive atmosphere for healing – that is, for righting wrongs, seeking forgiveness, harnessing the power of remorse and creating a genuine sense of human connection.

It is important to emphasize that peacemaking circles are not intended to be a form of trial, nor are they simply a meeting or case conference in the conventional sense. They are something very different from the usual approaches to bringing people together. The process involves the following elements:

- The participants sit in a circle so that there is no sense of hierarchy. The intention is that people in the circle are to all intents and purposes equals.
- A 'talking piece' is used. This is a symbolic item that has a strong emphasis on the power of listening. What is expected to happen is that no one will speak unless they hold the talking piece. Before someone is allowed to talk, they must wait their turn for the talking piece to be given to them. This is parallel with the rule of no interruptions as used in mediation (Lewis, 2009). This involves giving people the opportunity to give their side of the story without fear of being contradicted by the other person in the mediation, and is therefore a very powerful tool for enabling people to ventilate their concerns as a basis for moving forward constructively.
- Two respective members of the community ('elders') act as 'keepers'. These are not formal chairpersons, but help to maintain a sense of safety and security within the circle to encourage trust, openness and sharing.
- The focus is on helping everybody involved in the circle to recognize their own responsibility and to take ownership of what they have done and what they need to do. In this way, it is a strong basis for reparation. So, if somebody has done something that they regret and

for which they are able to show remorse, they are given the opportunity to express that remorse to the people concerned (for example, to the victims of a crime). This can also be useful in terms of conflict resolution where, often as a result of the tensions involved in a conflict situation, people may behave in unproductive ways and especially in disrespectful ways towards one another. A focus on taking ownership helps people to move away from such behaviours and to focus on conciliation and moving forward constructively. This emphasis is also important in terms of recognizing that, in many problem situations, the behaviour of one or more people may be unwittingly sustaining the problem situation. This creates the opportunity for people to recognize this, to take ownership of that fact and to change the situation without there being any sense of blame which can be counterproductive, creating ill-feeling, rather than encouraging healing.

- Circles like this can create a sense of community and 'connectedness' and can therefore be seen as a form of spiritual approach, recognizing healing as a spiritual process, a personal transformation.

It is vitally important that peacemaking circles are based on a genuine commitment to positive outcomes through open and constructive dialogue and that they do not become just another form of bureaucratic meeting.

▶ **Confronting without being confrontational** ▶ **Educating** ▶ **Principled negotiation** ▶

Positive strokes

Building confidence

When we are involved in helping people to sort out their problems, we face the risk of what is known as an occupational bias. That is, because we can so easily become engrossed in problems, we may have a tendency to concentrate primarily on problems and difficulties without necessarily balancing them out with positives (see the discussion of 'SWOT analysis' below). Being able to balance positives and negatives is a key skill for people problem solvers. However, because of the occupational bias we face, it is often necessary for us to make sure that we are accentuating the positives, that we are highlighting strengths and assets and valuing these as fully as we can. This can be particularly important when we are dealing with people whose confidence or self-esteem levels are low – a situation quite common when people are experiencing problems, as the problems themselves may be a source of low self-esteem (or may have been caused in part at least by pre-existing low self-esteem).

The idea behind positive strokes is that we should take every reasonable opportunity to accentuate the positives in a particular individual or group's life. The term 'strokes' refers to giving somebody a reassuring touch – a hand on the arm, for example. It is often used in a metaphorical sense to refer to anything we can say or do that will be geared towards boosting somebody's confidence. This is an important activity to undertake because people embroiled in problems can often lose sight of the bigger picture, as we have discussed earlier. People who are worried or anxious can understandably see nothing but the negatives at times. They can feel deskilled and devalued. Giving people positive strokes – that is, pointing out their strengths, abilities and positives – can have a tremendous benefit, but it has to be done carefully.

Simply stating positives in a mechanistic or unfeeling way is not likely to help. It will come across to the person or persons concerned as if we are simply following a mechanical routine or technique. It will have the effect of distancing us from people and can thus potentially be very counterproductive. Positive strokes need to be given genuinely, with warmth. They need to be based on a genuine concern for helping this particular individual to appreciate his or her strengths and to feel better about the situation they face. Blandly uttering positives in a random way will not help. It needs to be part of a skilful process of engaging with the people concerned, showing a genuine concern for the problem they face, but seeking to balance the anxieties they have against the strengths and positives they bring to the situation. This has to be done in a way that is not patronizing or belittling.

Sometimes this can be achieved by the careful use of questions. For example, instead of simply saying: 'I think you are good at X', questions can be asked which lead the individual concerned to conclude that he or she is good at X. Practice focus 2.11 illustrates this.

PRACTICE FOCUS 2.11

Lisa had got to the point where she was despairing about being able to sort her problems out. She felt worn down, deskilled and largely incapable. Reba was keen to help her but was beginning to feel overwhelmed by the strong sense of negativity she was getting from Lisa. She decided that she would need to inject some degree of positivity into the situation if she was going to be able to make progress in helping Lisa. She therefore decided to spend some time looking at what Lisa had going for her – what her strengths were. She thought of using a SWOT analysis, but felt Lisa was too demotivated to go along with that. She therefore decided to try positive strokes by using questions:

REBA: What do you see as your strengths?
LISA: What strengths? What are you talking about?
REBA: Well for a start, wouldn't you say you are a good mother?
LISA: Oh yes, I've always put my children first.
REBA: Well, that strikes me as not just one strength, but a whole set of strengths, wouldn't you say?
LISA: I suppose so.
REBA: Right. So let's see, what other strengths are there we can identify? ...

In addition to using positive strokes appropriately ourselves, we can help other people to do so – for example, where somebody is responsible for the well-being of another person (this could be a parent in a family or a supervisor in a workplace). Problems and tensions may be arising because of the lack of positive strokes. It could therefore be very beneficial, in some circumstances, to help certain people to appreciate the benefits of positive strokes and perhaps even to teach them how to use them appropriately (although we have to feel fairly confident in using this technique ourselves before we can realistically start teaching it to others).

One important point to consider is timescales. In some situations, positive strokes can make an almost instant improvement in the situation. In other circumstances, it may take longer. For example, in a situation where there are entrenched, long-term problems, the use of positive strokes is not likely to have an immediate impact. It may take a while for positive strokes (and other interventions) to undermine the culture of negativity, defeatism and cynicism that is so often associated with entrenched problems.

▶ **Giving feedback** ▶ **Know your enemy** ▶ **Providing an anchor** ▶ **SWOT analysis** ▶

Principled negotiation

Constructive ways of reaching agreement

This is an approach to conflict management that seeks to move away from the traditional process of 'positional negotiation' – that is, instead of trying to batter each other into submission, we try and find common ground and establish win–win solutions.

Principled negotiation involves a much more subtle process of negotiation than the long-standing method of adopting a position and then defending it. It requires us to adopt a holistic perspective, being able to get the big picture as it were. We may then be able to trade off concessions. So, in a conventional trade union scenario, we may have employers saying something along the lines of: 'We will give you a 2 per cent pay rise, provided that you drop your objection to x' and, in return, the staff side may respond: 'We will accept a 2 per cent rise and drop our objections to X, provided that you agree to Y'. This means that there is a broader approach to the negotiation table. It is based on the idea that there will be different concessions that can be traded, rather than just simply a fight to see who can hold on for the longest to their entrenched position. That is why this approach is called principled negotiation, rather than positional negotiation. It is not simply a matter of defending a position for as long as possible but, rather, looking at what are the principles on which we can agree a way forward.

This approach is built on respect, which has to be earned, of course. That respect comes from showing a clear commitment to achieving mutually satisfactory outcomes (win–win), rather than one party defeating the other (win–lose or even lose–lose). Success in the use of principled negotiation depends on at least three things:

1. *Good communication skills.* In order to earn the respect that is needed and to create the trust and credibility on which success depends, negotiators need to be able to communicate very skilfully.

2. *Reflective practice.* There are two aspects to this. First of all, there is a need to think holistically, rather than focusing narrowly on winning. A holistic perspective involves seeing the big picture and looking for the principles for potential agreement that can be used. The second aspect of reflective practice is to be able to react sensibly as situations change, and to avoid getting stuck in tramline thinking. This is an example of what Schön (1983) referred to as a 'reflective conversation with the situation'.

3. *Assertiveness.* Getting the balance of not creating problems for others by forcing them into something they are not happy with on the one hand, and not allowing them to force us into a situation we are not happy with, on the other – that is the basis of assertiveness (see *People Skills*, 2009a).

It is important to recognize that principled negotiation is not simply a process of compromising; it is a much more subtle and sophisticated undertaking than this. It involves a range of skills, and a degree of confidence in being able to put those skills into practice effectively. The skills and confidence involved can be developed over time, and the time, effort and energy needed to develop them can be a very worthwhile investment.

▶ **Elegant challenging** ▶ **Naming the process** ▶ **Negotiating expectations** ▶

Promoting realism

Getting the balance between optimism and pessimism

This tool involves finding the balance between naïve optimism on the one hand and defeatism-inducing pessimism on the other. In recent years there has been a growth of emphasis on what has come to be called 'positive psychology' (Seligman, 2003). This psychological theory emphasizes the importance of optimism. It argues that people who are optimistic are found to be more successful, for example, in terms of confidence and higher levels of self-esteem. According to this approach, pessimism is seen as a problem, a drawback to be avoided.

However, this approach, which has become quite popular, is increasingly being criticized for being too one-sided. For example, research has shown that pessimism is often a more accurate understanding of the situation, and an emphasis on optimism at the expense of pessimism is likely to lead to situations being distorted at times (Dienstag, 2006). One example of this is what is known in the child protection field as the 'rule of optimism' (Dingwall, Eekalaar and Murray 1983). It refers to situations where people are wanting to see signs of progress and adopt too positive an approach to the situations they are assessing, resulting in an awareness of risk factors that is at too low a level and therefore potentially very dangerous.

An emphasis on optimism can also mean that we are ill-prepared for major life challenges, such as a significant loss. People who are constantly optimistic can feel that they have been badly done to when they experience a major loss, because this is beyond their sense of what is right and fair, rather than the more realistic recognition that loss is part and parcel of life.

Because of the distortions involved in artificially setting up optimism as a good thing and therefore pessimism as a bad thing, we need to have a more balanced approach. That approach is known as realism (Thompson, 2009a). It involves seeing the glass is *both* half empty *and* half full, instead of having an artificial perspective which sees it as either one or the other. Realism enables us to capitalize on positives in a situation but also to prepare for the negatives. It gives us a more holistic and more balanced perspective on the realities that we face, instead of the one-sided distortions of either optimism, which tends to see only the positives, or pessimism, which tends to see only the negatives. It is a case of moving away from such either/or thinking towards what I would call both/and thinking – recognizing that both optimism and pessimism are unhelpful in their pure forms and that what we need is the balance of these two sets of issues in the form of realism.

What is involved in the tool of promoting realism is learning when it is important to be hopeful and persistent and when it is wise to accept defeat and move on. This is something that the people we seek to help can often struggle with. We can get people, for example, who are overly optimistic, and we need to balance that out to ensure that they are not heading for a major disappointment, while others may be overly pessimistic, an approach that also needs balancing out to prevent a sense of hopelessness leading to defeatism and thus reduced levels of motivation.

This need for balance can be linked to the CIA framework discussed earlier. There are certain things that we can control, other things that we cannot control, but that we can influence, and things that we can

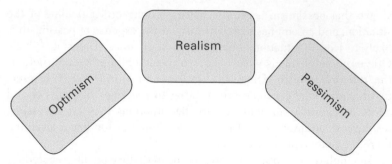

Figure 2.11   Promoting realism

neither control nor influence, and which we therefore need to accept. This is a form of realism, an alternative to relying on optimism which would give us too unbalanced a perspective on what can be done or pessimism which would give us too defeatist an approach to such matters. Promoting realism therefore involves not uncritically accepting positive psychology and jumping on the bandwagon that has developed in recent years.

▶ **CIA framework** ▶ **Challenging cognitive distortions** ▶ **Finding the growth zone** ▶

Providing an anchor

Providing security in times of instability

Sometimes people go through some very difficult circumstances with perhaps an accumulation of events adding pressure upon pressure, with the result that the people experiencing all this feel that they are under siege. Sometimes the situation can involve major losses, such as the death of somebody close to us, and this can be exacerbated by other problems arising at around the same time. Consequently, what is often necessary is for people to 'ride the storm'. What I mean by this is that, in many sets of circumstances, there is not going to be an easy short-term answer. It is going to take time to unravel the problems even though the individuals concerned may be in great distress and experiencing great pain in the process. Sometimes we have to acknowledge this by making it clear to people that we cannot take their pain away, but we can try to be with them while they go through it. Indeed, simply being with someone while they experience such difficulties can be an important steadying influence upon them – perhaps especially with young people who are likely to have less experience of having encountered such situations.

To some people this may sound sentimental, but it is a reality. When people are having to ride the storm, knowing that there is somebody there who is offering moral support at least can be of tremendous value. This is what is meant by anchoring.

I use this term to refer to situations where people may feel that they are in very stormy seas and in danger of being completely overwhelmed or washed away. The idea of an anchor is that it cannot stop the seas from being stormy. It cannot take away the worries and the difficulties, but it can provide some degree of stability and support. It can provide some sense of holding on to get through the difficult times. In some situations, this anchor role could be the difference between somebody coping and not coping, or 'going under'. I once received a thank you card from a student. I was surprised by this, as I had not done anything to help her other than simply to listen carefully to her on two or three occasions when she had come to see me about the terrible times she was going through at home. When I asked her about why she had sent me the card, she said it was because having those little chats with me gave her an anchor. She felt that she got through that very difficult situation without giving up the course because she knew there was at least one person there who was willing to listen and to offer support.

On many occasions, we will be the ones who are called upon to be anchors for other people. As problem solvers, we are the ones who will be seeking to ensure that, while we may not be able to resolve certain difficulties, we can at least provide some sense of stability and anchoring through the stormy seas. However, there may be times when we need an anchor ourselves, and it is an important self-care skill to think about who could fulfil that role for us if we needed it.

PRACTICE FOCUS 2.12

Salif had done very well on his course and he was looking forward to building on the learning he had achieved. He felt confident he would do well in his career. However, there was one thing he felt uncomfortable about, namely his feelings of unease when dealing with people who were expressing high levels of emotion –

particularly people who were grieving. His supervisor had emphasized the importance of being an 'anchor' for people when they needed it, but Salif knew that this was something that did not come easily to him. He worried that he might back away and protect his own feelings at a time when somebody needed him to 'attend', just to be present and not abandon them. However, he was determined not to let this happen and wanted to get enough experience of dealing with such issues to make him feel confident to see them through without backing off.

In addition, anchoring can be something that we can teach others to do. For example, many people feel very anxious when they are alongside people who are distressed, and have a tendency to back off (this is especially the case when somebody is grieving). While this sense of helplessness is understandable, the result can be very unhelpful. If somebody backs away from another person they care about who is expressing pain or distress, then that apparent rejection can often add to the sense of pain and distress. From time to time we may therefore be called upon to help somebody to deal with their own feelings of anxiety about supporting somebody else, perhaps by making it clear that, at the moment, it is the other person who has the greater need and so we should try to make sure that our own feelings do not prevent their distress from being recognized and addressed.

▶ **Capitalizing on crisis** ▶ **Know your enemy** ▶ **Responding to feelings**
▶ **SARAH** ▶

Pushing the buttons

Acting as an advocate

Power is an important issue in people work, partly because power relations (or at least the abuse of them) are often a source of problems. Similarly, the use of power is often part of the solution that is needed. If we think of power not in a narrow sense of something that we either have or do not have (depending on our position in society or in the organization concerned), but rather as a broader issue in terms of the ability of individuals and groups to influence others and to influence outcomes, then we can see that power is indeed a very relevant topic to people work. Indeed, much of our work as people problem solvers is around influencing others, either influencing the people we are trying to help directly or influencing others who have a bearing on the problem situation.

Pushing the buttons is a term I use to refer to the role of the people worker in trying to make things happen on behalf of the person they are trying to help. In some contexts, but not all, this would be referred to as advocacy. Acting as an advocate for somebody means drawing on our position of power to help them because their own position of power is such that they are not in a position to influence outcomes in the same way as we are. For example, if our position in society or within a specific organization is such that we are likely to be more respected than the person we are trying to help, then that can give us an extra degree of influence. An important notion here is what is known as the hierarchy of credibility. This refers to the fact that the higher somebody is in an organization (or indeed in society itself) the more likely that person is to be heard. Pushing the buttons refers to those situations where our position of authority, trust or respect can be brought to bear in a way that has positive influence on the outcomes we are trying to achieve. For example, a manager may be able to resolve difficulties within a team that individual members of that team are not in a position to tackle. This can also apply outside an employing organization. For example, a patient who is anxious because he or she feels the doctor is not listening to concerns being raised may find that when a nurse raises these concerns with the doctor, they are listened to.

In an ideal world advocacy would not be required, as people, regardless of their position in society, would be listened to and their concerns taken seriously. However, the reality is that it is often the case that people find themselves in difficulties and despair at finding a way out because they do not have the power to influence aspects of the situation that need to change. We, as professional workers, however, may be in a much stronger position to try and influence those factors.

Although 'pushing the buttons' can be very beneficial when used appropriately in the right circumstances, it also has dangers associated with it:

- If we are not careful, advocacy can create a sense of dependency. If we are helpful in one situation it may give the wrong message, namely that we can resolve other matters too.
- If we are not sufficiently skilful in the use of this technique, we may get a backlash that affects the position of the person we are trying to

help. For example, if we are tactless in trying to influence a situation, we may create ill-feeling if we alienate the people we are trying to influence. This may have unfortunate consequences in so far as that person may then adopt an even more negative approach to the person we are trying to help.

- We must be careful not to allow the use of power to go to our heads. I have come across situations where people have overstepped the mark and gone beyond using their position of power as a constructive tool to create a positive outcome and have thus strayed into the territory of abusing their power.
- We may set a precedent – that is, if we are very successful in helping one person resolve their difficulties through pushing the buttons, then we may find that others want the same help, even though, in their circumstances, it may not be entirely appropriate.
- The use of advocacy may bring us into conflict with other people who perhaps have a vested interest in the situation remaining as it is. As indicated above, pushing the buttons is about the appropriate use of power. We may therefore find that we enter into positions where other people are using their power against us. Consequently, we will have to be confident that we are sufficiently skilled and experienced to deal with any conflict issues that arise, or we will need to satisfy ourselves that we have sufficient backup from our colleagues and/or line manager to deal with any issues that may arise.

Pushing the buttons is clearly a potentially very effective tool but, as I have suggested, it is one that can also go wrong if we are not careful. If you are not already experienced in using this approach, I would encourage you to consider it and to explore in more detail what is involved in the process (see Part Three, 'Guide to further learning'). It is sad that many people who are trying to tackle people problems adopt a very narrow focus and concentrate solely on working directly with the individual or individuals concerned to make progress when it is often the case that change needs to occur elsewhere in order to facilitate progress. Pushing the buttons is just one way of trying to make sure that we adopt a broader focus, one that is more compatible with the complexities of people work.

▶ **Brokerage** ▶ **Dealing with objections** ▶ **Elegant challenging** ▶ **Principled negotiation** ▶ **The RED approach** ▶

RAID

Reducing problematic behaviours

This is a device for influencing behaviour. RAID stands for 'Reinforce the Acceptable, Ignore the Destructive'. This approach is commonly used in children's services, but can be more widely applied with adults in a variety of settings, provided that it is used with sufficient skill and sensitivity to do justice to the complexities involved.

RAID is an approach to dealing with behaviours that are destructive or problematic for the person concerned and/or for others. It is based on the idea that punishment does not work, unless it is constantly reinforced (Skinner, 1971). A focus on positive, desirable behaviours is deemed to be much more productive and effective. This fits well with the idea that positive goals are more effective. For example, consider the difference between 'I want to be slim' and 'I need to eat less'.

Focusing on negatives can be not only ineffective, but also counterproductive. For example, a child may become more prone towards particular behaviours if they receive attention for those behaviours, even if that attention is negative attention. For example, being reprimanded or chastised gives the child what would normally be perceived as unwanted attention. However, for many children (those who are neglected by their parents, for example), it is unfortunately the case this is better than no attention at all. We therefore have to be careful that, in focusing on negative behaviour, we are not actually unwittingly encouraging that behaviour.

The RAID approach involves first of all reinforcing the acceptable. That means that, where someone does something that is going in the direction that we regard as a positive, welcome direction, we encourage that, we reinforce it by giving praise and otherwise showing approval and endorsement. However, where behaviour is going in the 'wrong' direction, as it were, then rather than focusing on that, we should ignore it as far as possible. I need to emphasize the phrase 'as far as possible' because, in some circumstances, of course, it will not be possible to ignore destructive behaviour because of the risks involved. However, notwithstanding that limitation to the use of this tool, it can be a very helpful one for switching the focus away from an emphasis on negative behaviours to one that rewards and encourages the more positive ones. This can be highly effective in bringing about behaviour change, especially when the person concerned is aware of what is happening and is committed to trying to bring about that behaviour change.

The approach does raise certain ethical issues – for example, about who decides what is acceptable and desirable behaviour. This tool is therefore best used in partnership with the person(s) concerned who should be aware of what is happening and committed to bringing about positive change. If we are trying to use this contrary to a person's awareness and commitment, then it may be ineffective and potentially unethical.

▶ **Consequences** ▶ **Educating** ▶

REBT

Understanding anger

REBT stands for 'Rational Emotive Behavioural Therapy', but do not be put off by this rather grand-sounding term. It is actually relatively straightforward and, when used appropriately, can be very helpful. REBT is an approach associated with the work of Ellis (1962). It was originally called rational therapy, then was changed to rational emotive therapy and, later, to rational emotive behavioural therapy or REBT for short.

REBT is based on another three initials, namely **ABC**. **A** stands for an activating event. It can be an event or behaviour that triggers off a particular reaction in us. It can refer to an actual event (for example, somebody treating us badly at a particular moment) or to a memory of that event which triggers off a reaction in us.

C stands for consequence. Activating events will have consequences – that is, they will provoke a reaction. For example, referring back to the instance given above of somebody treating us badly, we may react to this angrily.

B refers to beliefs. Beliefs or cognitions are important elements that stand between activating events and consequences or reactions. REBT teaches us that we should beware of the common mistake of assuming that a trigger produces a reaction without there having been any cognitive process in between. To stick with the same example, if I react angrily to somebody treating me badly, then it is because I believe that I should not be treated badly. However, if my belief system were such that I did not have any such notion that I should not be treated badly, then I would not react with anger.

This is a very important theory that can be used as a most helpful tool. This is because unhelpful reactions will often arise as a result of irrational beliefs (**B**). For example, if I have the irrational belief that no one should refuse requests I make, then I am likely to react inappropriately on the occasion of somebody quite reasonably refusing the request I make. The problem thus can be seen to arise from my irrational belief.

This approach is widely used in anger management. It is used to show that a great deal of anger arises from our belief systems and, in particular, when those belief systems include irrational beliefs. To control anger, then, is not simply a matter of counting to ten, but rather of identifying what are the beliefs that trigger off an angry response and establishing whether or not they are reasonable and realistic in the circumstances.

However, anger management is not the only use for REBT. For example, it can be used to help boost self-esteem. If we encounter somebody whose belief system includes a belief that they are of little worth or value as a human being, then their reactions are likely to reinforce that view. What often occurs is a vicious circle in which a belief of one's own lack of value (**B**) results in actions (**C**) that then reinforce the notion that the person concerned has little worth. Practice focus 2.13 illustrates this.

PRACTICE FOCUS 2.13

Siân was the manager of a busy team that was under constant pressure. She made sterling efforts to keep things going as best she could in difficult circumstances. However, things went from bad to worse. The demands kept building up and the resources available to meet those demands were shrinking. Siân became increasingly stressed and felt she could not continue any longer. She therefore told her supervisor that she was considering leaving and taking up a less demanding job. Her supervisor was very concerned about this as she did not want to lose Siân, since she was an excellent manager for the most part. Siân's supervisor talked to her in depth about the situation and was able to identify that Siân had an irrational belief that, despite increasing demands and shrinking resources, she should be able to maintain both the quality and quantity of the team's work. This irrational belief meant that Siân was not looking at alternative strategies for managing a situation of work overload – instead, she was just working harder and harder and driving herself and her team into the ground. Her supervisor helped her to realize that she had to learn how to let go of the idea that she could achieve the impossible.

REBT can be used as a form of self-awareness. For example, if something produces a strong emotional response in me, I can look at my belief systems to identify which of my beliefs or values has been offended. I can then ask myself whether that is a reasonable or rational view that I am adopting and if not, seek to change that.

REBT can also be used as a therapeutic tool to help others, to review their beliefs and their reactions to situations, especially where there is an identifiable pattern of their reactions causing problems either for themselves, for others or both. For example, if someone reacts very strongly to even the smallest of failures at a particular task, then that can lead to a situation where the tensions and pressures are so high that the situation becomes difficult. It could then pay dividends to look at why this person reacts so strongly to minor failures by identifying what it is within their belief system that is triggering this reaction.

REBT can also be a very helpful tool in working with groups or teams. For example, it can be used as a team development exercise. A team can be asked to identify what its core beliefs and values are and then to see whether they are making reasonable, rational assumptions. It can also be done the other way round – that is, to begin with any problems that they may be experiencing and then try and trace those problems back to the possible inclusion of an irrational belief in their collective team system (or culture).

REBT can be a most effective tool and can be very thought provoking if used appropriately. Of course, it has to be used sensitively, as when we are talking about people's beliefs, we are addressing issues that are very close to home. We have to be very careful that we are not giving people the impression that we are 'psychoanalysing' them. We have to be sufficiently skilful in our use of this technique to make sure that it does not come across as intrusive.

▶ **Challenging cognitive distortions** ▶ **Reframing** ▶

Recognizing grief
Appreciating the significance of loss and grief

Loss and grief are significant aspects of human experience. They can have a drastic effect on our lives, perhaps when we least expect it. The fact that the word 'bereavement' means 'robbed' gives us some idea of how emotionally significant loss can be.

A major loss can affect us in the following ways:

- *Thoughts.* It is not uncommon for people who have experienced a major loss to find it difficult to 'think straight'. They may be dominated by thoughts about what has happened and may therefore lose sight of other important issues.
- *Feelings.* It perhaps goes without saying that our emotions will be significantly affected by a major loss. The emotional reaction can vary enormously depending on the circumstances (and the individual concerned), but a very common reaction is for the intense feelings generated to go either inwards (as depression and guilt, for example) or outwards (as anger or even aggression).
- *Actions.* Our behaviour can change dramatically as a result of loss. We can behave in ways that are out of character (a form of stress response, in effect). Our behaviour can also be unreliable – a drop in work performance, or even actions that are actually dangerous (neglectful operation of machinery, for example).

The three of these can combine to make a major impact on our relationships (and, indeed, other aspects of our lives). This can produce a very dangerous situation in which our experience of loss can put a major strain on relationships (especially where the loss has also affected the others involved in those relationships), thus putting those relationships at risk of breaking down, thereby adding further to the pressures being experienced and creating a situation where a grieving person loses support at the time they need it most.

There are two important points to emphasize about loss:

1. Although loss and grief are closely associated with death, we should not fall into the trap of concentrating on death-related losses only. Loss can occur in a variety of ways that are not linked to a death – for example, the breakdown of a relationship, the loss of a status or position, and the loss of opportunities or aspirations. If we draw too close a link between loss and death, we run the risk of missing a significant range of loss issues that are unconnected with death.

2. Different people react to loss in different ways. There is no standard, 'one size fits all' approach to grief. This is an important point to recognize because, if we do not take this message on board, we may find ourselves in a position where we are putting somebody under pressure to grieve in a particular way (in accordance with our own views of what constitutes 'healthy' grieving) that they do not feel comfortable with. This could amount to kicking somebody when they are down.

When we consider the two points above in combination, we can see that we have a situation where grief can often go unacknowledged because (i) if the loss is not death related, it may not register with us that we are dealing with a loss situation; and (ii) if we do not recognize certain thoughts, feelings or actions as being grief related (because they do not fit the stereotype of 'the grieving person'), it again may not register that we are dealing with loss issues. Consider the following examples:

- A woman who has worked in the same place for over 20 years is transferred to a new location. Normally highly motivated, she becomes withdrawn and lethargic after the move.
- A man becomes distant and distracted after his daughter leaves home to move in with her boyfriend.
- A couple become very aggressive towards one another after their close friends move away.
- A child begins to behave in a very disruptive and challenging way after being sexually abused.

The list could go on – loss (and our reactions to it) is much more common than most people realize. Consequently, it is possible for us to fail in our attempts to help people tackle their problems because we do not recognize the significance of loss and grief. In Part One above I emphasized the importance of 'problem identification' – that is, being clear about what the problem is before we attempt to tackle it. It is important that we should consider loss issues when identifying problems. If we do not, then there is clearly the danger that we will not be aware of key issues and our efforts to help could be wasted or, in certain circumstances, could do harm.

It is often the case that people who are grieving as a result of losses that are not death related do not realize the effect that grieving is having on them. For example, someone may become depressed without making a connection between their state of mind and their loss. Recognizing grief and its significance in our lives is therefore an important tool for us to use in dealing with a wide variety of problem situations.

It is something we need to consider in terms of how we make sense of situations and how we respond to them. It is also something we need to consider in terms of how we help others understand, and face up to, the problems they are experiencing. For example, making someone aware that their current situation may be largely due to an unrecognized grief reaction can, if handled sensitively and appropriately, be a huge step in helping people move forward. It is an example of 'catharsis', the freeing up of emotional blockages that can be preventing us from dealing with our problems.

Much the same can happen on a collective basis (families, teams, members of particular groups and so on). Indeed, there can be shared grief responses that can be very powerful influences on the actions of individuals within groups and on group dynamics.

Of course, loss and grief issues need to be handled very sensitively as they can relate to very sore points for people – and that includes us, as problem solvers. We are not immune to the effects of grief so we must make sure that, in dealing with loss and grief, we make sure that we have adequate support to fall back on should issues relating to our own experiences of loss arise.

▶ **Holding** ▶ **Grief audit** ▶ **Responding to feelings** ▶

The RED approach

Managing conflict

This is a tool I have developed that has proven to be a helpful method to use in the work I undertake around conflict management issues. Situations involving conflict tend to have a high level of tension associated with them. It can therefore be very helpful to have a clear systematic framework to adopt when dealing with conflict. It can help to create a greater sense of confidence and trust and thus dissipate some of the tension.

The RED approach can be broken down into its three component parts. **R** stands for 'Recognize the conflict'. This is an important point to emphasize for two reasons. First, there is a strong tendency for people to feel uncomfortable about conflict issues and perhaps to brush them under the carpet where possible, to hope that they will go away if they are ignored. Of course, that is a dangerous tactic and often leads to conflicts festering over time and therefore getting worse. Second, people may not recognize conflict because it is a much more common entity than most people realize. What they see as ordinary, everyday behaviour will often be based on an underlying conflict that is not being brought out into the open. For example, it may not be recognized that somebody's non-cooperation in a particular project is due to conflict between that person and one or more others who are also involved in it. As we noted in relation to 'PCS analysis', it is very easy to individualize the situation and regard such a person as being awkward or difficult rather than appreciate the wider context, which may have a lot to do with conflict. The first step towards dealing with conflicts, therefore, is to recognize where and when they occur.

E stands for 'Evaluate the conflict'. It would not be realistic for us to attempt to resolve every conflict we encounter – they are just so widespread. However, it is also dangerous to ignore significant conflicts, as they are likely to get worse rather than better if not addressed. The key task, therefore, is to evaluate conflicts, to weigh them up, so that we get an idea of how important or significant they are, how detrimental their consequences could be if allowed to develop, how likely or otherwise escalation of the conflict is, and so on. To a large extent, this involves using the assessment skills discussed in *People Skills* (2009a). Our ability to evaluate conflict can develop over time through experience and perhaps also through training. The important point to note is that we should not leave such matters to chance. We do not have a crystal ball at our disposal, and so we cannot know for sure that a particular conflict will prove very detrimental if not tackled, but there are tools available to us that will enable us to form an opinion as to how significant a particular conflict is (see, for example, the discussion of 'Risk assessment' below).

D stands for 'Deal with the conflict'. In a limited number of cases, simply being aware of the conflict (and those involved being aware that we know of it) can be sufficient to keep the conflict under control and make it manageable. However, in the majority of cases, it is dangerous to allow significant conflicts to remain live issues. If our evaluation has determined that a particular conflict is significant, then we now have the task of deciding how best to deal with it. There are various options open to us, but all of them are likely to involve some degree of attempting to get the parties to appreciate each other's point of view. Communication is therefore a key part of trying to resolve conflict. Encouraging open and clear communication can be an invaluable part of conflict management.

Handling conflict is a central part of dealing with people problems because it is so often the case that conflict is either the cause, in part at least, of such problems or is, again in part at least, the result of such problems. In tackling conflict issues, it is important to avoid the two destructive extremes. On the one hand, we do not want to fall into the trap of trying to pretend that the conflict is not there. This 'ostrich' approach is doomed to failure, of course. But, despite its dangerousness, it is still a very common reaction to conflict. At the other extreme, we also need to avoid overreaction. A panic reaction to conflict will only 'up the stakes', as it were, by increasing the tensions and thereby increasing the likelihood of a harmful outcome. Maintaining the healthy balance between these two destructive extremes is not always easy. However, it is to be hoped that the RED approach can be a helpful tool in assisting us to try and remain free from the problems associated with these two extremes.

At a personal level, the RED approach can be used to make us confident that we are responding appropriately to a situation characterized by conflict. It can therefore be a significant source of confidence and reassurance. It is likely to be less useful in dealing directly with people who are in conflict, but that is not to rule out its use altogether. As with any tool, the skill of the craftsperson in deciding when it is appropriate and how best to use it is paramount. One arena where it can certainly be helpful, though, is in working with groups of people. It can be used as a means of helping to identify any conflicts or tensions that exist, evaluating them in terms of their relative importance and, where appropriate, coming up with strategies for dealing with them. This can be done in a preventative way – that is, by anticipating conflicts and preparing the ground for preventing them or nipping them in the bud. It can also be used in a remedial way once conflicts have already begun to arise.

Whichever way it is used, the RED approach offers a clear and helpful way of dealing with some very demanding situations that could become major problems if not handled sensitively and appropriately.

▶ **Avoiding avoidance** ▶ **Confronting without being confrontational** ▶ **Risk assessment** ▶

Reframing
Redefining problem situations to allow people to move forward

The basic idea behind reframing is that sometimes we cannot change the objective circumstances in which we are working or living, but perhaps we can change our attitude towards them. Reframing is based on the psychological concept of 'cognitive restructuring', as Marshall puts it:

> Cognitive restructuring refers to a way of dealing with a problem where what are seen as acceptable solutions, or outcomes, cannot reasonably be expected. If the conditions cannot be changed then the only way forward is to change your conceptualisation of them and your own relation to them. This may mean lowering your expectations in some cases.
>
> (1998, p. 25)

Lowering our expectations is one way of achieving this but, of course, is not the only one. What it is about is renegotiating expectations. This is an important issue in relation to stress, as a very common cause of stress is either unclear or unrealistic expectations.

There is also a parallel here with assertiveness. It would be a mistake to see assertiveness (that is, seeking win–win solutions) as being simply a matter of compromising or reducing expectations. It is more a case of finding ways forward where both parties can be happy. Reframing is very similar. It is a way of finding an alternative approach that can be acceptable. I once came across a man who told me that his job was very stressful because it involved trying to find resources that were largely absent. He told me that his job was necessarily stressful because failure was an inherent part of his job. He was being asked to find resources that, in his view, did not exist. However, when I suggested that he should check and, if necessary, renegotiate his job description to make sure that it stated words to the effect that his job was to look for rather than find such resources, he was delighted with my comments. It gave him a way forward. By reframing his job description in this small but significant way, it changed it from being a job necessarily characterized by failure to one that could involve success. That is, if his job was to look for resources, he could still do an excellent job even though he might not find such resources, as that could be due to factors beyond his control.

Reframing can also be linked to pessimism and optimism. Sometimes reframing is needed because somebody is being unduly negative or unduly positive (in reality, the former tends to be more likely than the latter). Somebody who is prone to a pessimistic outlook may need help in reframing things in a more positive way while somebody who has an optimistic outlook may, on occasion, need help with reframing to be more realistic about what can be achieved in the circumstances or what outcomes can be expected. An example of positive reframing would be, 'I only managed to get it right three times out of five' being changed into 'I managed to get it right most of the time'. An example of reframing to move somebody away from an unrealistic version of optimism might be, 'we are bound to get this contract' being changed to 'we're in with a good chance of getting this contract'.

The technique can be used directly and explicitly. For example, we can say to somebody, 'I think it would be helpful if we reframed the situation' and then explain what we mean by that. Alternatively, we may do it implicitly. For example, when someone talks to us in a way that we feel is in need of reframing, we can feed it back to that person in a more realistic way. For example, if someone says: 'I don't know anything about that sort of thing', then a useful reply could be: 'I take it by that that you mean you will need training before undertaking this role and we would certainly want you to undertake such training.' In a way, this is a form of gentle challenging and indeed this is often what is required – a way of challenging something that needs reframing (see the discussion above of elegant challenging). Such challenging can be done in a variety of ways – for instance, a counter example can be given. If someone says: 'Nobody has ever managed to do that', then this can be challenged by the response of 'What about Sarah – didn't she do that?'

Naming the process, as discussed above, can also be used to good effect. If someone is being too self-centred about a particular issue, this can be gently challenged by 'We always seem to be coming back to the implications for you and I can see why that's important, but I think we have to look at the bigger picture here in terms of the implications for everybody concerned'.

Reframing is also something that can apply to groups of people or teams. It may be, for example, that one source of conflict is that different people within a group are conceptualizing the same issues in different ways and, in order to reach some sort of workable consensus, it will be necessary to come up with a shared reframing of the issues. Coming up with such a shared reframing may be a long and difficult job, but it can be one that is well worth the time and effort invested in it if it means that a team or group of people can move forward away from problems they have been experiencing.

Some people in the past have been a little cynical about reframing and see it as a form of cheating or self-delusion: 'If you can't have what you want, just kid yourself into believing you never wanted it anyway.' However, this is a gross oversimplification of what reframing is all about. How we react to events in our lives will depend not only on those particular events, but also on our beliefs about them and about ourselves. This is what is known as a phenomenological perspective – that is, one that emphasizes the importance of perception and meaning. Often, such perceptions are based on habit, and when we examine those habits, we may well be prepared to change our perspective. For example, if someone who has worked with children for many years were to move to a job that involved working with adults, then there may be a number of ways in which he or she would need to adjust. There may be habits that have developed over the years that are quite appropriate in working with children but which need to be reframed when working with adults.

▶ **Challenging cognitive distortions** ▶ **REBT** ▶ **The three Hs** ▶

Releasing the scapegoat
Avoiding the destructiveness of blame

This involves identifying 'scapegoating' processes where they are occurring and trying to establish their ineffective and even counterproductive nature. It is often the case that someone in a family, team or group bears the brunt of criticism. They are identified as 'the problem' or as the weak link who is 'letting the side down'. It is generally the least powerful member of the family or group who is identified as the scapegoat. This reflects the complex power dynamics that tend to operate when groups of people come together. The person least able to defend him- or herself is likely to become the person who is 'picked on'.

The term 'scapegoat' refers to a sacrificial goat – that is, to someone who is sacrificed, who suffers for the sake of the wider benefit of the group. This is a process that groups can find helpful up to a point, as it gives them a pressure release valve, but it is of course unfair and oppressive for the person who is scapegoated in this way and is therefore a destructive process that needs to be challenged and prevented where possible. It can also be problematic for the group, as it is likely to distract attention from the real sources of their problems and thereby prevent group members from developing the understanding they need to tackle those problems effectively.

Scapegoating can be deliberate, as in bullying, where a particular person is identified as someone who will be criticized and who will be made to feel responsible for problems that are not directly the result of their actions. They are, in effect, being victimized because they are perceived as an easy target.

However, the process can also be the unintentional result of how power operates in subtle multidimensional ways (but the results are, none the less, the same in terms of the harm done). Often at the heart of the problem is avoidance. More powerful group members may not be prepared to face up to difficult or sensitive issues (a phenomenon known as 'anxiety avoidance') or to matters that would involve them in losing face. Blaming a less powerful member of the group becomes an attractive alternative to facing up to such difficult and potentially embarrassing matters.

I use the term 'releasing the scapegoat' to refer to the various ways in which we can try to change this type of situation. It can be broken down into two types. In the first type, we are looking at scapegoating as an organizational issue. If the scapegoating appears to be deliberate, then we will need to consider legal and policy issues relating to bullying and victimization. If the person being bullied is prepared to address the matter formally in accordance with a particular policy of the organization concerned, then we will need to support them sensitively through the process. Second, if the bullying is in a family context, rather than an organization, then we need to think in terms of, first of all, safeguarding procedures if the matter relates to a child or a vulnerable adult. If the person being scapegoated is not a child or vulnerable adult, then we need to consider helping them to make a decision about whether they want to remain in that situation or move on. If they choose to remain in that situation, we can explore with them ways in which they can be supported in trying to guard against scapegoating, to challenge it where necessary. If the scapegoating is not deliberate and is a reflection of complex family or group dynamics, then there are various steps that can be taken to try and change these. There is, for example, a significant literature base in relation to family therapy (Dallos and Draper, 2010) and to groupwork (Doel, 2006) which can be drawn upon to help us to make releasing the scapegoat a useful and viable tool for problem solving.

▶ Responding to feelings ▶ Risk assessment ▶

Responding to feelings

Taking account of the emotional dimension

Emotion is often presented as if it were an exception to the rule, something that represents a change from the normal state of affairs – for example, when somebody says 'when I mentioned the subject, he became emotional'. In reality, everything we do has an emotional dimension. For example, being agitated may be seen as being emotional, but is calmness not an emotional state too? It is far too simplistic and misleading to think that life is basically a rational undertaking and that occasionally emotions creep in. Emotions, in one form or another, will affect everything that we do, as there is no neutral, non-emotional state.

This has quite significant implications. It is not just a technical matter of definition of what constitutes emotional and what does not. Rather, it is a case of realizing the profound and far-reaching implications of recognizing that emotions play at least a small part in shaping everything we do. We must therefore move away from the idea that emotions apply only during exceptional circumstances – for example, when somebody is particularly happy or unhappy. Being neither particularly happy nor particularly unhappy is in itself an emotional state.

PRACTICE FOCUS 2.14

Karen was a training officer whose duties involved not only commissioning some training from specialists, but also delivering part of the annual training programme herself. There had been a request for training in relation to emotional intelligence, and so she took the opportunity to deliver this herself, as it was a topic that had interested her for some time. The first course went very well, but she was surprised how some members of the group seemed very reluctant to talk about emotional issues – they seemed very uncomfortable. Karen had expected that people who felt uncomfortable with such matters would not have signed up for the course, so she could not understand the level of discomfort on some people's part. This taught her an important lesson – not to underestimate the extent to which the emotional side of life can present significant challenges.

The concept of emotional intelligence is one that has become quite popular in some areas, even though the concept itself is quite confusing, as the notion of emotion does not sit easily with that of intelligence. But, terminology aside, the point that it is important to recognize and respond appropriately to feelings is an extremely significant one, and that, after all, is the basic tenet of emotional intelligence. To many in the people professions, emotional intelligence is old wine in new bottles, in the sense that the importance of recognizing feelings (our own and those of the people we are working with) and responding appropriately to them is an idea that has a much longer history and much firmer foundations than the relatively new notion of emotional intelligence.

An important part of responding to feelings, particularly the feelings of others, is to be able to read body language. This is something we can practise. When we have some spare time we can watch other people and think about what emotions they are indicating through their non-verbal communication and how precisely this is done. For example, we can look at how closely people stand in relation to each other and work out whether this reflects the closeness of the relationship. We can also look at such matters as eye contact. The more we develop these observation skills, the more skilful at reading body language we can become. We can do this in live action, as it were, by watching people in our ordinary lives, but we can also do the same through television and film. Indeed, in these latter examples, body language is sometimes exaggerated for dramatic effect in order to make a point to ensure that viewers do not miss out on a crucial part of the story line. This means that TV and film can be particularly useful at highlighting the relationship between body language and emotion.

The other side of this coin is that we need to make sure that our body language is appropriate. What type of emotional message are we trying to convey in the way we use nonverbal communication? This can be at a very simple level (for example, are we showing interest through smiling?) or at much more complex and intricate levels. The more aware we become over time of these important issues, the more skilful we can become at making sure that we are using body language appropriately and not giving people the wrong message. For example, we may be very interested in what somebody is trying to say and very keen to help them, but if our anxiety leads us to refrain from making eye contact, the actual message we may be giving in emotional terms is that we do not care, that we are not prepared to engage with this person.

Of course, a key part of emotional response is being able to understand and identify our own feelings. This is a matter of self-awareness. How much do you know about what makes you tick emotionally? How tuned in are you to what pleases you, what annoys you, what enthuses you, what turns you off, and so on? This is not a recommendation that you should psychoanalyse yourself, but rather a plea for a major focus on self-awareness. It is unrealistic to expect to be able to respond appropriately to other people's emotions if we do not have a clue about our own.

It is important to be able to respond to other people's emotions in a constructive way. This means being able to reinforce positive emotions. For example, if somebody is commenting on how their confidence is beginning to grow, then this is something we can encourage further. However, if somebody is expressing destructive emotions, our challenge is to be able to respond to those feelings positively and constructively, not by pretending they are not there, nor by reacting inappropriately ourselves. In between those two unhelpful extremes is a constructive and helpful balance. A major part of responding appropriately to other people's feelings is to have a certain degree of awareness of the importance of emotions, how they influence individuals and interactions between people or, in short, emotional intelligence.

▶ **Holding** ▶ **SARAH** ▶ **Think–Feel–Do** ▶ **Tuning in** ▶

The right person for the job
Matching skills and aptitudes to task

This can be seen to apply in two ways. First of all, it applies in its usual sense – relating to the workplace and employment matters. A lot of stress can arise because somebody is in the wrong job. That is, their particular employment role at the moment is not suited to their talents, experience or interests (Thompson, 1999). For example, having a creative person in a mundane role that is basically routine and does not require any creativity can be soul destroying for the individual concerned, whereas having somebody who enjoys the security and structure of routine, mundane work, may feel very threatened in a job that requires creativity and reflective practice.

This is a matter of selection and recruitment as well as job design. Any good manager will know that trying to fit a square peg into a round hole is asking for trouble. Care therefore needs to be taken to ensure that people being asked to undertake particular tasks are the best people to do so in the circumstances. We should be very wary of a blanket approach that assumes that any competent individual should be capable of any task. Life is, of course, not that simple.

While the employment issues related to the notion of the right person for the job are clearly important, we should not neglect the other side of the coin when it comes to people problem solving. Helping people to solve their problems often involves asking individuals to undertake particular tasks or to fulfil certain roles. We can therefore apply the same logic and look at who is the best person for the job, who is the best person to undertake a particular role or to complete a particular task within a problem-solving framework. For example, in a fraught, volatile situation that requires calm, it would be wise to entrust certain tasks or duties to the person or persons within the problem situation who appear to be the most stable, calm and collected. At the other extreme, if we were to ask somebody who is easily excitable to undertake certain roles, this may lead to a counterproductive situation where his or her actions actually increase the level of instability and concern rather than reduce tensions and anxiety.

Another implication of this is that we should be careful not to set people up to fail. For example, if we are dealing with somebody with a low level of confidence who is very anxious about particular aspects of their life or work situation, then it could be disastrous to ask that person to do something that involves a lot of confidence or even courage. Simply encouraging or cajoling somebody to do something that they feel they are unable to do is not only insufficient, it can actually be very unhelpful indeed as it may undermine that person's confidence still further.

A positive approach can be based on first of all mapping or scanning the situation, working out what needs doing, and then moving along to look at who is the best person for each of the items that have been identified from this scan. We should, of course, not seek to impose our view on other people as that, in itself, can be unhelpful, but rather to try and positively influence developments in the right direction. Often the people we are seeking to help will have enough self-awareness to know that they are not cut out for certain jobs, or are keen to adopt certain jobs, as the case may be. However, at times, certain individuals may volunteer for tasks that they are not suited for. This is clearly a situation that will need to be handled sensitively and carefully. It will require us to draw on our interpersonal skills.

Finding the right person for the job does not have to be a duty that falls solely to you. It is something that, in many circumstances, can be done collectively. There can be group discussion about who is the best person to undertake particular tasks or fulfil certain roles. Do not make the mistake of assuming that it is all down to you individually.

In summary, the idea of the right person for the job can be seen as something to consider as part of our assessment – are the problems being experienced, in part at least, due to somebody undertaking roles or duties that they are not well suited to or feel uncomfortable with? It can also be an important part of our intervention – that is, as a problem-solving tool in its own right. Even if the problem situation does not derive from an inappropriate allocation of job roles, reallocating may, none the less, be an important part of the solution or a step towards finding the solution.

▶ **Creative tension** ▶ **Doing the right things vs. doing things right** ▶ **Giving feedback** ▶ **Negotiating expectations** ▶

Risk assessment

Analysing the risks involved in a given situation

More or less everything we do in life involves a degree of risk. Even if we play things safe and try to keep risks to a minimum, we run the risk of missing out on some important opportunities (perhaps opportunities to solve problems we have been wrestling with for quite some time). Risk, then, is not something we can avoid altogether – it is something we have to learn to manage. Or to be more accurate, it is something that we need to manage better, as basic risk management is something that we can all do (it is something we learn as part of growing up), even though some people may be better at it than others.

Risk management is something we do in an informal way every day of our lives. When we are crossing the road, we are weighing up whether it is safe to do so, making a judgement about the speed of vehicles, the time it will take us to get across the road and so on. For most of the risks we take, this informal approach based on years of experience is perfectly adequate. However, there will come times where we need a more formal approach – one where we explicitly identify the risk factors we are dealing with, partly to make sure we have considered them carefully and are fully aware of them and partly to make sure we have a record of them for the benefit of others in the future (for example, a colleague trying to tackle the same issues in helping someone and therefore facing the same – or similar – risks as those you faced and explored carefully).

A key part of risk management is having a clear picture of the risks we (and the people we are seeking to help) face and their implications. This is where risk assessment comes in. There are various approaches to risk assessment, but one I have found particularly helpful is the Brearley model. Paul Brearley (1982) developed his model by exploring the risks faced by older people living in the community. However, his model has been adapted to apply in a wide variety of settings and is now recognized as a generic risk assessment tool. It can be summarized as follows:

1. *Begin by considering the context we are working in.* Are there, for example, any cultural differences that may influence how we interpret the situation or how we respond to it?
2. *Identify the dangers.* A danger is what we want not to happen. That is, if there is a loose stair carpet, the danger is that someone will fall down the stairs and be injured or even killed.

3. *Identify the hazards.* These are the risk factors that will make the danger more likely to occur (in the above example, the loose stair carpet would be a significant hazard). Other common hazards may be the influence of alcohol (people are at more risk when they are drunk), the use of machinery, someone having a 'short fuse' and being prone to violence, and so on.

4. *Divide the hazards into two types: situational and predisposing.* Situational hazards are those which relate to the specific circumstances at the moment. For example, the stair carpet is not normally loose, but has become loose because the tacks holding it in place have worn away over time. Situational hazards are therefore related to specific time periods. Predisposing hazards, by contrast, are the ones that persist over time. They relate to particular predispositions (for example, Alan's tendency to run up the stairs). It may be the case that he has been running upstairs for years but has never had an accident. However, the combination of a situational hazard (the loose stair carpet) with a predisposing one (his tendency to run up the stairs) may well be what produces the danger – the actual accident of Alan falling down the stairs.

5. *Identify the strengths.* What aspects of the situation make it less likely that the danger will occur? What are the counterbalancing features? For example, if we have someone who is prone to violence (predisposing hazard) in a situation of high tension (a situational hazard), the combination of the two may be potentially explosive. However, there may be other factors (the strengths) that tilt the balance against the danger occurring (for example, someone present who has skills in defusing fraught situations, someone with aggression prevention skills).

6. *Identify gaps in your knowledge.* What do we not know about the situation? Is there anything that could significantly change the situation that we are not aware of? Considering these issues will help to prevent us from making decisions that we may later regret because we acted too soon without first trying to fill some of the gaps in our knowledge. Sometimes the situation is so dangerous that we have to act without the luxury of gathering extra information or delving into the situation further, but even then, being aware of what gaps there are in our knowledge could be helpful – for example, by warning us about which aspects of the situation need extra caution.

7. *Consider what actions are needed.* This means that risk assessment is not just about gathering information – it also involves making sense of that information and developing a realistic action plan based on it.

This is not, of course, a foolproof approach to risk assessment, but it does give a very useful framework and structure to work to. I have used it many times and have found it useful both for clarifying my own think ing and for giving the person(s) I am trying to help a degree of confidence and security in what I am doing.

In what circumstances can it be used? Well, it can be drawn upon in basically any situation which involves sufficient risk to justify a formal approach. The precise circumstances will vary from setting to setting and situation to situation, but the key indicator is: sufficient concern to warrant looking closely and explicitly at the risks involved in the situation concerned.

▶ **Capitalizing on crisis** ▶ **Consequences** ▶ **SWOT analysis** ▶

Role reversal

Seeing the situation from someone else's point of view

It is often the case that people who are experiencing problems become so engrossed in the challenges they face, and the anxiety that so often accompanies them, that they do not take account of other dimensions of the situation or of key issues. This tendency to adopt a narrow, partial view is a recurring theme in dealing with people problems, although we should not be surprised by this, as the pressures involved can often prevent people from thinking clearly or looking at the wider picture.

One way of tackling this is through role reversal. This can be done in one of two ways, directly or indirectly. By directly I mean situations where people actually carry out another person's duties. For example, in a situation of conflict, it may pay dividends to ask each of the two parties to undertake the other's role for a limited period (although this may have to be closely supervised to prevent one or both of them sabotaging the other's work). In this way each party can be helped to understand the pressures the other faces and to begin, perhaps, to see the situation from their point of view.

However, situations where this direct approach may be used are likely to be fairly limited, which brings us to the indirect use of role reversal. This involves enabling the benefits of direct role reversal to be achieved through discussion. This can be two separate discussions (one with party

A and the other with party B) to try and get each one of them to appreciate the other's point of view or, if we have the skills and confidence to
do so, one joint discussion involving both parties where we enable them
to explore each other's perspective. This is very close to what happens in
the process of mediation as a form of dispute resolution.

One interesting approach to role reversal is what has come to be
known as 'Garfinkeling'. This refers to the work of the sociologist
Harold Garfinkel who was interested in the 'unwritten' rules of particular societies (the assumptions that go to make up core elements of a
culture). According to Garfinkel (1967), we can identify these very
important unwritten rules by breaking them – and we can break them
by a process of reversal. For example, if we consider unwritten social
rules about gender roles, we can identify these rules by reversing the
gender. Morgan makes apt comment when he makes the point that:

> Garfinkel elucidates our taken-for-granted skills by showing us what
> happens if we deliberately attempt to disrupt normal patterns of life.
> Look a fellow subway passenger in the eye for a prolonged period of
> time. He or she will no doubt look away at first but get increasingly
> uncomfortable as your gaze continues. Perhaps he [sic] will eventu-
> ally inquire what's wrong, change seats or get off at the next stop.
> Behave in your neighbor's house as if you live there. Disrupt the
> smooth and continuous line of your walk down a crowded street
> with a series of random stops and turns or with the shifty manner of
> a suspicious character. In each case, you will gradually discover how
> life within a given culture flows smoothly only insofar as one's behav-
> iour conforms with unwritten codes. Disrupt these norms and the
> ordered reality of life inevitably breaks down.
>
> (1997, p. 139)

Another example would be rules about how people address one another
in a power relationship. For example, if Lyn is used to addressing her
line manager as Mr Davies, while he calls her Lyn, imagine how strange
(and awkward) it would seem, if she called him by his first name or how
unfriendly it would seem if he addressed her by her title and surname.
Switching things round in this way helps us to realize that unwritten
rules are operating and that we are making assumptions – assumptions
which may be part of the problem we are trying to solve or which may
be acting as obstacles to solving that problem.

Garfinkeling can be used to inject a note of humour and lighten a
tense situation, but it also has a serious role to play in bringing out

assumptions that can be problematic. Consider the dialogue in Practice focus 2.15.

PRACTICE FOCUS 2.15

FACILITATOR: Why did Sarah get upset with you?
PAUL: I don't know.
FACILITATOR: What did she say to you?
PAUL: She said I had sexually harassed her.
FACILITATOR: And you feel you didn't?
PAUL: No, it was just a bit of fun. I didn't mean anything by it. I thought she'd be flattered. [Pause] I don't know why women can't take a joke.
FACILITATOR: If it was the other way round, if it were women making jokes about men and treating them mainly as sexual objects, as if that were the only thing about them that is important, do you think men would like it?
PAUL: Yeah, sure, it would be a laugh.
FACILITATOR: Really? Even if it were day in day out? Don't you think it would get wearing after a while, particularly if it meant that other strengths you've got get overlooked?
PAUL: Yeah, I suppose you've got a point. I hadn't thought about it like that.

This type of dialogue will not in itself sort out the problem of sexual harassment, but the 'switching' involved in Garfinkeling will have laid the foundations for developing awareness and making the individual concerned think more about his actions and their potentially detrimental effects than would otherwise have been the case.

Role reversal can be used as a way of clarifying our own thinking (If somebody accused me of sexual harassment, how would I react? How would I feel?) and thus broadening it out – putting ourselves in someone else's moccasins, as it were. It can also be used to help others, to enable them to appreciate other people's perspectives, and it can even be used as a development tool for teams or groups – to promote partnership working by encouraging and supporting people in seeing the situation from other people's point of view.

The effective use of role reversal involves careful planning. It is not a tool that should be used unthinkingly, as it can complicate matters significantly. For example, if it is used in a situation of hostility, it could heighten the hostility if one party chooses to use it as a weapon against the other. Like any tool, role reversal only works where it is used in the appropriate circumstances and with the appropriate skill.

Role reversal can be a very effective way of understanding complex underlying dynamics that are shaping a particular situation. It can be used in a very straightforward way at times, but can also be part of a very complex multilevel assessment that enables us to develop a more sophisticated understanding of what can often be very destructive situations.

▶ **Challenging cognitive distortions** ▶ **The empty chair** ▶ **Encouraging creativity** ▶

SARAH

Coping with emotional intensity

This is a tool designed to help people deal with raised levels of emotion. Sometimes people problem solvers can feel ill-equipped when they encounter a degree of emotional intensity. This tool is presented as a useful, structured way of trying to make sure that we respond in a positive and helpful manner.

SARAH is an acronym introduced by Lambert (1996b) who argues that: 'When things start to go off the rails and signs of roused emotions appear, think SARAH' (p. 37). SARAH can be explained as follows:

S *stop talking* This emphasizes the importance of listening. If, for example, someone is becoming agitated, carrying on talking may make the situation worse, whereas showing that we are listening should help to calm things down by demonstrating that we are taking seriously the concerns of the person concerned.

A – *active listening* Simply listening is not enough – it needs to be active listening. That is, we need to show we are listening through our body language. This may be simply a nodding head (don't overdo it!), but can also be conveyed in other subtle ways. It is essential that we make the point loud and clear that we are 'attending' to the person. If we do not, we risk aggravating the situation.

R – *reflect content or feeling* This involves feeding back some aspect of our understanding of the situation. This may involve paraphrasing a key point that has been made, but it should not be simply a case of 'doing parrot-like imitations', as Lambert puts it (1996b, p. 38). It is a question of making it clear that we have understood (or an opportunity to seek further clarification if we have not understood). When reflecting feelings it is important not to put words into people's mouths. In particular, you should avoid saying: 'I know how you feel' because, of course, you do not know how another person feels. It is much better to say something more neutral like: 'I can understand why you might be annoyed by this situation, but ...'.

A – *act with empathy*   It is important to distinguish between empathy and sympathy. The latter involves sharing feelings with someone (if they are sad, we are sad). Empathy, by contrast, involves recognizing and acknowledging someone's feelings without necessarily feeling them ourselves. This distinction is important for two reasons:

1. If you share the feelings of the various people you seek to help it is only a matter of time before you will become burnt out – overloaded by an excess of negative feelings. For self-care reasons you need to keep a certain distance and not take on board other people's feelings through sympathy.
2. Sympathy can intensify someone's feelings. For example, if someone is expressing anger about the way a third party has treated them, then if we show that we are angry too, we may unwittingly contribute to an escalation of those feelings.

H – *handle objections*   Lambert sums this up well when he comments that:

> When your calm, sensitive handling of the situation has made it easy for your client to listen to reason again, deal with any objections raised. Always deal with what your client says. Never try to second guess 'what they really mean'. You will almost certainly get it wrong. Even if you were to get it right, you will destroy the belief that you have been listening carefully and with empathy and understanding.
>
> (1996b, p. 39)

This tool can be used in one-to-one encounters, but is also valuable when dealing with a number of people expressing high levels of emotion. This can be a family context, a team within an organization or indeed any situation involving more than one person. The more people there are involved, the greater the danger that emotions will escalate – with one emotional reaction triggering off another. However, the more demanding the situation is because of the number of people involved, the more useful this tool can be.

It is not expected that people can demonstrate the skills involved in SARAH without the opportunity to practise, but the technique does provide a platform from which skill development can take place over time. An important factor in terms of such skill development can be confidence. Dealing with people displaying high levels of emotion can be very daunting, and so it is not surprising that many people may feel very unconfident about tackling such situations. However, it is important to realize that a lot of very effective problem solving happens because the person trying to help 'weathered the storm' of high emotions and, in so doing, won respect and professional confidence. People are much more likely to trust us and our judgement if they know that we have the skills and courage to weather some emotional storms with them, whereas they are likely to have little respect for, or confidence in, someone who shrinks away when emotions are to the fore. There is therefore much to be gained from building on the platform that SARAH provides.

▶ **Handling objections** ▶ **Responding to feelings** ▶

Serendipity

Making the most of chance occurrences

This is the process of capitalizing on chance happenings, being alert enough to draw out the positives as situations evolve. Many things happen for a reason or combination of reasons – they are the result of deliberate, often concerted, efforts to make them happen. But, sometimes things just happen; circumstances conspire to produce situations by chance. Sometimes such situations are very negative where people are in the wrong place at the wrong time, and a disaster may befall them. For example, this can apply to road traffic accidents where somebody may be injured or even killed through no fault of their own. It was just chance circumstances that came together to produce such an undesirable situation.

However, sometimes the chance happenings provide very positive situations where people are fortunate enough to be in the right place at the right time. When such good fortune arises, it is important that we do not 'look a gift horse in the mouth'. If we are not careful, we may fail to recognize the benefits to be gained from a particular set of circumstances, or if we do recognize them, then we may not react quickly enough to be able to take full advantage of them. If we are too slow on the uptake, then we may miss significant opportunities to make a positive difference to the problems people are currently facing.

Another possible problem with the use of serendipity as a tool is that we may be too inflexible in our approach and not be prepared to change our original plan. This is where reflective practice is important, as this involves having a reflective conversation with the situation – in other words, being able to identify changes and respond to them, rather than just unthinkingly pressing on with plans when the circumstances have changed.

We may encounter resistance from people who have suffered great misfortune and have therefore developed a pessimistic outlook on life and/or have low self-esteem, which can lead them to assume that they are not worthy of good fortune. Others, by contrast, may be only too ready to capitalize on a 'lucky break'. The idea of *carpe diem* (seize the day) is what serendipity is all about. It involves striking a balance between, on the one hand, recklessly abandoning plans without proper consideration or risk assessment and, on the other, sticking rigidly to existing plans and being unwilling to consider chance opportunities that arise serendipitously.

To make full use of serendipity requires a certain degree of flexibility and creativity that come with confidence and experience. It is therefore likely that inexperienced problem solvers may struggle at first with the idea of serendipity, but, over time, may become more used to it and more adept at capitalizing on the opportunities it presents.

▶ **Capitalizing on crisis** ▶ **Encouraging creativity** ▶ **Lateral thinking** ▶

The six thinking hats

Looking at the different angles

Edward de Bono is well known for his work on lateral thinking, as discussed earlier in this book. However, he has also made a major contribution to our understanding of effective thinking processes through his work on the 'Six Thinking Hats' (de Bono, 2000). The basic idea behind this approach is that individuals and groups can gain a helpful overview of a situation by looking at it from six angles – that is, wearing in turn six different thinking hats. These hats are as follows:

- *The white hat.* This refers to analytical thinking. It involves taking a logical, rational look at the situation to try and make sense of it.
- *The red hat.* This involves looking at the emotional dimension, considering the feelings involved in a situation in order to counterbalance the rational elements of the white hat.
- *The black hat.* This involves identifying weaknesses, limitations and pitfalls. In effect, it sounds a note of caution. It prevents people from moving forward too quickly without considering the potential ways in which things could go awry.
- *The yellow hat.* This is the counterbalance to the black hat. It is about positive thinking, optimism and being energized. It looks at what the benefits of a particular plan are. It looks at the positive points that can be capitalized upon in a particular situation.
- *The green hat.* This is the hat of creativity and innovation. It involves looking imaginatively at a situation and trying to explore new and different ways of approaching the challenges involved, rather than being stuck within conventional tramlines.
- *The blue hat.* This involves focusing on control and co-ordination. It is about pulling together the various elements of our understandings of the situation, so that we have a very coherent and meaningful whole, rather than just separate perspectives that do not gel or make sense together.

By looking at each of these hats in turn, an individual can get an overview of a situation which can be very useful as a means of understanding that set of circumstances and considering how best to move forward. It can also be used in a group setting – for example, at a meeting or a series of meetings as part of a project plan where the people involved can look in turn at each of these elements in order to get a helpful holistic perspective on the situation.

However, it could also be used as a problem-solving tool directly with individuals, families, teams or other groups of people where the problem solver is helping the people involved to see the situation from the six different angles. Of course, it would be necessary to choose the situations in which it is used very carefully, as it would not necessarily be applicable in all circumstances. For example, to some individuals or families it may seem an artificial approach that is not helpful to them. As with any tool, it is important to have the knowledge of the craft of problem solving to be able to choose the appropriate tool to be used at that time.

While de Bono's work has been influential and very successful, my

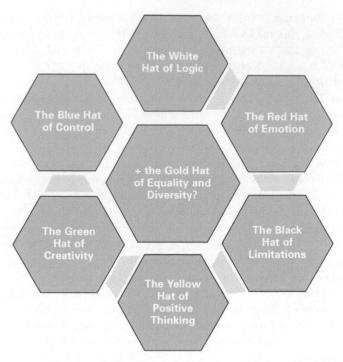

Figure 2.12   Seven thinking hats

view is that he omits a significant seventh hat. It is what I like to refer to as the gold hat of equality and diversity. Given the importance of such matters, it can be seen as very helpful to include consideration of discrimination and the need to prevent it as part of what can in effect become a Seven Thinking Hats approach.

▶ **Chunk up or chunk down** ▶ **Helicopter vision** ▶

SMART objectives

The importance of having clear goals

In Part One of the book, the importance of systematic practice was emphasized. That is, it was argued that it is important to be clear about what we are trying to achieve, how we intend to achieve it and how we will know when we have achieved it. This involves having clear objectives. If we are not clear about what specific objectives we are aiming for, then we will struggle to know whether or not our work has been successful and we can bring it to a conclusion. We will also not be clear about what steps we need to take during our intervention if we are not sure where that intervention is supposed to be taking us. Systematic practice is not a rigid approach that does not allow for change and variation over time but if we are not clear what our objectives are to begin with then, when they change, we will be even more confused. Clarity about objectives is therefore paramount in objective people problem solving.

The SMART approach to objective setting is one that has become quite popular in many quarters. SMART is an acronym:

- **S**pecific;
- **M**easurable;
- **A**greed;
- **R**ealistic; and
- **T**ime bound.

O'Connell comments that: 'SMART objectives date back to the 1950s and are part of "management by objectives" school credited to Drucker (1954)' (2003, p. 38).

Over the years, there have been slight changes to the use of SMART in terms of what the letters refer to. For example, in some versions of SMART the **A** stands for 'achievable' rather than 'agreed'. However, there is then an overlap with the **R** for 'realistic'.

Let us now look in more detail at each of the five specific parts of SMART:

1. *Specific.*   This refers to the need to make sure that our objectives are not too general or vague. For example, if we say that our objective is to help someone or support someone, that is not sufficiently specific for us to be able to work out at the end of the day whether or not we have achieved what we set out to do. While our overall aim may be that of helping or supporting somebody, our objectives need to be more specific under the general aim we are pursuing (namely to help someone). The objective of 'boosting Mark's confidence' is not sufficiently specific, whereas 'boosting Mark's confidence to the point where he can achieve tasks x, y and z unaided' is far better.

2. *Measurable*. This refers to the need to make sure, as far as possible, that we can measure the progress made. That is, we can clearly identify the actual progress made. The term measurement implies the use of numbers. Where we can realistically attach a number to something, this can be very helpful in determining whether or not we have made the progress we wish to. For example, if we are trying to eradicate or reduce the occurrence of an unacceptable behaviour (aggression, for example), then it can be very helpful to be able to measure the incidence of such behaviour before we intervene and after we have intervened. If a particular unacceptable behaviour is recorded as happening on average five times a day, and a month later we are able to record that it is happening no more than twice a day, then this will tell us that (i) we have made good progress, and (ii) we still have further work to do. Note, however, that not everything is measurable and sometimes it can be very artificial to try and attach a numerical scale to something which does not lend itself to that sort of approach. Attempting to make sure that our objectives are measurable is a worthy pursui,t but we should not overdo this to the point of making the use of numbers meaningless in certain circumstances. For example, if our objective is to improve somebody's commitment to a particular role, then it may not be possible to measure progress in any precise way because a numerical scale would not be appropriate in such cases. However, there may be other ways of determining whether or not that goal has been achieved, other ways of showing that success has been reached – for example, recognizing clear signs that the role is being fulfilled appropriately.

3. *Agreed*. The point has already been made in this book that the best form of change is agreed change. That is, if we try to impose our view on people, we are likely to engender resistance that can be unhelpful if not actually counterproductive. It is important to make sure, then, that we are consulting adequately with key stakeholders in any decision making around the objectives we are working towards. In many cases it is unlikely that somebody will be motivated towards pursuing a particular objective if they have not played a part in determining what it should be.

4. *Realistic*. 'Nothing succeeds like success' is an important adage to remember. Setting objectives that are realistic can produce a virtuous circle, that is, once the person concerned has achieved that objective, it will motivate them to move on to achieve the next objective. However, if the objectives are unrealistic, then the opposite can occur, a vicious circle. That is, if somebody is given an unrealistic task to achieve and they fail to do so, then they may give up on any future tasks

as well. Setting unrealistic objectives is therefore a significant demotivator and can lead to significant problems. We therefore have to be very careful to ensure that the objectives we are setting are realistic in the context in which they are to be pursued.

5. *Time bound.* It is very easy for objectives to drift, for other priorities to take over and for our initial plans to get lost in a confusing welter of other demands and circumstances. Setting a deadline can help to avoid this. Of course, there is no guarantee of success. Deadlines are often not met, but setting a specific deadline for an objective to be achieved will play a part in motivating people to work towards that objective within the defined timescales. Where no timescale is set, then there is a danger that the work to be done will fall to the bottom of the priority list and perhaps be forgotten about in the short term at least. However, in setting timescales, we must remember the **R** of SMART and make sure that such timescales are realistic. There is no point in setting an unrealistic timescale as that will not help at all.

Like so many other tools, the SMART objectives approach can be used in a variety of ways. It can be used on an individual basis to clarify our thinking and make sure that we are being sufficiently focused in our work. It can also be used to help others to be focused in what they are doing. This could apply in a management setting as part of a supervisory relationship, for example, or it could operate in similar fashion in a variety of other settings where there is a professional worker trying to help somebody resolve particular difficulties. The SMART objective framework can be useful in such circumstances to remove confusion and provide a focus for our energies. In my experience, I have found that this sort of focus can be very helpful for people who are either anxious or depressed or both. By providing a clear framework and focus, we can help to reduce the negative feelings that are so often part of the situations we deal with as people problem solvers.

SMART objectives can also be used at a group or team level. When there is a particular project being planned, then it can be very useful to apply SMART objectives to the planning and, of course, at a later stage to the review of the project and ultimately to its evaluation at its conclusion.

One final note of caution about the use of SMART objectives: we should not allow the benefits of a focused framework to degenerate into the disbenefits of a rigid approach. It is not uncommon for objectives to change because the circumstances in which we are working change. If the objectives do change, then this should signal that it is time for us to review our SMART approach rather than abandon it. It is relatively easy to look again at our objectives if we feel that the circumstances are dictating that they need to change (for example, because it has become apparent that a particular objective is no longer achievable or appropriate). Equally, we should not hold on to our original SMART plans simply because they have the benefit of being clear and focused. If they are no longer appropriate, then they should be changed. Focus and structure should not be confused with rigidity.

▶ **Objectives tree** ▶ **Visioning** ▶ **Working backwards** ▶

SOLER

Managing interpersonal relations

This is a tool deriving from the work of Gerard Egan, a very well-respected author in the people work arena. He presents SOLER under the heading of 'The Microskills of Attending'. It is an acronym, designed to help with face-to-face interactions. Egan captures the basis of SOLER well when he argues that:

> The main point is that an internal mind-set in which you are with a client might well lose its impact if the client does not see this internal attitude reflected in your nonverbal communication.
>
> (1994, p. 93)

The technique can be summarized as follows:

* **S** – Face the client *squarely*.
  Posture is an important part of 'engaging' with people. If we adopt a posture that does not give a clear message that we are interested, then we should not be surprised to find that we are having little influence. Facing somebody squarely should not be interpreted as 'squaring up' to someone. Rather, it is a matter of showing interest by avoiding a posture that shows that our attention is not being directed elsewhere.
* **O** – Adopt an *open* posture.
  This reinforces the importance of posture. An open posture should give a clear message that we are not being defensive, nor are we

seeking to attack. Egan points out that open can be used literally or metaphorically – literally, as in not having our arms or legs crossed and metaphorically, as in adopting an open attitude towards the person(s) you are engaging with.

- **L** – *Lean* towards the other person where appropriate.
  Leaning forward is another way of showing interest. However, it has to be done selectively. This is because leaning forward too much can come across as intrusive. There is also the danger that it will be seen as something you are doing for effect, rather than a skilled worker using an interpersonal skills tool appropriately.

- **E** – Maintain good *eye* contact.
  Good eye contact should not be equated with constant eye contact – in other words, staring. Indeed, this is an easy mistake to make, to be so concerned with showing interest that we overdo it and end up staring, with the result that we can come across as threatening or at least as unnerving. Good eye contact basically means balanced eye contact – not too much, not too little.

- **R** – Try to be relatively *relaxed*.
  It is important to remember that our involvement with a particular individual is to help him or her (even though this may indirectly help us in some way), and so you need to give a clear message that you are there to help and can be relied upon to do so. Fidgeting or other signs of nervousness can not only be distracting and irritating, they can also give the message that our needs or our concerns are more important than those of the person we are trying to help.

SOLER can be a useful mnemonic to help us focus on effective communication. We should not underestimate just how important interpersonal interactions tend to be. Indeed, if we are not skilful in this area, then our skills in other respects may be of little use to us. That is, if we are not able to do a good job of getting the basics right, then our advanced-level skills (for example, mediation skills in a conflict management situation) are likely to be seriously undermined.

Egan writes from a US perspective, but he acknowledges that it is important to adopt these guidelines cautiously in multicultural settings. This is an important point to make, as nonverbal communication does vary from culture to culture. However, the fact that he talks about 'North-American culture' in the singular suggests that he is not taking full account of issues of cultural diversity.

Cultural differences can apply at a number of levels. For example, one aspect of culture that is often forgotten is that of class. Sometimes there can be class differences that affect how interactions take place. For example, someone from a middle-class background trying to work with someone from a working-class background may find that there are barriers that need to be overcome.

In my view, SOLER can be useful in its own right as a tool for 'attending', as Egan intended. However, it can also be very useful as a basis for developing self-awareness. To connect with other people in order to engage in problem-solving activities, we need to have a good understanding of how we come across to other people. SOLER can be a helpful means of considering these issues. For example, we can look at how we use posture and eye contact and see how we can come across as 'natural' and relaxed, rather than as wooden or nervous.

We should be looking to move through three stages. The first stage is understandably one where we feel nervous and show it indirectly if not directly. The second stage is where we still feel nervous, but we manage to control it or at least disguise it to a certain extent. The third stage is where we are sufficiently experienced and confident that we no longer feel nervous, although we may still have a heightened level of awareness at times (when we are 'on our toes').

If someone goes into this type of work without first feeling nervous, we may be left wondering whether they appreciate what is involved in what they are doing or just how important it is. Some degree of nervousness is to be expected, then, especially in the early stages of our career in this type of work. SOLER can help us to guard against nervousness getting the better of us.

▶ **Responding to feelings** ▶ **SARAH** ▶

Stop trying!

Taking a break from our efforts can sometimes be helpful

At times we can be trying so hard to solve a problem that we cannot see the wood for the trees and/or we are sustaining the problem dynamic (that is, something we are doing is unwittingly keeping the problem alive). It can therefore often be of benefit to take a break, to pause our work and review the situation carefully before recommencing our efforts.

This can simply involve putting the matter on hold for a while (if its seriousness and/or urgency make this possible and safe). We therefore need to choose which situations we apply this approach to very carefully, as it will not apply to all. What it entails is getting some degree of distance between ourselves and the problem that we are facing, as, particularly with some long-standing and deeply rooted problems, we can get too close to them over time and we can therefore not see the broader picture. In terms of using the 'stop trying' technique, what it amounts to is returning to the situation after a break from trying to make any difference to it and then, once we do return, establishing:

1. Does the distance give us a fresh perspective? If so, how can this help us to move forward?
2. Has anything changed in our absence? If so, is this because of our absence or is it just coincidence (although we may not be able to tell whether or not it is due to our absence in many cases)? If it is due to the change brought about by our absence, what does that tell us about what we need to do differently? For example, have we been sustaining the problem in some way? If, for instance, people are reluctant to move forward, is it because our presence in the situation is encouraging dependency and magical thinking, so that they are in some way expecting us to be able to produce a magic solution for them?

Even if we cannot identify anything to do differently, taking time out from a problem can give us some breathing space and allow us to return to it with renewed energy. That in itself can be a very valuable commodity, and can make a positive difference to many situations.

Also, if the person we are trying to help is not highly motivated, then being left alone with their problems may mean that they are less resistant to moving forward when we do return to pick up where we left off. However, this is far from guaranteed; it will only apply in certain circumstances and certainly not in all.

It may seem strange to think that we can help people by stopping trying, but the reality of the situation is that our efforts to help can be enhanced if we take a break from them provided that we choose the situations carefully that we apply this to, so that we do not create further problems in pulling out temporarily at what could potentially be a key time, leaving the people we are trying to help feeling abandoned.

▶ **Encouraging creativity** ▶ **Lateral thinking** ▶

Stress audit

Getting an overview of pressures, coping methods and support

A stress audit is a means of developing a picture of the stresses and strains in a situation, and it can be very helpful in forming the basis for reducing stress quite significantly.

Stress is the term we use to refer to the experience of facing pressures that exceed our current ability to cope with them. The Health and Safety Executive define stress as: 'The adverse reaction people have to excessive pressures or other types of demand placed on them at work' (http://www.hse.gov.uk/stress/furtheradvice/whatisstress.htm).

Stress is traditionally seen as a two-dimensional phenomenon. These two dimensions are: (i) stressors – that is, the pressures that we face; and (ii) coping methods – that is, our various ways of trying to cope with those pressures. According to this traditional approach, whichever is the stronger of the two (the stressors or the coping methods) will determine whether or not stress is experienced. One problem with this approach is that it is too individualistic. It ignores the wider social and organizational context and assumes that the person experiencing stress is at fault, that it is the individual concerned who is responsible for their own problems (Thompson, 2011d).

PRACTICE FOCUS 2.16

Kaldip had been worried about the strain his team seemed to be under. He could see that things were getting worse. It seemed to be the case that the more pressure the team came under, the less confident people became about coping with the pressures and the less they seemed to support each other. He could see that it was developing into a vicious circle of increasing stress. He decided to speak to his line manager about this and he was glad he did, as she explained to him about how a stress audit could be used to develop a clear understanding of the team's situation. He could see how potentially useful this could be for getting the issues firmly on the agenda and for giving the team a basis for working together to tackle the difficulties they were experiencing.

It is therefore important to include the third dimension of stress, namely that of support. There are three sets of relationships set up when we include the dimension of support, so it is not only the relationship between pressures and coping, but also, secondly, the relationship between pressures and support. With good support, our pressures seem more manageable, more in proportion, but without such support, those pressures can loom large and seem even greater. Thirdly, there is the relationship between support and coping. Where we have good support, that can enhance our coping ability and strengthen our resolve. However, where there is an absence of support, we can struggle to cope, feeling less confident, feeling less valued in terms of tackling the challenges that we face. Adding this third dimension of support is therefore a very significant part of developing the more sophisticated and more realistic understanding of stress (Thompson, 2009c).

The stress audit tool involves reviewing these three aspects and using them as a basis of planning how to move forward. It means drawing up a list of the stressors involved in this situation. This is complemented by drawing up a list of what coping methods can be used and finally what sources of support can be drawn upon to help to tackle the circumstances involved. By identifying these three sets of factors, we then get a picture that will enable us to consider how we can reduce pressures, increase coping methods or introduce new, more effective ones and also, just as importantly, how we can increase the level of support available to people.

This tool can be used by an individual to clarify their own thinking as a form of reflective practice. It can also be used directly with someone who is experiencing difficulties as a result of stress, or it can be used with families, teams and other groups in order to get an overview of the situation and therefore lay the foundations for developing a clear and helpful plan for tackling the stress issues involved.

▶ Avoiding avoidance ▶ Culture audit ▶ Eating an elephant ▶

SWOT analysis

Balancing positives and negatives as an aid to decision making

SWOT analysis is a decision-making tool that has its roots in marketing theory. It was originally developed by the Boston Consulting Group for the purpose of helping companies to make decisions about marketing plans. However, over the years, it has become widely used as a general decision-making tool.

It can be used in a wide variety of situations and settings. It can be used as a framework for informing decisions about plans, developments and projects. It can also be used as a team development tool, for self-analysis (clarification of one's own thinking) or even a tool of intervention in working directly with people experiencing problems.

However, before going into too much detail about how it can be used, we should first examine what is involved in undertaking a SWOT analysis. As Figure 2.13 illustrates, SWOT analysis involves dividing a sheet of paper into four sections by drawing a line across the middle and a line down the middle. The top left-hand corner is headed 'S' which stands for strengths. The top right-hand corner is headed 'W' which stands for weaknesses. The bottom left-hand corner is headed 'O' which stands for opportunities and the bottom right-hand corner is headed 'T' which stands for threats.

If we look carefully at the resulting framework, what we can note is that the left-hand side of the page focuses on the positives – strengths and opportunities. The right-hand side of the page focuses on negatives – the weaknesses and threats. This is useful because it helps us to provide a balanced overview of the situation we are analysing. Sometimes people

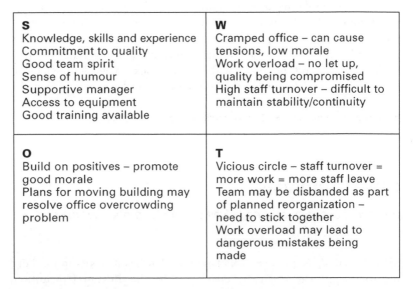

S Knowledge, skills and experience Commitment to quality Good team spirit Sense of humour Supportive manager Access to equipment Good training available	**W** Cramped office – can cause tensions, low morale Work overload – no let up, quality being compromised High staff turnover – difficult to maintain stability/continuity
O Build on positives – promote good morale Plans for moving building may resolve office overcrowding problem	**T** Vicious circle – staff turnover = more work = more staff leave Team may be disbanded as part of planned reorganization – need to stick together Work overload may lead to dangerous mistakes being made

Figure 2.13   SWOT analysis from a team development day

are biased in one direction or another. For example, people who are used to dealing with problems may tend to focus on the negative side and pay relatively little attention to the positives. A sales rep, by contrast, may be occupationally inclined to focus on highlighting the positives and playing down the negatives. So, regardless of our occupational background, SWOT analysis should be a useful tool for helping to provide a more balanced approach that takes account of both positives and negatives.

The top half of the diagram can be seen to represent the present (strengths and weaknesses now). The bottom half of the diagram can be seen to represent the future (opportunities and threats for the future). This temporal dimension to the framework is what makes it a useful decision-making tool. It can balance the present situation against likely future outcomes, divided into positives (opportunities) and negatives (threats).

The analysis is carried out by first of all entering the appropriate words in the four boxes. Second, we should look at the resulting outcomes from this in terms of any patterns which emerge. Are there any themes which are giving us warning signs, for example? Are there any positive themes that we can build on and make the most of? In short, what does this overview of strengths, weaknesses, opportunities and threats tell us about the situation we are analysing?

The tool can be used by a single individual to clarify his or her thoughts. For example, we could use SWOT analysis to analyse a particular situation we are currently dealing with and, in so doing, we may obtain a better view of the situation. It is amazing how, by writing words into four boxes on a sheet of paper like this, we can recognize patterns and issues that otherwise may not have become apparent to us.

SWOT analysis can also be used in direct intervention. For example, we could sit down with a particular individual or group of people and ask them to undertake a SWOT analysis of the situation they currently face. This is likely to bring out the negative aspects, fears and problems, for example, but if it is done properly, it should also bring out potential solutions in terms of strengths and opportunities. It is very easy for people who are experiencing problems to adopt a very negative mindset and not take account of positives, thus blocking progress towards potential solutions. SWOT analysis can help to counterbalance this. Of course, it will not solve problems in itself, but it can be a useful tool for helping the individuals concerned to gain greater insight into the situation they face and may point up ways forward.

SWOT analysis can also be used as a management tool – for example, by inviting a group of staff involved in a particular project to undertake an analysis of that project. Once again, this can help to identify strengths to be built on, opportunities to be capitalized on as well as weaknesses to be wary of and threats to avoid or remove.

Similarly, SWOT analysis can be used as part of a team development process. I have used this technique a number of times myself in running team development workshops. I divide teams of staff into sub-groups, issue each sub-group with flipchart and pen and ask them to undertake a SWOT analysis of their particular team. After a while, we place the flipchart papers on the walls of the training room and invite members of the team to circulate and compare notes across the different SWOT analyses that have been produced. In my experience, this often produces a lot of commonality across the different analyses, which helps to reinforce the message that can be deduced from the analysis. However, it can also be very useful when conflicts or differences of perspective between sub-groups emerge and this can identify issues that the team needs to address.

One note of caution about the use of SWOT analysis: in some quarters it has become well established as a working tool. However, this can lead to problems. I have encountered situations where undertaking a SWOT analysis becomes a routine process, and then is simply reduced to a bureaucratic issue rather than a genuine decision-making tool. For example, I recently came across a situation where somebody undertook a SWOT analysis in just a few minutes, recorded the points on paper very briefly, but then passed on to the next part of the process without making any attempt whatsoever to look at what the SWOT analysis told us. SWOT it may have been, analysis it was not.

It is also important to note that SWOT analysis is something that gets easier and better over time. The more experience you have of using this technique, the easier you will find it and the more you will get out of it. My advice, therefore, is to take every opportunity you can to practise your SWOT analysis skills. The beauty of this particular technique is that it can be applied to such a wide variety of situations. There is therefore no shortage of opportunities for practising your SWOT analysis skills.

As a footnote, it is worth noting that Tom Lambert, in his book *Key Management Solutions* (1996b), proposes a variation on the theme of SWOT analysis. He writes about COST analysis with 'C' standing for company concerns, 'O' for opportunity analysis, 'S' for company strengths and 'T' for threat analysis.

▶ **The CIA framework** ▶ **Mind mapping** ▶ **Objectives tree** ▶

Think–feel–do

Taking account of the three dimensions of human behaviour

This is a framework that I used to underpin my *People Skills* (2009a) book. It is a longstanding, well-established approach to human psychology. Basically, what it refers to is the idea that any complex human action will involve three dimensions: thoughts, feelings and actions or, to give them their technical terms, the cognitive, affective and behavioural dimensions.

Over the years, I have found this to be a very helpful framework for helping problem solvers to get an overview of the situation. What the technique involves is making sure that we consider all three dimensions in our work. There is no compensation involved here. For example, to concentrate on 'think' and 'feel', and to do so superbly, will not compensate for failure to address the 'do' dimension. It is a bit like a car. An effective car has to have working engine, brakes and steering. The absence of one will not be compensated for by the others. If we are going to do justice to the complexities of the problems we encounter in people work, then we have to make sure that we are covering all three aspects of Think–feel–do.

What can often happen is that pressures can lead us to concentrating on those aspects of Think–feel–do that we feel most comfortable with. For example, some people feel very comfortable with emotional issues and may concentrate on these at the expense of the other aspects. By contrast, some people may feel uncomfortable in dealing with feelings and will run the risk of not addressing this dimension adequately. We have to be very wary, then, of falling into the trap of sticking more closely to the aspect(s) of this three-dimensional model that we feel most comfortable with and avoiding the aspect(s) we feel least comfortable with. We have to become well-rounded practitioners in this respect, being able to address all three elements.

A pattern I have noticed over the years is for excessive work pressures to have an adverse effect on the use of Think–feel–do as a framework. In my experience, the feelings dimension is the most vulnerable. Often, when people become very busy, they can forget to take account of people's feelings (their own and those of other people). You may well have been on the receiving end of this yourself where perhaps, in dealing with somebody from a particular organization, that person is so busy that they fail to take account of your feelings and your needs. This can lead to feelings of anger, thus upping the emotional stakes and perhaps leading to a vicious circle in which the problems escalate.

When pressures get very high, the think dimension can also fail to feature. It means, in effect, that the people concerned are operating on 'automatic pilot'. They are not thinking about what they are doing. They are not thinking about what the appropriate response to their situation is – they are just reacting. This sort of knee-jerk approach is really very dangerous and can have highly detrimental consequences for all concerned.

However, in some extreme circumstances, it is also possible for the 'do' dimension to be neglected. People, in some cases, can become so pressurized that they become paralysed, temporarily at least, by the pressures they face. I have come across examples of people who sit at their desk with a stack of paperwork in front of them but do not feel able to pick up their pen and deal with it. They have become stuck in a very difficult set of circumstances as a result of the pressures they face.

The Think–feel–do framework can therefore be a very useful tool for trying to make sure that we are taking account of all three important dimensions and not allowing ourselves to be drawn into focusing on one or two at the expense of the overall picture. What is needed is a well-rounded problem solver to make sure that all three dimensions are being considered.

As with many of the tools presented here, this technique can be used either as a means of self-checking, making sure that we are on the right track, or as a direct tool of intervention. We can actually sit down with somebody who is experiencing problems and talk to them about their thoughts, their feelings and the actions involved (what has happened plus what needs to happen). It can be used as a general tool or specifically in those circumstances where someone is failing to address one of the issues. For example, if somebody is in a very complex situation involving a wide range of feelings, it is understandable that they may concentrate very heavily on the feelings dimension and may need some help to broaden it out to take account of the thoughts and actions that also need to be considered. On the other hand, some people may concentrate in a very pragmatic manner on thoughts and actions and fail to address the emotional dimension, thus running the risk of causing problems for other people (through insensitivity to their feelings, for example) or for themselves by not taking account of the role of their own emotional reactions in the situation.

However this technique is used, it should be borne in mind that it is a tool and much depends on the skills used in putting that tool into use. Think–feel–do can be a very helpful framework, but it needs to be used with skill and sensitivity.

One final note of caution: some people have made the mistake of seeing Think–feel–do as a process rather than a framework. They have assumed that Think–feel–do should be used in a linear fashion – that is, think then feel then do. This is a misunderstanding and a distortion of the Think–feel–do framework. It is not implied within the framework that there should be any order to how these issues are addressed. The point, rather, is to make sure that all three are addressed.

▶ **Chunk up or chunk down** ▶ **Educating** ▶ **Helicopter vision** ▶

The three Hs

Understanding what motivates people's behaviour

This is a tool that has a lot in common with 'Think–feel–do'. Its basic premise is that our behaviour is governed by three sets of factors, each beginning with the letter **H**:

1. *Head.* Of course, although we are not entirely rational creatures, much of what we do will depend on our thought processes, our reasoning. For example, in deciding to pursue a course of action, much will depend on what I think of the situation, the likely outcomes, and so on. That is, my brain will be engaged in a process of trying to make sense of the situation I am in and deciding the most appropriate way forward.
2. *Heart.* As Pascal (1995) put it: 'The heart has its reasons which reason knows nothing of'. Of course, while rational thinking will play a significant part in decision making, emotional factors will also feature. Emotion can play a part in holding us back (fear and

anxiety, for example) or in pushing us forward (desire and enthusiasm, for example).

3. *Habit.* Despite the strong influence of both head and heart, we
must take account of the very powerful influence of habit. Habit is
probably one of the most important influences on a person's behaviour. This is largely because habit tends to develop a momentum of
its own. That is, if there is nothing to indicate that we should
change what we are doing today, then the chances are we will do
what we did yesterday – in other words, the habit will continue. The
longer it continues, the more established it becomes and the
stronger it will be in its influence over us.

The three Hs tool can be used in a number of different ways. It can
help us with decision making, for example, and this can apply in terms
of our own personal decisions; decisions we make jointly with the
people we are trying to help (those whom we are working in partnership
with); and in helping groups or teams of people to make decisions. As
a decision-making tool it can be very useful in clarifying the factors that
are shaping our decision making. We can ask ourselves: 'To what extent
is our decision making being influenced by head – that is, rational
thought; to what extent by heart – that is, the influence of the
emotions; and to what extent habit? A wise decision is likely to be one
that takes account of all three of these factors. It will be one that
considers carefully the rational side of the decision being made. Are we
being logical about this? Are we taking account of the relevant issues?
Have we thought it through properly? It will also take account of the
emotional dimension of heart. Will this decision motivate or de-moti-
vate people? Will it make them feel good or will it create ill-feeling and
resentment? Are we being sufficiently sensitive to emotional issues in
making this decision? And, of course, it will also have to address the
habit dimension. Are there any strong habits that will scupper this decision? Are there any habits that will support it? Do we have to do any
preparatory work in changing or reinforcing habits?

The three Hs can also be used as an analytical tool for understanding complex situations without necessarily being part of a formal decision-making process. The process is very similar to that described above
in relation to decision making, but its focus is not so much on making
a decision but rather on understanding the complexities of a situation
– for example, as part of an assessment. In particular, the three Hs can
be useful for exploring people's motivation. What rational thoughts
motivate them in a particular direction? What feelings reinforce that

motivation? What habits reinforce or block that motivation? In looking at motivation in this way, steps can then be taken to increase motivation in the desired direction or decrease motivation where it is something that we are trying to discourage (an inappropriate or destructive behaviour, for example).

Many people are used to thinking in terms of head and heart or thoughts and feelings and how these affect our behaviour. However, the dimension that is often missing is that of habit. Habit can be seen to apply at two different levels. First of all we have individual habits. Each of us will have a set of habitual behaviours, things that have developed over time that we have become comfortable with. In this respect, habits are very positive. They help to get us through the day. Imagine how difficult it would be to try and get through our lives without having comfortable habits to rely on. However, there is also a downside to habits at this personal level, in so far as we can over-rely on them. We can, for example, adopt a habitual response to an unusual situation and therefore deal with it inappropriately. Too great a reliance on habit can also mean that our creativity and our propensity to work in an innovative way to develop new solutions can be severely limited.

Second, habits can also apply at a broader level and this is usually what we refer to as culture, whether this is a team culture or an organizational culture, or a culture relating to any other collection of people over time. A culture is, in effect, a set of shared assumptions or unwritten rules and this leads to habits forming within that culture. That is, if you are part of a particular culture (say an organizational culture), then it is likely that there will be a certain set of habits associated with this. Think, for example, about your current organizational situation. How would you describe the culture of the organization that you are associated with at present? What are its unwritten rules? What habits are the bread and butter of that culture?

It is important to recognize that habits operate at individual and broader levels. To make sure that, where habits need to change in the spirit of problem solving, then we should not focus just on individual habits, as often collective cultural habits can be much more powerful and also, at times, much more destructive. Some people may feel that the idea of pursuing culture change is overly ambitious. However, it is not a question of changing the whole culture, but rather the more realistic aim of focusing on specific elements – that is, specific habits within that culture that need to be addressed.

One of the lessons that 'Think–feel–do' teaches us is that it is not enough to look at thoughts and feelings without also looking at what has happened and what needs to happen. This lesson should also be applied to the three Hs. While the three Hs can be a very useful decision-making or analytical tool (especially in relation to motivation) we should not lose sight of the fact that actions will need to follow on from our analysis.

▶ **Think–feel–do** ▶ **Culture audit** ▶ **Inviting innocent questions** ▶

The three Rs

Drawing on strengths

This is an approach I introduced in my *Practising Social Work* book (Thompson, 2009b), although it is applicable across the people professions and not restricted to social work. The three Rs to which the title of this tool refers are: **R**esourcefulness, **R**obustness and **R**esilience.

The three Rs can be seen as a good way of identifying three sets of factors that can usefully be strengthened where there is a lack of one or more of them or which can be drawn upon fruitfully where they exist in abundance. Let us now consider each of these in turn.

Resourcefulness

This refers to how creative or imaginative somebody is, how good they are at being able to find ways forward, so that they are not limited to a narrow focus and a small number of potential solutions.

Robustness

This refers to how hardy people are in the sense of how well they manage not to be knocked over, as it were, by adverse circumstances they encounter, how strong they are in being able to press on regardless of the difficulties and obstacles they encounter.

Resilience

This refers to a person's ability to bounce back from adversity, the ability to get ourselves back up on our feet and try to get over any difficulties we have had and not allow them to continue to influence us negatively.

PRACTICE FOCUS 2.17

Sonia had been qualified for almost two years and was still unsure whether she had made the right career choice. She felt her work was very routine and uninteresting, very different from what she had expected. She was wondering whether she should consider making a radical career change. One night, she met up with an old friend and explained to her that she was very dissatisfied with her current work because she had 'got into a rut'. Her friend talked to her about the three Rs she had read about and suggested that this might be something helpful for Sonia to consider. Sonia was not convinced at first, but gradually warmed to the idea. She started to realize that it could actually be quite helpful to work on developing her resourcefulness and resilience. She started to understand that her own defeatist attitude about what she could achieve at work was an important part of what was holding her back in terms of getting satisfaction from her work.

These three sets of factors each play an important role in terms of problem solving. What can be very helpful indeed is to focus on developing each of these three areas as fully as possible. It can apply to ourselves, in the sense that developing our own capabilities and confidence in relation to each of these can make us much better problem solvers. However, there is more to it than this, because we can also use the three Rs in terms of recognizing where one or more of these are lacking in the people we are trying to help. What we would then need to do is look at how we can introduce an element of resourcefulness, robustness or resilience – as the case may be – to boost them where they exist already, but perhaps are at too low a level to be helpful, or develop them where they do exist, so that we can make the most of what is available. Thirdly, we can also use the three Rs to recognize where one or more of these factors exist already in the people we are helping, and then try to build on these, exploiting them positively in making progress and celebrating them. This can be very important in terms of self-esteem to help people recognize the strengths they do have and then to work with them to capitalize on them as much as possible.

Overall, then, the three Rs is potentially a very useful tool for strengthening our own abilities, for recognizing where people are struggling with a lack of certain abilities and help them to fill those gaps as far as possible, or recognizing where people already have strengths, and then building on them as much as we possibly can.

▶ **Educating** ▶ **Encouraging creativity** ▶

TOTE

Testing out the changes we make

This is an approach drawn from neuro-linguistic programming (or NLP for short). As a tool, it involves testing the current situation (**T**), changing it in some way (= Operate or **O**), testing again (**T**), and then leaving the situation (exit = **E**). It is drawn from the work of Alder (1996) and is linked to how scientific research is done. It involves what is known as 'isolating the variables'. For example, if we change three things at the same time, and that combination produces a positive difference, then we will not know which of those variables made the difference. Was it: (i) one the three factors operating in isolation? (ii) a combination of any two of them and, if so, which of the three possible combinations: AB, AC or BC? or (iii) was it the interaction of all three that produced the positive change?

What this teaches us is that it can be very wise to change one factor at a time and then see what happens as a result of changing that factor. In that way, we can get a clearer picture of what is actually making a difference. This can be seen to be helpful in a number of ways. It involves four steps, and these are as follows:

1. Identify what the potential variables are. This involves being clear about which aspects of the situation could potentially be changed.
2. Prioritize the factors in terms of likely positive impact. This means we are not just selecting from among a range of potential variables at random, but have a logic as to why we are choosing one over the others. Prioritizing involves considering which of the variables is likely to have the most positive impact if we change it.
3. Undertake a risk assessment. Making changes to a situation can improve it, but, of course, there is also the risk that it will make it

worse. We therefore need to be clear about what the risk factors involved are.

4. We then use Alder's TOTE method: **T**est, **O**perate, **T**est, **E**xit. In other words, for each of the variables, we will test them, act accordingly, test the situation (that is, see what changes if any have been produced) and then exit – that is, bring that phase of the operation to a close. We can then repeat this for other variables until we are satisfied that we have made enough of a difference to the situation.

In using TOTE in this way, we should be able to identify what makes a difference to the situation and what does not. This can then – in many circumstances, but not all – give us a platform for helping the individuals concerned to make at least some of the changes they need to bring about in order to improve their situation.

However, what can also happen at times is that the tool gives the individuals concerned enough insight as to what has been troubling them that they are now able to proceed to address their problems with little or no professional input into the situation. In this way, TOTE can be a very empowering tool.

▶ **Consequences** ▶ **Risk assessment** ▶

Transactional analysis

Understanding interpersonal dynamics

Transactional analysis, or TA as it is commonly known, is a theoretical perspective that is widely used in the caring professions, but can also be used in a management context in any setting. Space does not permit a detailed exposition of it here, so I must limit myself to looking at how one of its basic tenets, ego states, can be helpful in understanding and, where appropriate, changing interpersonal interactions.

According to TA, we can understand how people relate to one another by reference to the interactions of three basic ego states: parent, adult and child. The interactions can take the following forms:

- *Parent–child.* If I adopt a parental, authority figure attitude towards you, I am putting you under pressure to adopt a subordinate role – to be a child to my parent. This can also occur the other way round. If you behave in a childish way, not taking responsibility for your actions, then I may well feel the need to adopt a parental mode in order to 'bring you into line'.
- *Parent–parent.* If I adopt a parental attitude towards you, and you are not prepared to accept this, then we may enter a power battle in which you try to 'parent' me in return. If we are not careful, this can become very destructive, with both parties adopting childlike attitudes towards the other and to the situation (see child–child below).
- *Adult–adult.* This is a good balance to aim for. Each party treats the other with respect and thus creates a sound platform for collaboration and mutual assistance. This does not mean that both parties are necessarily on an equal footing – there may still be significant power differences between the two – but they none the less treat each other with respect. This has much in common with the idea of assertiveness and seeking 'win–win' outcomes.
- *Parent–adult.* This too has much in common with assertiveness. In this combination, one person is trying to pressurize the other into a child role, but he or she is refusing to do so, but without falling into the trap of entering a parent–parent conflict situation. The person adopting the adult ego state remains calm, treats the other person with respect and thus puts him or her under pressure to step down from the parent role to adopt the more reasonable and respectful one of adult.
- *Child–child.* This is where neither party in an interaction is taking responsibility. An example of this I have come across many times is staff working in an environment where they are not happy but, instead of raising the issues through the channels available to them (as adults), they prefer to indulge in gossip and moaning. Constructive (adult) action to make positive changes in an unsatisfactory situation is rejected in favour of potentially destructive 'whingeing'. A little ventilation of ill feelings or resentment can be quite appropriate and helpful, but if it is allowed to dominate, then child–child interactions can become quite corrosive of morale, trust and teamwork (see also the discussion above of 'The drama triangle').

Understanding interpersonal interactions in terms of these various combinations can be quite helpful. It can give us a great deal of insight into what is happening between people. It can help us understand how we are relating to other people and how they are relating to us. Similarly, we can use it to make sense of interactions between others (for example, colleagues or members of a family).

Once we have used the tool to help make sense of the interactions, then we may also be able to use it to try and change those interactions where necessary or where it would be helpful to do so in order to tackle a particular problem or set of problems. Sometimes we may get a very clear message that we need to adjust our own ego state. For example, in working with someone who has a low level of self-esteem and therefore little confidence or assertiveness, we may be drawn into a parental mode. Of course, this could create a vicious circle in which we trap the individual we are trying to help in a cycle of low confidence. That is, if we adopt a parental mode and start 'looking after' them, we are likely to be encouraging a childlike response, which in turn will encourage a further parental reaction on our part. We can be a supportive adult and, in the process, encourage others to be adult, without falling into the trap of being 'parental'.

We may also use this approach to help others adjust their ego states to create more harmonious relationships. However, if we do use it in this way, we will need to be careful about the language we use. For example, some people may be insulted if anyone suggests they are being childlike, while others may feel flattered to be described as 'parental'. We will therefore have to find other, more indirect means of getting the point across.

TA can be helpful in making sense of group or team dynamics. For example, some people may be adopting parent roles while others are playing the child, rather than all aiming to be 'adults'. In some circumstances it can also be used to help change those dynamics, although this is a very skilful and advanced-level task.

Transactional analysis does not have all the answers and should not be overused. However, when used appropriately it can cast a lot of light on relationships. It can provide a good foundation on which we can build our knowledge, skills and experience.

▶ **The CBC approach** ▶ **Circular questioning** ▶ **The drama triangle** ▶

Tuning in

Making connections with the people we are trying to help

We have already noted that many of the problem situations we are called upon to deal with are characterized by some degree of conflict. Sometimes this is 'real' conflict, in the sense that the interests of the parties concerned are in opposition or at odds with one another. However, it is often the case that the conflict is a perceived conflict, in so far as there is no underlying difference of interest, but the perceptions of one or both parties lead to a conflict situation arising. In other circumstances, there is no conflict – real or perceived – but there may be tensions and anxieties that have a similar effect, namely to put barriers between people. It would be very naïve to assume that everybody we are seeking to help will welcome our involvement. Even in those situations where we can be of enormous benefit to someone, he or she may none the less react in a negative and rejecting way, to begin with at least. This may be a defensive reaction on their part because of the pressures and threats involved in the problems they are experiencing, or it may be that they do not understand our role or are suspicious that we have some sort of hidden agenda that could be to their detriment.

In seeking to work with people in a problem-solving way, we must therefore make efforts to ensure that we engage or connect with them in the early stages of the process. This is what is known as 'tuning in'. It generally involves establishing some sort of common ground. This may be on a personal level – for example, establishing that you attended the same school or have an interest in the same sport or hobby, or it may be on a professional level (for example, by clarifying what you both have to gain by working together to resolve the problems being encountered). This can involve clarifying your role in some detail. This is particularly important if your role is one that may not be widely understood. For example, there may be stereotypical assumptions associated with your role that will need to be cleared away for you to have a positive working relationship. Stop for a moment and consider your role. Are there any negative connotations associated with it? For example, if you are a personnel officer, would people possibly assume that you are trying to make them redundant? If you are a social worker, would the stereotype of 'child snatching' stand in the way of good working relations? Even counsellors who generally have no powers to deprive people of their jobs or of their children, may still be viewed with suspicion and mistrust because of the common misguided notion that anyone who needs the help of a counsellor is experiencing psychiatric problems.

How, then, do we 'tune in'? A lot will depend on our interpersonal skills. However, the following pointers should prove helpful:

- *Nonverbal communication.* Are you making appropriate use of body language? For example, are you smiling appropriately? If seated, are you leaning slightly forward to show interest?
- *Time and place.* Have you chosen a venue or a time that may be distracting and thus undermining of your efforts to connect? For example, sitting in a formal office setting may create a degree of formality that acts as a barrier to tuning in.
- *Role and purpose.* Have you clarified your role and the purpose of your involvement? If the individual concerned is unclear about or, worse still, suspicious about your role, this will create further barriers.
- *Pleasantries.* Begin with some small talk to establish a connection. Be careful not to overdo this, as this may make the person nervous. They may feel that you are avoiding getting down to brass tacks, perhaps because you are anxious about giving them bad news. Too much small talk can create these sorts of fantasies in the mind of the person you are trying to help. However, if you launch straight into the business of the day without some sort of attempt to 'lubricate' the interaction, you may find that you are perceived as being cold and uncaring and, in this way, tuning in will not have worked.
- *Listening.* There is no substitute for effective listening. If you want somebody to feel that you are genuinely trying to help them, then it is imperative that you listen, and listen carefully.

Although the emphasis has been on how we can use tuning in to work effectively with others, it is also something that we can teach others to do once we feel comfortable with the technique ourselves. For example, we may find that there are tensions in a family or in a work group because of this failure of tuning in. Helping people to develop the skills involved in tuning in can be very beneficial in dealing with those problematic situations that involve a breakdown of interpersonal relations or a failure of individuals to develop effective working relations. Sometimes the situations are far more complex than simple tuning in can deal with but, on many an occasion, all that will be required is for one or more individuals to develop the skills of tuning in. Some people do not get past first base because of their lack of skills in this area. For example, on more than one occasion, I have come across managers who have generated considerable resentment within the teams they are supervising because they have not practised skills of tuning in and have simply launched into giving instructions on work-related tasks.

It has to be remembered that problem solving is something that we do with people, not to them (remember that the **P** of PRECISE practice refers to 'partnership based'). To be able to help people, we have to be on the same wavelength as them, to a certain degree at least. Establishing that common ground through tuning in is therefore an activity that is well worth practising. The more we do it, the more skilful we can become and the more advanced a level we can practise at, thereby becoming even more effective over time.

▶ **The CBC approach** ▶ **Positive strokes** ▶ **Recognizing grief** ▶ **Responding to feelings** ▶

Using dissonance

Challenging ingrained views

'Cognitive dissonance' is an important psychological concept. It refers to situations where our brain is telling us that there is a contradiction between two ideas (or 'cognitions'). For example, imagine a situation where you have known somebody for a long time and you have great trust in them. You feel that they would not do anything to harm or betray you, but then imagine that new information comes to light that strongly suggests that this person has acted in a way that is contrary to your interests, that they have let you down in some way or acted against you (for example, spreading rumours about you). In such a situation dissonance is created. That is, there is a lack of congruence between the idea that you can trust this person and the new information that has come to light.

This creates a very uncomfortable feeling that we are not able to tolerate for long. We will want to take some steps to resolve this dissonance. To resolve this dissonance and thus rid ourselves of this very uncomfortable feeling, we will have to either:

1. abandon our original cognition – that is our idea that this person is trustworthy; or
2. disregard the new information – 'No, that can't be the case; he/she would not do that to me'.

This is not only a useful concept in helping to explain a great deal of human behaviour in certain circumstances, it can also be used as a technique to create change, particularly attitudinal change. Consider the following dialogue in the context of an investigator dealing with a complaint of sexual discrimination:

GODFREY: I didn't appoint her because I didn't think she was strong enough.

INVESTIGATOR: Strong in what sense?

GODFREY: In this line of work you have to deal with a lot of difficult and demanding people and I didn't feel that she was up to that.

INVESTIGATOR : Because she's a woman?

GODFREY : Well, yes, to a certain extent. We all know that men tend to be more robust than women in this sort of thing.

INVESTIGATOR : In what way?

GODFREY : Men tend to be less intimidated in these difficult circumstances that our staff face.

INVESTIGATOR : Am I right in thinking that your organization's chief executive is a woman?

GODFREY : Yes, that's right.

INVESTIGATOR : Is she easily intimidated?

GODFREY : No, certainly not.

INVESTIGATOR : So, if your chief executive had applied for this post, you would have had no difficulty in appointing her to it? You wouldn't have thought that, as a woman, she would be too easily intimidated?

GODFREY : No.

INVESTIGATOR : Then how do you know that the particular woman you rejected would have been easily intimidated?

Here, the investigator is making very clever use of cognitive dissonance. He is creating a situation where the assumption that Godfrey is making (that women are too easily intimidated for his purposes) is contradicted by the idea that his organization's chief executive, as a woman, is not easily intimidated. This clever juxtaposition of the contradictory elements will make it more difficult for Godfrey to hold on to his prejudicial assumption about women.

Much of the work a people problem solver gets involved in includes an element of entrenched attitudes that can be obstacles to progress. These may be discriminatory attitudes, as in the example above, or may be self-defeating attitudes, such as a lack of confidence or self-respect. Specifically in relation to the latter case, cognitive dissonance can be put to good use to help raise self-esteem and boost confidence. For example, when someone claims: 'I don't have any skills to draw on', helping them to identify examples of skills they do actually have can create a degree of dissonance that will help to undermine their self-defeating view of themselves as unskilled and therefore incapable.

Using dissonance to create change is a very subtle process. It involves first of all recognizing an attitude or an assumption that is counterproductive or blocking progress, and then skilfully identifying contradictory elements which will create a feeling of dissonance. This needs to be done sensitively, as simply throwing contradictions into the pot in the hope that dissonance will be created is leaving far too much to chance and is therefore a dangerous option. A much safer course of action is to use this technique only where we feel confident that we have been able to identify:

1. the problematic attitude or assumption;
2. an opposing cognition that is likely to create dissonance, and that we are able to put the two together in a way that will not alienate the person concerned and will have a constructive and positive effect.

Interestingly, dissonance can also be used in reverse, as it were. That is, if we encounter a situation where somebody appears to be feeling very uncomfortable, then the concept of cognitive dissonance can be used to try and explore why that is. We can try, for example, to identify whether there are any elements of dissonance in the situation. This can then be used to help the person deal with their uncomfortable feelings. This is particularly helpful in those situations where cognitive dissonance exists, but the individual concerned has not identified the actual contradiction where he or she simply feels uncomfortable, but is confused about the reasons for it. This is not to say that discomfort is always as a result of cognitive dissonance. There can be other causes, but cognitive dissonance is one that is well worth exploring as a possible, if not likely, cause.

▶ **Challenging cognitive distortions** ▶ **The paradoxical approach** ▶ **Role reversal** ▶

Using personal constructs

Developing our own theories

This is a tool based on the work of George Kelly, a psychologist, who developed a theory of people as scientists, in the sense that we make sense of the world by developing hypotheses and then testing them out.

For example, my hypothesis may be that I can trust Peter. I will therefore trust him and, if my trust is rewarded, I will then see him as a trustworthy person, but if he does not reward my trust and lets me down, then I will categorize him as untrustworthy and will not trust him again. The idea of personal construct theory is based on Kelly's work (1955). It refers to the way in which a construct enables us to place aspects of our experience near one pole or another of a continuum. For example, in relation to trusting Peter, there would be a continuum between, at one end, finding him trustworthy and, at the other end, finding him untrustworthy. Personal construct theory is therefore based on the idea that such constructs are sets of opposites – for example, happy/sad, safe/unsafe – and, of course, trustworthy/untrustworthy.

The idea behind the theory is that we rate people, situations and other aspects of our experiences in terms of these constructs and from this we develop our model of the world, our outlook on life. By having a set of constructs that create a picture of the world, we are able to live our lives with some degree of understanding by slotting people or other aspects of our lives into the continuum between one pole of the construct and the other.

Kelly developed the idea of the repertory grid which is quite a detailed, almost mathematical way of analysing and mapping someone's repertoire of constructs. This has reached the point now where it has become so complex that many psychologists use computer software to enable them to construct a repertory grid. Such a grid will give a picture of somebody's model of the world as characterized by the range of constructs they use and where they place different aspects of their life experience in terms of the two poles of each of those constructs.

However, we do not have to go that far. A simpler and more flexible use of personal construct theory can be very helpful as a basis for problem solving. It involves asking such questions as: What constructs are shaping the current problem situation, and how can changes to these constructs be made to bring about an important improvement in the situation? For example, it has been known for quite some time that people who are abused are less likely to trust other people. We can therefore use personal construct to identify that a particular individual who has been abused (perhaps in their childhood) who is likely to be scoring people at the untrustworthy end of the trustworthy / untrustworthy construct. This can help us to then develop a plan for how we can help that person to become more trusting without placing themselves at risk by becoming too trusting.

Personal construct theory is based on a more sophisticated understanding of empathy (drawing on phenomenological theory). It involves understanding a situation from the point of view of the person experiencing the problem and helping them to recognize how particular changes in their outlook (construct system) can help them to address their problems. While empathy is a useful concept in itself, it tends to be used at a fairly general level, with no specific focus. Constructs, by contrast, enable us to develop this more sophisticated understanding of empathy by breaking down our understanding of the other person's outlook on the world in terms of specific constructs.

▶ **Educating** ▶ **Naming the process** ▶ **REBT** ▶

Visioning

Developing a vision of the place we want to get to

One of the benefits of 'SWOT analysis' is that it provides a bridge between the present and the future (the top half of the page and the bottom half of the page). It helps us to think about moving forward and, in situations where we are dealing with people and their problems, that is a very important undertaking. This is partly because people experiencing difficulties can often feel as though they are stuck or trapped, and thus not able to make progress or resolve their difficulties. The sense of defeatism and helplessness that can arise from this can be very counterproductive. It is therefore important to have a focus on positive future outcomes.

There are various ways of doing this, but they can all be grouped under the general heading of 'visioning'. What visioning refers to is the ability to foresee a positive future. This approach is often used as part of strategic management – for example, when the question 'where do you expect your organization to be in three years' time?' is asked. However, while this type of visioning clearly is a useful tool for strategic management, it should not be restricted to this domain.

Visioning can be used in a wide variety of situations. What it involves is trying to help people think about how the future might look. One particularly helpful method of doing this, deriving from solution-focused therapy (de Shazer, 1985, 1991), is what is known as 'the miracle question'. In practice situations, the question is phrased in a variety of ways, but in essence, it asks:

Suppose tonight while you sleep, a miracle happens. When you awake tomorrow morning, what will you see yourself doing, thinking, or believing about yourself that will confirm that a miracle has taken place in your life?

Its aim is to instil a focus on a future minus the problems currently being experienced and thus to begin to develop a positive outlook. Some people may find this difficult to do (particularly anyone who is depressed), but with a little bit of gentle perseverance, support and skilful help, they can be assisted to come up with a vision of the ideal situation. Of course, it is highly unlikely that we will be able to achieve that ideal situation but, by having this vision, it is possible to look at how we can plot a route to get as close to that ideal situation as possible. Also, by identifying the differences between the current situation and the future situation, it is possible to identify what needs to change. This can sometimes be helpful in setting priorities. In some circumstances, there is just so much that needs to change that we can feel overwhelmed by the situation. However, by undertaking this visioning, we can gain an overview that can help us make decisions about which issues to tackle first.

PRACTICE FOCUS 2.18

Mark had worked with young people in a deprived area for almost a year and was having mixed results. He felt very comfortable in forming a rapport with them and recognized that this was one of his strengths. However, he often struggled to make any inroads with the young people in terms of what he wanted them to achieve. He had noticed that they seemed to lack any sense of purpose. He was at a loss as to how to tackle this strong sense of aimlessness.

However, things changed when he attended a training course where he was introduced to the idea of 'visioning'. He soon realized that this was what was missing from his work with young people. He had been encouraging them to move forward with their lives, but without helping them to develop a clear picture of where it was they wanted to get to. He knew that it would not be an easy task to get them to develop that vision, but he was already looking forward to making a start on trying to use his relationship-building skills to encourage the young people to develop a sense of direction.

A key element of the solution-focused therapy approach (as discussed in Part One) is the need to focus more on solutions than on problems; to try and develop a mindset that focuses on solutions. It is sometimes assumed that, in order to solve a problem, we need to know what has caused it. However, the solution-focused approach challenges this view and argues that, in many circumstances, the solution may have little connection with the cause.

Another approach to visioning is what is known as task-centred practice (Marsh and Doel, 2005). This involves identifying where we are now plus where we want to be and then plotting the route from the former to the latter in terms of the tasks that need to be achieved in order to make progress. An important underlying principle of this approach is that 'nothing succeeds like success'. What this means is that, when beginning to identify tasks that need to be achieved to make progress, we should focus primarily on the easiest tasks in order to boost confidence to give a clear message that progress is possible and to establish a basis of success. Another important principle of task-centred practice is that the tasks that need to be achieved can be shared out – it can be a co-operative effort. Instead of the problem solver simply being an adviser or counsellor, he or she can actively engage in the process by trading off tasks. For example, a problem-solving helper could agree to undertake tasks A, B and C on condition that the person being helped achieves tasks X, Y and Z. Some practitioners take this a step forward by actually producing a written contract – an agreement outlining the goals being aimed for, and the tasks required to achieve them, and who will be responsible for what over what timescale. My own view on this is that it can be very helpful if undertaken skilfully and sensitively. However, if not handled properly, it can simply add an extra layer of bureaucracy and formality that can stand in the way of progress. This is not to rule out the use of written agreements but rather to issue a warning that they need to be handled carefully and sensitively.

Visioning can be used at a range of levels. It can be used as a personal clarification tool. You can sit yourself down and ask yourself where you want to be and how you are going to get there. It can be used as a tool of intervention (as in the example of task-centred practice given above). It can be used as a team development tool for teams to identify where they want to be and how they are going to get there. It can also be used as a strategic planning tool for whole organizations or sub-sections of organizations.

Visioning is recognized as an important part of leadership. It is a skill of established leaders that they are able to identify a vision and work towards achieving it, motivating, or even inspiring, others to share in creating that vision and working towards it. In my view, there is a close link between leadership skills and problem-solving skills. This is because good leaders are often able not only to solve problems that stand in the way of progress towards the identified vision, but may actually, because of their leadership skills, also be in a position to anticipate the problems and 'head them off at the pass'. The other side of the coin is that problem-solving skills in a wide variety of settings, undertaken by people who are not necessarily in leadership positions, may none the less, draw on leadership skills.

▶ **Chunk up or chunk down** ▶ **Helicopter vision** ▶ **Working backwards** ▶

Working backwards

Keeping a clear focus on outcomes

This is a technique that has much in common with the idea of vision-ing discussed earlier. The notion of 'beginning with the end in mind' is one of the seven principles discussed in Stephen Covey's (2004) book *The Seven Habits of Highly Effective People: Powerful Lessons in Personal Change.* What this technique refers to is the idea that, before we go about our business, we should have a fairly clear picture of what we are trying to achieve. In this respect, this technique has much in common not only with visioning, but also with systematic practice. As Covey sees it, there are two layers of creation. First, something is created in our minds. Then we have to translate that mental creation into a phys-ical creation. We have to make it happen. There are two key issues involved in this: planning and motivation.

In terms of planning, it is important that we are clear what we are trying to achieve – where we are trying to get to. As the saying has it, if we do not know where we are going, any road will take us there. As we noted in Part One, not having clarity about what we are doing can sap morale and waste a lot of time and energy. The principle of 'begin with the end in mind' is a useful way of keeping this to the forefront of our efforts, trying to make sure that in whatever we do we have clarity about the end product that we are trying to produce.

In terms of motivation, the important thing to recognize here is that it is often our future goals that provide us with motivation. Much of the psychological literature places a great emphasis on the importance of the past (our upbringing, for example) in shaping our present actions and desires. However, it would be a mistake to place too much empha-sis on the role of the past and not take account of the role of the future, as part of what motivates us to do what we do today is our desire to be in a different place tomorrow, to achieve particular ends.

The idea of beginning with the end in mind is therefore an important motivational tool. It can be used in two ways. First of all, it is something that we can incorporate into our own actions and thoughts (and in this way is parallel with systematic practice). But we can also use this as a direct technique with the people we are trying to help (either on an individual basis or collectively with groups or teams). We can ask them to work backwards – to 'begin with the end in mind'. This is often referred to as goal setting, the process of identifying specific goals to be achieved. However, goal setting in many quarters has often become a pale imitation of what it should be. It has become a bureaucratic process by which putative goals are identified but, in my experience, it is often the case that these goals rarely drive actual practice in the organization concerned. The connection between the goal and the action is often not maintained. This is where the technique of 'begin with the end in mind' can be helpful. It can help us to move away from the mechanistic process of setting goals for the sake of setting goals and maintain a clear link between the end we are trying to achieve and the actions we need to take to get there.

De Bono captures the idea of beginning with the end in mind when he describes what he calls 'working backwards':

> One of the most powerful problem-solving methods is to work backwards from the hoped-for solution. It is not unlike end-play in chess: 'What preceding state could have led to this position; what pre-preceding states could have led to that state, etc.?' The possible states preceding the solution state are taken as destinations and we look for states that might have preceded each of them … and so on back, until we are within range of where we start. Imagine a car journey from Edinburgh to London. London is the destination so we work backwards from London. 'If only I could get to Hatfield then the journey from there to London is easy. Now I could get to Hatfield easily from Baldock, so now I need to get to Baldock …' all the way back to Edinburgh. Although the process is powerful it is by no means easy to use because it requires a very great deal of imagination and conceptual skill. The steps must be small and concrete. It is also necessary to define the desired end-state very clearly.
>
> (1983, p. 59)

Two sets of problems are commonly associated with beginning with the end in mind. First, some people may struggle to identify the end they are working towards. This is often a reflection of the problem situation they find themselves in. It may be a very complex and confusing situation, with a lot of pressures and strains. In such circumstances, we should not be surprised to find that many people will struggle to identify the goals they are trying to achieve. Where this occurs, some of the techniques discussed under the heading of visioning can be of value. However, whatever technique we adopt, the important principle to bear in mind is that we must go at his or her pace. There is little point in trying to force somebody into identifying the goal. If this happens, it is likely that, either they will become resistant, thus blocking progress, or they will mechanistically come up with goals to reduce the pressure they are feeling from us. Of course, neither of these is a helpful approach.

Even when we have identified the goals, there may be a problem in coming up with ways of achieving them. This can be for the same reasons: the complexity, the confusion, the pressure, and so on. Here, as a problem-solving helper, we have an important role to play to act as a support through difficult circumstances, to be helpful and constructive, but without taking over. Once we make the mistake of trying to force the issue, we become part of the problem rather than part of the solution. We become an extra pressure for the person concerned to deal with, rather than a support in dealing with the pressures and problems they already face.

In terms of application, working backwards is something that can be used at any time in our attempts to solve people problems. It is something that we should bear in mind at all times as, without this focus on what we are trying to achieve, there is the danger that we will drift away from our purpose, and thus waste time, energy, effort and even money (a risky thing to do in these resource-strapped days). However, there will also be times when this principle is one that is particularly relevant, for example in circumstances where people feel they have lost their way or where they feel stuck and trapped.

▶ **Helicopter vision** ▶ **Objectives tree** ▶ **SMART objectives** ▶ **Visioning** ▶

Worst case, best case

Getting things in perspective

By exploring the extremes of a situation, we can get a perspective on a problem that in turn can help develop a sense of clarity and control and thus a degree of confidence.

This is a tool that helps us to map out the boundaries (or 'parameters') of a problem situation. This can then help to provide a useful overview of what we face and provide us with some potential insights into how best to tackle the issues involved.

It involves first of all identifying the worst case scenario. By this, what I mean is, what is the worst that could happen in this situation? Just how bad could it get if things were taken to the extreme? We then need to look at what the key factors are that are likely to lead to this worst case scenario if it were to happen. What are the likely suspects, as it were, that will produce the most negative outcome that we can imagine?

We then need to balance this by thinking about the best case scenario. In other words, what is the ideal outcome that we could hope for from this situation? We would then need to think about what are the key factors that are likely to lead to this more positive outcome and consider what can be the positive factors to explore?

Once we have mapped out the worst case and best case scenarios, we can then revisit the worst case scenario and ask ourselves the following two questions:

1. What positives need to be promoted to avoid the worst case from materializing? That is, what steps can we take that will enhance the positive elements of the current situation in a way that makes the worst case scenario less likely to come about?
2. What negatives need to be avoided? In other words, what are the aspects of the situation that are pushing in a negative direction that are likely to produce a deterioration in the situation? What can we do to tackle these negatives, to remove them or at least to reduce them or their impact?

We would then need to move on to revisit the best case scenario and ask ourselves two similar questions:

1. How do we promote the positives to make the best case scenario more likely to happen? What this means is that we need to be clear about what steps would need to be taken if we are to be able to move in the direction of the best case scenario.
2. How do we avoid the negatives that will make it less likely that the best case scenario will be achieved? This reflects the situation in relation to the worst case scenario, but approached from the opposite angle. What we are trying to do here is to look at what factors

will stand in the way of progress and consider what we can do about them.

By undertaking this 'worst case, best case' analysis, we can look at what patterns emerge from examining the situation in this way. By looking at such patterns, we may be able to consider what our priorities should be. In other words, we can identify the factors that are most significant in either taking us forward positively or potentially moving us in a negative destructive direction. As such, this can be a very helpful technique for casting light on a complex set of situations. It maps out the territory, in the sense that we are dealing with, and gives us some very strong clues about what the positive and negative factors are in that situation, so that we can intervene as constructively as possible by working on those sets of factors.

Although this is a useful tool in its own right, there is also a useful bonus, in the sense that it can be an excellent basis for partnership working. By making sense of the situation together, we have a good basis for creating a good working relationship. This in itself can offer considerable reassurance and thus can be quite empowering for people.

▶ **Promoting realism** ▶ **SWOT analysis** ▶

PART 3

Guide to further learning

Introduction

In this final part of the book, I present some ideas for follow-up study. The point was made in Part One that the ideas presented in this book draw upon an extensive theory base. While you do not have to be au fait with the theoretical underpinnings before you can use the tools presented in Part Two, I would argue strongly that the deeper your understanding of the ideas on which the tools are based, the better equipped you will be to make best use of the tools. The more informed you are about the theoretical issues, the greater the insight you will have when it comes to using the tools at an advanced level. You should be wary of falling into the trap of seeing practical tools as an alternative to theoretical understanding. As the discussion of reflective practice in Part One confirms, we should be seeking to integrate theory and practice, rather than to reject one in favour of the other. The more you understand the theory base linked to the various tools, the stronger a position you will be in, not only to practise at an advanced level, but also to continue learning and developing over time (Thompson, 2000).

Not all of the tools have a literature associated with them, and so this part of the book is organized under themes, rather than in relation to specific tools – although individual tools are mentioned where appropriate. Following the guidelines on further reading, there is a short section which provides details of relevant websites and organizations.

The ideas that inform the discussion about problem solving presented in Part One, combined with the ideas underpinning the specific techniques in Part Two are, as mentioned above, part of a huge theory base that draws on decades of research, theory development and professional experience in psychology, sociology, social work, counselling and management. Drawing specific, detailed links between the guidance provided in this book and the huge theory base on which it draws would be a major undertaking, requiring a book in its own right. What follows, then, is by no means a comprehensive exposition of the underlying theory base but, rather, simply a basic guide to pursuing further study to develop your understanding of the complex issues the book covers.

Further reading

Communication

My own book on effective communication (Thompson, 2011c) presents a review of theoretical issues in Part One and then draws out many of the practice implications in Part Two.

Other useful sources include: Rosengren (2000) and Schirato and Yell (2000) which offer good theoretical perspectives, while Hargie, Dickson and Tourish, (2004), Clutterbuck and Hirst (2003) and Turner (2003) offer a management perspective. Jandt (2007) provides a helpful discussion of communicating across cultures.

Congruence is a concept deriving from NLP – see Knight (2002) and/or O'Connor and Seymour (2003).

Conflict

Chapter 19 of *People Skills* (Thompson, 2009a) is a good starting point. Lewis (2009) and Doherty, Steffan and Guyler (2008) are helpful texts on workplace conflict. Mediation is covered from a family perspective in Roberts (2008), and from a management perspective in Crawley and Graham (2002). McConnon and McConnon (2004) is also informative. Commercial mediation is discussed in Mackie, Miles and Marsh (1995). De Bono (1986) is also well worth looking at.

Elegant challenging is a concept deriving from neuro-linguistic programming (NLP), a topic explored in some detail in Knight (2002) and O'Connor and Seymour (2003).

Peacemaking circles are discussed in Pranis, Stuart and Wedge (2003) and McCaslin (2005).

Teamwork in specific contexts is covered in Payne (2000) and Onyett (2003), although both contain material that can be helpful in understanding teamwork across a wide range of settings. In addition, see Dearling (2000) which also has wider applicability than its title implies. Parker (2008) is also an informative guide.

Crisis and change

The basics of crisis intervention are explained in Thompson (2011b). Managing change is a topic with a large literature basis. John Kotter is generally recognized as a leading thinker in this field – see Kotter (1996) and (2002).

Change involves loss, which is well covered in Thompson (2002b), a collection of readings about loss and grief. The Introduction is particularly helpful in understanding loss and grief in the context of tackling people problems. See also Thompson (2012b) for a discussion of the challenges associated with grief. Thompson (2009b) discusses problems in the workplace in relation to loss, grief and trauma.

Force-field analysis was introduced in Lewin (1947) and is also explored in Thompson and Bates (1996). (Cognitive) dissonance is a concept arising from the work of Festinger (1957). Hughes (2010) is a fairly comprehensive text on managing change in organizations.

Decision making

A good starting point for this subject is Tschäppeler and Krogerus (2011). Making the most of meetings is the subject of Barker (2006) and Pincus and Miller (2004). A classic work in relation to risk assessment is Brearley (1982). See also Carson and Bain (2008) and Gigerenzer (2003). Buzan and Buzan (2003) is an excellent introduction to mind mapping.

Equality and diversity

PCS analysis is discussed in Thompson (2011a) and Thompson (2012a). These are also both good introductions to issues in relation to discrimination, equality and diversity. Texts about specific areas of discrimination include: Solomos (2003) on racism; Wilson (2003) on sexism; S. Thompson (2005) on ageism; Swain et al. (2004) on disablism; DePalma and Atkinson (2008 on heterosexism in relation to working with children and Morland and Willox (2005) more broadly; and Moss (2005) on elements of religious discrimination.

Managing pressure

The CIA framework is discussed in Thompson (1999). Thompson, Murphy and Stradling (1996) also contains a lot of useful information about pressure and stress. Other texts include: Sutherland and Cooper (2000), Schabracq et al. (2001) and, on the legal implications, Earnshaw and Cooper (2000).

Motivation and influencing skills

Adair (2009a) is a widely used text on motivation. Adair (2009b) is also of interest. Pink (2011) offers a very helpful overview of motivation. Influencing skills are discussed in Chapter 16 of Thompson (2009a). See also Dent and Brent (2006) and Cialdini (2007). Negotiation skills are discussed in Gates (2010). REBT is covered in Dryden (2006).

Problem solving (general)

Part Three of *People Skills* (Thompson, 2009a) covers a range of problem-solving issues under the heading of 'Intervention Skills'. I have found Egan (2009) very helpful, although he does tend to focus on counselling-style interventions for the most part, which does narrow its scope somewhat.

Covey (2004) is a very popular text which contains a lot of useful insights, although its theoretical base is questionable in places due to its reliance on 'biological reductionism' – that is, the tendency to try and explain psychological and sociological factors in biological terms. Isaksen, Dorval and Treffinger (2011) is an interesting resource relating to creative approaches to problem solving, as is Higgins (2006).

If you are approaching people problems from a social work point of view, Thompson (2009b) is very good for setting the context of such work.

Relationships

Egan (2009) is again a useful source here. Other helpful texts include: Willerton (2010) and Duck (2007).

The ability to respond to feelings, or 'emotional intelligence' is covered in Goleman (1996), Merlevede, Bridoux and Vandamme (2001) and McBride and Maitland (2002). However, none of these texts does justice to the complexity of emotion, particularly its sociological dimensions. More sophisticated analyses of emotion are to be found in: Fineman (2000), Howe (2008) and Payne and Cooper (2004). A text that is particularly good on gender and emotion is Fischer (2000). Transactional analysis is covered in Berne (2010), a classic text.

The drama triangle is explained in Karpman (1968), downloadable from www.itaa-net.org/TAJNET/articles/karpman01.html

Organizations and websites

The British Association for
Counselling and Psychotherapy
1 Regent Place, Rugby, CV21 2PJ
T 0870 443 5252
F 0970 443 5160

www.counselling.co.uk

The Chartered Institute of
Personnel and Development
151 The Broadway, London, SW19 1JQ
T 020 8971 9000
Information and publications relating to workplace issues.

www.cipd.co.uk

MIND
15–19 Broadway, London, E15 4BQ
T 020 8519 2122
F 020 8522 1725
An important mental health organization.

www.mind.org.uk

The Work Foundation
Peter Runge House
3 Carlton House Terrace
London, SW1Y 5DG
T 0870 165 6700
F 0870 165 6701
A source of useful information about workplace issues.

www.theworkfoundation.com

humansolutions
A site offering free information and advice on a range of workplace well-being issues.

www.humansolutions.org.uk

References

Adair, J. (2009a) *Effective Motivation: How to Get Extraordinary Results from Everyone*, 2nd edn, London, Pan.

Adair, J. (2009b) *Leadership and Motivation: The Fifty-Fifty Rule and the Eight Key Principles of Motivating Others*, London, Kogan Page.

Adair, J. (2010) *Effective Leadership Skills: How to Develop Leadership Skills*, 2nd edn, London, Pan.

Alder, H. (1996) *NLP for Managers: How to Achieve Excellence at Work*, London, Piatkus.

Anda, R. F., Brown, D. W., Felitti, V. J., Bremner, J. D., Dube, S. R. and Giles, W. H. (2007) 'American Adverse Childhood Experiences and Prescribed Psychotropic Medications in Adults', *Journal of Preventive Medicine*, 32(5).

Argyris, C. (1995) 'Action Science and Organisational Learning', *Journal of Management Psychology*, 10(6).

Barker, A. (2006) *How to Manage Meetings*, London, Kogan Page.

Bateson, G. (2000) *Steps to an Ecology of Mind*, 2nd edn, Chicago, University of Chicago Press.

Berne, E. (2010) *Games People Play: The Psychology of Human Relationships*, London, Penguin.

Bono, E. de (1983) *Atlas of Management Thinking*, Harmondsworth, Penguin.

Bono, E. de (1986) *Conflicts: A Better Way to Resolve Them*, Harmondsworth, Penguin.

Bono, E. de (1990) *Lateral Thinking: A Textbook of Creativity*, Harmondsworth, Penguin.

Bono, E. de (2000) *Six Thinking Hats*, London, Penguin.

Brearley, P. (1982) *Risk and Social Work*, London, Routledge.

Brown, J. (1997) 'Circular Questioning: An Introductory Guide', *The Australian and New Zealand Journal of Family Therapy* 18(2).

Buzan, T. and Buzan, B. (2003) *The Mind Map Book*, London, BBC.

Carson, D. and Bain, A. (2008) *Professional Risk and Working with People: Decision-Making in Health, Social Care and Criminal Justice*, London, Jessica Kingsley.

Cialdini, R. B. (2007) *Influence: The Psychology of Persuasion*, London, HarperBusiness.

Clarke, M. and Stewart, J. (2003) 'Handling the Wicked Issues', in Reynolds et al. (2003).

Clutterbuck, D. and Hirst, S. (2003) *Talking Business: Making Communication Work*, Oxford, Butterworth Heinemann.

References **255**

Congress, E. P. (2002) 'Using the Culturagram with Culturally Diverse Families', in Roberts and Greene (2002).

Covey, S. R. (2004) *The Seven Habits of Highly Effective People: Powerful Lessons in Personal Change*, 2nd edn, London, Simon & Schuster.

Crawley, J. and Graham, K. (2002) *Mediation for Managers: Resolving Conflict and Rebuilding Relationships at Work*, London, Nicholas Brealey.

Dallos, R. and Draper, R. (2010) *An Introduction to Family Therapy*, 3rd edn, Maidenhead, Open University Press.

Dearling, A. (2000) *Effective Use of Teambuilding in Social Welfare Organisations*, Lyme Regis, Russell House Publishing.

Dent, F. E. and Brent, M. (2006) *Influencing: Skills and Techniques for Business Success*, Basingstoke, Palgrave Macmillan.

DePalma, R. and Atkinson, W. (eds) (2008) *Invisible Boundaries: Addressing Sexualities Equality in Children's Worlds*, Stoke on Trent, Trentham Books.

Dienstag, J. F. (2006) *Pessimism: Philosophy, Ethic, Spirit*, Princeton, NJ, Princeton University Press.

Dingwall, R., Eekalaar, J. and Murray, T. (1983) *The Protection of Children: State Intervention and Family Life*, Oxford, Blackwell.

Doel, M. (2006) *Using Groupwork*, London, Routledge.

Doel, M. and Marsh, P. (1992) *Task-Centred Social Work*, Aldershot, Ashgate.

Doherty, N., Steffan, B. and Guyler, M. (2008) *The Essential Guide to Workplace Mediation and Conflict Resolution: Rebuilding Working Relationships*, London, Kogan Page.

Drucker, P. (1954) *The Practice of Management*, London, Heinemann.

Dryden, W. (2006) *Getting Started with REBT*, 2nd edn, London, Routledge.

Duck, S. (2007) *Human Relationships*, 4th edn, London, Sage.

Earnshaw, J. and Cooper, C. L. (2000) *Stress and Employer Liability*, 2nd edn, London, Chartered Institute of Personnel and Development.

Egan, G. (1994) *The Skilled Helper: A Problem-Management Approach to Helping*, 5th edn, Pacific Grove, CA, Brooks/Cole.

Egan, G. (2009) *The Skilled Helper: A Problem-Management Approach to Helping*, 9th edn, Pacific Grove, CA, Brooks/Cole.

Ellis, A. (1962) *Reason and Emotion in Psychotherapy*, New York, Lyle Stuart.

Festinger, L. (1957) *A Theory of Cognitive Dissonance*, Stanford, CA, Stanford University Press.

Fineman, S. (ed.) (2000) *Emotion in Organizations*, 2nd edn, London, Sage.

Fischer, A. H. (ed.) (2000) *Gender and Emotion: Social Psychological Perspectives*, Cambridge, Cambridge University Press.

Forsyth, P. (1998) *Making Meetings Work, London*, Chartered Institute of Personnel and Development.

Garfinkel, H. (1967) *Studies in Ethnomethodology*, Englewood Cliffs, NJ, Prentice-Hall.

Gates, S. (2010) *The Negotiation Book: Your Definitive Guide to Successful Negotiating*, Chichester, John Wiley & Son.

Gergen, K. (2009) *An Invitation to Social Construction*, 2nd edn, London, Sage.

Gigerenzer, G. (2003) *Reckoning with Risk: Learning to Live with Uncertainty*, Harmondsworth, Penguin.

Goleman, D. (1996) *Emotional Intelligence: Why it Can Matter More Than IQ*, London, Bloomsbury.

Hargie, O., Dickson, D. and Tourish, D. (2004) *Communication Skills for Effective Management*, Basingstoke, Palgrave Macmillan.

Higgins, J. M. (2006) *101 Creative Problem Solving Techniques: The Handbook of New Ideas for Business*, 2nd edn, Winter Park, FL, New Management Publishing.

Hopkins, J. (1986) *Caseworker*, Birmingham, Pepar Publications.

Howe, D. (2008) *The Emotionally Intelligent Social Worker*, Basingstoke, Palgrave Macmillan.

Hughes, M. (2010) *Managing Change: A Critical Perspective*, London, Chartered Institute of Personnel and Development.

Isaksen, S. G., Dorval, K. B. and Treffinger, D. J. (2011) *Creative Approaches to Problem Solving*, London, Sage.

Jandt, F. E. (2007) *An Introduction to Intercultural Communication: Identities in a Global Community*, London, Sage.

Janis, I. (1982) *Groupthink: Psychological Studies of Policy Decisions and Fiascoes*, 2nd edn, Boston, MA, Houghton Mifflin.

Karpman, S. (1968) 'Fairy Tales and Script Drama Analysis', *Transactional Analysis Bulletin*, 7(26).

Kelly, G. (1955) *A Theory of Personality: The Psychology of Personal Constructs*, New York, W. W. Norton.

Knight, S. (2002) *NLP at Work: The Difference that Makes a Difference in Business*, 2nd edn, London, Nicholas Brealey.

Kotter, J. P. (1996) *Leading Change*, Boston, MA, Harvard Business School Press.

Kotter, J. P. (2002) *The Heart of Change*, Boston, MA, Harvard Business School Press.

Lambert, T. (1996b) *Key Management Solutions*, London, Pitman.

Larrick, R. and Klayman, J. (1998) 'Not Beyond Repair', *FT Mastering Management Review*, December.

Lewin, K. (1947) 'Feedback Problems of Social Diagnosis and Action', *Human Relations*, 1.

Lewis, C. (2009) *The Definitive Guide to Workplace Mediation and Managing Conflict at Work*, Weybridge, RoperPenberthy Publishing.

Mabey, C. and Iles, P. (eds) (1994) *Managing Learning*, London, Routledge.

Mackie, K., Miles, D. and Marsh, W. (1995) *Commercial Dispute Resolution: An ADR Practice Guide*, London, CEDR

Magnus. B. and Higgins, K. M. (eds) (1996) *The Cambridge Companion to Nietzsche*, Cambridge, Cambridge University Press.

Marsh, P. and Doel, M. (2005) *The Task-Centred Book*, London, Routledge.

Marshall, P. (1998) *Unlocking Your Potential*, Oxford, How To Books.

McBride, P. and Maitland, S. (2002) *EI Advantage: Putting Emotional Intelligence into Practice*, London, McGraw-Hill.

McCaslin, W. D. (2005) *Justice as Healing: Indigenous Ways*, St Paul, MN, Living Justice Press.

McConnon, S. and McConnon, M. (2004) *Resolving Conflict: How to Manage Disagreements and Develop Trust and Understanding*, 2nd edn, Oxford, How To Books.

Merlevede, P. E., Bridoux, D. and Vandamme, R. (2001) *Seven Steps to Emotional Intelligence*, Carmarthen, Crown House.

Miller, W. R. and Rollnick, S. (2002) *Motivational Interviewing: Preparing People to Change Addictive Behaviour*, 2nd edn, New York, Guilford Press.

Moore, B. (1996) *Risk Assessment: Practitioner's Guide to Predicting Harmful Behaviour*, London, Whiting & Birch.

Morgan, G. (1997) *Images of Organization*, 2nd edn, London, Sage.

Morland, I. and Willox, A. (eds) (2005) *Queer Theory*, Basingstoke, Palgrave Macmillan.

Moss, B. (2005) *Religion and Spirituality*, Lyme Regis, Russell House Publishing.

Myers, S. (2007) *Solution-Focused Approaches*, Lyme Regis, Russell House Publishing.

O'Connell, A. (2003) 'The Transfer of Training to the Workplace', *British Journal of Occupational Learning*, 1(2).

O'Connor, J. and Seymour, J. (2003) *Introducing NLP: Psychological Skills for Understanding and Influencing People*, London, HarperCollins.

Onyett, S. (2003) *Teamworking in Mental Health*, Basingstoke, Palgrave Macmillan.

Parker, G. M. (2008) *Team Players and Teamwork: New Strategies for Developing Successful Collaboration*, 2nd edn, Jossey-Bass.

Pascal, B. (1995) *Pensées*, Harmondsworth, Penguin.

Payne, M. (2000) *Teamwork in Multiprofessional Care*, Basingstoke, Palgrave Macmillan.

Payne, R. L. and Cooper, C. L. (eds) (2004) *Emotions at Work: Theory, Research and Applications for Management*, Chichester, Wiley.

Pincus, M. and Miller, R. F. (2004) *Running a Meeting that Works*, London, Barron's Educational.

Pink, D. H. (2011) *Drive: The Surprising Truth About What Motivates Us*, Edinburgh, Canongate.

Pranis, K., Stuart, B. and Wedge, M. (2003) *Peacemaking Circles: From Crime to Community*, St Paul, MN, Living Justice Press.

Renzenbrink, I. (ed.) (2011) *Caregiver Stress and Staff Support in Illness, Dying and Bereavement*, Oxford, Oxford University Press.

Revans, R. (1998) *An ABC of Action Learning*, London, Lemos & Crane.

Reynolds, J., Henderson, J., Seden, J., Charlesworth, J. and Bullman, A. (eds) (2003) *The Managing Care Reader*, London, Routledge.

Roberts, A. R. and Greene, G. J. (eds) (2002) *Social Workers' Desk Reference*, Oxford and New York, Oxford University Press.

Roberts, M. (2008) *Mediation in Family Disputes: Principles of Practice*, 3rd edn, Aldershot, Ashgate.

Rogers, C. (1960) *On Becoming a Person*, London, Constable.

Rosengren, K. E. (2000) *Communication: An Introduction*, London, Sage.

Sartre, J.-P. (1989) *No Exit and Three Other Plays*, New York, Vintage.

Schabracq, M., Cooper, C., Travers, C. and van Haanen, D. (2001) *Occupational Health Psychology: The Challenge of Workplace Stress*, Leicester, BPS Books.

Schirato, T. and Yell, S. (2000) *Communication and Culture: An Introduction*, London, Sage.

Schneider, J. (2006) *Transforming Loss: A Discovery Process*, East Lansing, MI, Integra Press.

Schön, D. F. (1983) *The Reflective Practitioner*, New York, Basic Books.

Scollon, R. and Scollon, S. W. (2001) *Intercultural Communication*, 2nd edn, Oxford, Blackwell.

Seligman, M. E. P. (2003) *Authentic Happiness*, London, Nicholas Brealey.

Senge, P. M. (1994) 'The Leader's New Work: Building Learning Organizations', in Mabey and Iles (1994).

Shazer, S. de (1985) *Keys to Solutions in Brief Therapy*, New York, W. W. Norton.

Shazer, S. de (1991) *Putting Difference to Work*, New York, W. W. Norton.

Skinner, B. F. (1971) *Beyond Freedom and Dignity*, New York, Random House.

Solomos, J. (2003) *Race and Racism in Britain*, 3rd edn, Basingstoke, Palgrave Macmillan.

Sutherland, V. J. and Cooper, C. L. (2000) *Strategic Stress Management: An Organizational Approach*, London, Macmillan – now Palgrave Macmillan.

Swain, J., French, S., Barnes, C. and Thomas, C. (eds) (2004) *Disabling Barriers – Enabling Environments*, 2nd edn, London, Sage.

Thomas, W. I. and Znaniecki, F. (1958) *The Polish Peasant in Europe and America*, New York, Dover Publications.

Thompson, N. (1995) *Age and Dignity: Working with Older People*, Aldershot, Arena.

Thompson, N. (1999) *Stress Matters*, Birmingham, Pepar.

Thompson, N. (2000) *Theory and Practice in Human Services*, Buckingham, Open University Press.

Thompson, N. (ed.) (2002) *Loss and Grief: A Guide for Human Services Practitioners*, Basingstoke, Palgrave Macmillan.

Thompson, N. (2006) *Promoting Workplace Learning*, Bristol, The Policy Press.

Thompson, N. (2007) *Power and Empowerment*, Lyme Regis, Russell House Publishing.

Thompson, N. (2009a) *People Skills*, 3rd edn, Basingstoke, Palgrave Macmillan.

Thompson, N. (2009b) *Practising Social Work: Meeting the Professional Challenge*, Basingstoke, Palgrave Macmillan.

Thompson, N. (2009c) 'Stress', in Thompson and Bates (2009).

Thompson, N. (2011a) *Promoting Equality: Working with Diversity and Difference*, 3rd edn, Basingstoke, Palgrave Macmillan.

Thompson, N. (2011b) *Crisis Intervention*, 2nd edn, Lyme Regis, Russell House Publishing.

Thompson, N. (2011c) *Effective Communication*, 2nd edn, Basingstoke, Palgrave Macmillan.

Thompson, N. (2011d) 'Workplace Well-Being: A Psychosocial Perspective', in Renzenbrink (2011).

Thompson, N. (2012a) *Grief and its Challenges*, Basingstoke, Palgrave Macmillan.

Thompson, N. (2012b) *Anti-Discriminatory Practice*, 5th edn, Basingstoke, Palgrave Macmillan.

Thompson, N. and Bates, J. (1996) *Learning from Other Disciplines: Lessons from Nurse Education and Management Theory*, Norwich, University of East Anglia Monographs.

Thompson, N and Bates, J. (eds) (2009) *Promoting Workplace Well-Being*, Basingstoke, Palgrave Macmillan.

Thompson, N. and Gilbert, P. (2011) *Supervision Skills*, Lyme Regis, Russell House Publishing.

Thompson, N., Murphy, M. and Stradling, S. (1994) *Dealing with Stress*, Basingstoke, Macmillan – now Palgrave Macmillan.

Thompson, N., Murphy, M. and Stradling, S. (1996) *Meeting the Stress Challenge*, Lyme Regis, Russell House Publishing

Thompson, S. (2005) *Age Discrimination*, Lyme Regis, Russell House Publishing.

Thompson, S. and Thompson, N. (2008) *The Critically Reflective Practitioner*, Basingstoke, Palgrave Macmillan.

Thomson, P. (1996) *The Secrets of Communication: Be Heard and Get Results*, London, Simon & Schuster.

Tschäppeler, R. and Krogerus, M. (2011) *The Decision Book: Fifty Models for Strategic Thinking*, London, Profile Books.

Turner, P. (2003) *Organisational Communication: The Role of the HR Professional*, London, Chartered Institute of Personnel and Development.

Wilde, J. (2002) *Anger Management in Schools: Alternatives to Student Violence*, 2nd edn, Lanham, MD, Scarecrow Press.

Willerton, J. (2010) *The Psychology of Relationships*, Basingstoke, Palgrave Macmillan.

Wilson, F. M. (2003) *Organizational Behaviour and Gender*, 2nd edn, Aldershot, Ashgate.

Index